READY FOR LIFE

# Ready for Life

David R. Veerman, editor

Contributing Writers: Linda M. Washington
Jeanette A. Dall
Betsy Todt Schmitt
Carol J. Smith
Betsy Rossen Elliot
Mary Ann Lackland

Tyndale House Publishers, Inc.
WHEATON, ILLINOIS

Visit Tyndale's exciting Web site at www.tyndale.com



This book was produced by The Livingstone Corporation.

Designed by Melinda Schumacher

Edited by Kathryn S. Olson



---

**Library of Congress Cataloging-in-Publication Data**

Ready for life / David R. Veerman, editor : contributing writers, Linda M. Washington . . . [et al.].
p. cm.
Summary: Presents devotions with discussion questions and Bible verses centering on such topics as friendship, decision making, money management, school, truthfulness, and more.
ISBN 0-8423-5199-X
1. Children—Religious life. 2. Teenagers—Religious life. 3. Children—Conduct of life. 4. Teenagers—Conduct of life. [1. Prayer books and devotions. 2. Christian life. 3. Conduct of life.] I. Veerman, David. II. Washington, Linda M.
BV4571.2.R4 1998
248.8'3—dc21 98-5776

---

Printed in the United States of America

04 03 02 01 00 99 98
7 6 5 4 3 2 1

# Contents

# Getting Ready for *Ready for Life*

*(The "How to" for the "How to's")*

The junior-high/middle-school years are tough. Everything is changing—bodies, minds, friends—and emotions and hormones are running wild. Clearly, early adolescence is a time of stress for the whole family. Young people need help understanding themselves and learning how to adapt to the changes in themselves and in the world. Their parents want to know what's going on and how to help lead their kids in the right direction.

Psychologists and sociologists agree that the pressure point for early adolescents is competency. That is, in the middle of all the changes, young people want to feel that they can do something well, that they are good at something. So they sign up for activities and try a variety of sports, lessons, and experiences. They want to learn "how to."

This is the ideal age, therefore, to teach skills. A skill, by definition, is the ability to perform a specific task, to do something adequately. Baseball skills, for example, would include pitching, fielding, throwing, and batting. Gardening skills would include preparing the soil, planting, fertilizing, and weeding. And computing skills would include word processing, programming, and surfing the Internet.

A clue that a skill is being taught is the introduction of that skill with the words *how to,* as in "how to pitch," "how to plant," and "how to program." More basic and much more important than skills needed for sports and hobbies, however, are what social scientists have labeled "life skills." In short, these are the skills needed to live successfully, to interact with others, and to make a positive contribution to society. As Christians, we would quickly add that *spiritual* life skills are even more important.

Clearly, early adolescents want and need to learn "how to" in a wide range of areas involving school, friends, family, God, and the world.

This brings us to this book—its purpose and "how to" use it. Designed for families with at least one early adolescent (approximately ages eleven to fourteen), *Ready for Life* contains forty separate life skills. Each of these skills has five related lessons—two hundred lessons in all.

A quick survey of the contents will reveal a wide variety of life skills, including "How to Help a Friend," "How to Manage Money," "How to Get Organized," "How to Have Fun," and everything in between. Looking closer, you will also see a number of decidedly spiritual life skills such as "How to Worship," "How to Understand the Bible," and "How to Know What You Believe."

Each of the lessons for a life skill begins with a **story.** These stories feature young people in interesting, real-life dilemmas. The story's purpose is to help you and your family feel the need for and create an interest in the skill. In each story an authority figure will teach the main point.

**Questions** follow each story. Interesting, progressive, and personal, the questions seek to involve the whole family, check on understanding, and reinforce the teaching.

Next you will find **Bible Discovery,** selected verses that teach the biblical principle and reinforce the skill. All verses quoted are from the New Living Translation (NLT) of the Bible.

**Bible Point** follows Bible Discovery. A short summary of the Bible readings, the Bible Point will underline the main point of the lesson.

Each lesson ends with **Bottom Line,** a one-sentence wrap-up of the teaching. Each daily devotion should take only ten to twenty minutes to complete, depending on how long you spend in discussion.

You may want to use *Ready for Life* as the basis of your family devotions for a year. You can begin with Life Skill #1 and go all the way through #40. You may, however, want to use this book with other devotional books such as *Sticky Situations* or *Life Application Family Devotions.* This would keep the life skills fresh and inviting.

Some families may choose the skill to read based on a current need or interest. For example, if a child is struggling with a troublesome friendship, you may want to spend a week learning "How to Make Friends" or "How to Handle Arguments." If your family has had questions about church, you could read "How to Worship" or "How to Get the Most out of Church." You can skip around in the book, as long as you follow through all five lessons for the life skill you're learning.

Thank you for buying this book. I trust that God will honor your efforts to help your family become *ready for life.*

*Dave Veerman*

# 1

# How to Be a Good Friend

## *Make the First Move*

"I don't have any friends," Cheryl complained to her mother. "Everyone hates me." Cheryl's mother knew better than to believe that statement. Their family had just moved to that city about a month ago, and everyone was struggling with the new adjustment. Cheryl was in seventh grade, and that was tough enough. Getting used to a new town and a new school had really pressured Cheryl. In her old hometown, she knew everyone and had very nice friends. She missed them so much it made it difficult to even want to get to know anyone new.

"What kind of friends do you want to have?" Cheryl's mother asked.

"Like my old friends," Cheryl whined.

"OK," her mother continued, "what things describe your old friends back home?"

Cheryl began to think about her old friends. Loyal. Polite. They were funny and fun to be around. They made her feel loved and cared about, and they never put her down.

"Let's list some of these qualities on paper, Cheryl," her mother suggested. After Cheryl had jotted down some of her ideas, her mother asked, "Have you tried to be this type of friend to the kids at your new school?"

Cheryl's first response was to say that no one at the school even gave her a chance to be a good friend.

Cheryl's mother gingerly continued. "Maybe it's time for you to make the first move. Take the initiative and try to be friendly first. You can't wait for others to find out who you are. To have good friends, first you have to be one."

Cheryl knew her mother was right. She really hadn't tried that yet. "OK. I'll try being a good friend, and maybe, just maybe, someone will return the favor."

"That's more like the Cheryl I know," her mother said as she patted her daughter on the shoulder. "You're on your way to discovering a good friend. I just know it!"

#### Questions

- Why is it difficult to make new friends?
- What would your list of important qualities of a friend look like?
- Why should you try being a good friend in order to have a friend?

#### Bible Discovery

Read these Bible verses: Romans 13:9; 1 Corinthians 13:4-8.

#### Bible Point

God wants his people to love others just as they love themselves.

#### Bottom Line

In order to have good friends, you must first be willing to be a good friend.

### *Don't Tell*

Before the youth group meeting, Sandy's youth leader, Donna, pulled her aside and asked her to be a volunteer in that night's group game. Donna secretly gave her a dollar bill and told her not to tell anyone about it. "It's a secret," Donna said and winked at Sandy. Sandy winked back and excitedly joined the rest of the group.

Donna opened the meeting and gave instructions. "Welcome everyone! Tonight we're talking about keeping confidences. So I've secretly given someone in this room one dollar. Your challenge is to find out who that person is. Ready? Go!"

Sandy nervously clenched the dollar in her pocket as she talked with others, pretending to discover who had the money. It wasn't long before Sandy just couldn't stand it. She had to tell! So she blurted out to the next person who asked her, "Yes! I have it!"

After the game, Donna got the group seated and quiet. After thanking Sandy, she asked, "How many of you would have kept the dollar a secret?"

Some raised their hands. Next she asked, "How many of you are more like Sandy—you just have to tell?"

Some others raised their hands. Then she said, "Of course, keeping a secret about a dollar and keeping a friend's deepest, darkest confidence are two different things. But this game can help us think about what it takes to be a trustworthy friend. When people put their trust in us, we want to prove that we're worthy of that trust!

"You all know that there are some secrets that *shouldn't* be kept, such as when a friend is hurting someone or is being hurt by someone else. But most of the time, personal information your friends share with you is just that—personal."

After the lesson, Sandy talked with Donna some more about being a trustworthy friend. Donna asked, "Instead of giving you the dollar, if I had shared some very personal information with you, would you have had a tough time keeping the secret?"

Sandy had to admit that she probably would have kept the secret, but it wouldn't have been easy. Donna explained how trust is lost between friends when one person fails to keep a confidence. Donna also explained how the opposite is also true. "Remember when you told me about your problem with your mother. We had a good talk, and I haven't told anyone else about your problem. Because of that, I'll bet you know you can tell me other personal information too. You know you can trust me."

Sandy agreed, and Donna continued, "When we keep a friend's innermost thoughts to ourselves, we build trust between each other."

Sandy was glad she was learning to be a trustworthy friend.

### Questions

- How would you have responded in the game if you were Sandy?
- How do you feel when someone betrays one of your secrets?
- What causes you to tell secrets that someone has entrusted to you?
- How can keeping a confidence build trust between friends? When can it cause problems?
- Why is trust an important part of a good friendship?

### Bible Discovery

Read these Bible verses: Psalm 101:6; Proverbs 11:13; 20:6.

Bible Point

If we want to have faithful friends, we need God's help to be trustworthy when it comes to keeping confidences.

Bottom Line

If you want to keep good friends, keep their confidences.

## *Listen Up*

"I'm going to pass back your tests today, class. Some of you did well. But some of you have a long way to go!" the teacher explained as he began to distribute the tests.

Samantha knew which category she would fit into as soon as the teacher spoke. School always seemed to be a struggle for her. No matter how hard she studied for tests, she just couldn't remember the information when she needed it.

As expected, when Samantha received her test, she saw a bright red D on the top. She sighed and hastily put the paper in her notebook. Now she had to face her parents at home later that day. They would be so disappointed.

At lunch, Samantha barely touched her sandwich and chips. *Who can eat at a time like this?* she thought to herself. Her friends at the table were laughing and cutting up together. But Samantha didn't feel like laughing.

"What's your problem, Samantha?" someone finally asked.

"Oh, I'm sort of having a bad day," she said in a quiet voice.

Her friends looked blankly at her as if they couldn't come up with anything to say. Finally Kelly piped up in a sarcastic voice, "Well, get over it! You're making me depressed!" Everyone at the table cracked up at Kelly's remark and resumed their chatter.

Samantha cleared away her stuff and headed out of the cafeteria. "Wait!" She heard a voice behind her. It was her friend Heather— Samantha and Heather went to the same church, and both were active in the youth group. "I heard you say you were having a bad day. Want to talk about it?" Heather asked.

Relieved, Samantha told her all about the test and how she dreaded seeing her parents when she got home. Heather gave Samantha her full attention. She didn't offer any easy answers or interrupt her with advice. She just listened. "I feel better already, though," Samantha said afterward.

Heather smiled and said, "I didn't say much. I just listened! But my mom says sometimes that's all we need—a good listener."

"You're a good friend and a great listener. Thanks!" Samantha said to Heather. When nobody else seemed to want to listen, Heather had been there for her!

Questions

- How do you feel when it seems there's no one to listen to you?
- Why is it important to listen to your friends?
- How did Heather show she was a good listener?
- Why is listening a sign of a good friend?

Bible Discovery

Read these Bible verses: Proverbs 11:12; 18:13; James 1:19.

Bible Point

God says that listening is the mark of a good friend.

Bottom Line

Good friends listen to each other without interrupting.

## *Through Thick and Thin*

"Did you hear what Brian did?" someone asked. The question rang out in the school hallway.

"I can't believe it," another said.

"It must have been pretty bad, whatever it was," piped in another. Several students were standing around outside their lockers after school, discussing the fact that their friend Brian had been called out of class to the principal's office just before school was out for the day.

Suddenly Brian's closest buddy, Brad, walked up to his locker. "What are you guys talking about?" he asked as he reached inside his locker.

Several of the boys looked at each other like, "Where has this guy been?"

"Hellooooooo!" teased Mike. "Haven't you heard? Brian got called into the principal's office. I heard it was for fighting or something. But Jason says he heard it was about—" Mike looked around suspiciously and lowered his voice—"drugs."

Before Mike could say anything further, Brad interrupted everyone. "Hey! You guys don't really know why Brian was called in.

And neither do I. But I *do* know that Brian is my friend, and he wouldn't get caught dead fighting or dealing drugs. So you can just take your gossip and get out of here."

"Well said," came a deep voice behind the crowd. Startled, the group looked around only to be face-to-face with the principal himself. And behind him stood Brian—grinning widely at Brad. The principal continued. "For your information, Brian was called into my office to accept an award for Student of the Month. It's just too bad he had to find out who his real friends are the hard way."

The principal glared at the now-embarrassed crowd and put his arms around both Brad and Brian. "A loyal friend is the best kind of friend. Congratulations, Brian. Today you are a winner in more than one way."

### Questions

- How was Brad's response to Brian's mysterious situation different from the others?
- What is gossip?
- What does it mean to you to be loyal?
- When have so-called friends believed the worst about you?
- Why is loyalty an important part of being a good friend?

### Bible Discovery

Read these Bible verses: Proverbs 3:3; 17:17; 1 Corinthians 13:6-7; 1 John 3:16.

### Bible Point

God says that a mark of love and friendship is loyalty.

### Bottom Line

Good friends are loyal to each other, sticking together through thick and thin.

## *J.O.Y.*

Hannah and her sister, Lisa, had always been close friends. Sure, they had their disagreements. But even then, they rarely lost their tempers. The two had to share a room growing up, so they learned early what it meant to share. And sometimes they learned it the hard way. Since the girls were both growing older and wanting their own space, they became irritable and argumentative more and more often.

One day Lisa, the older of the two, came home from a week-long summer camp with their church. She was eager to show off her photographs and tell Hannah all the details. The girls laughed together at all the photos, and Lisa told her what they had learned about God that week. "And now for your special prize . . . ," Lisa said, her voice filled with anticipation. Usually whenever the girls traveled, they would bring each other some sort of memento from the trip—candy, a pen, etc. This time, Lisa brought something extra special for her little sister.

Hannah closed her eyes and held out her hands. "Here it is!" Lisa said and placed a metal key chain with the letters *J-O-Y* printed on it into Hannah's hand.

Hannah looked at the key chain curiously and quietly asked, "What is it?"

"It's the secret to our friendship!" Lisa said with a laugh. "The *J*, *O*, and *Y* stand for Jesus, Others, Yourself. At camp this week we learned that when these are placed in the right order, they spell *JOY!*" Lisa went on to explain that one of the things she learned during the week was how special her relationship with Hannah was and how she didn't want to mess it up by arguing all the time.

"I know we have our fights and all, but whenever we try to think about the other person first, we end up getting along. I know that a lot of times I think of myself first—my schedule, my clothes, my space. But I learned that when Jesus is first in my life, he frees me to put others before myself. And that's what I want to do, Hannah. I value our friendship, and I want to consider your needs before my own. I know that when we live like that, we're happy. We have 'joy', I guess you might say."

"Yeah, and if we get the letters out of order—what a mess!" Hannah laughed. "It would be something like *yoj*—all backwards. I'd rather have joy!"

The girls kept the key chain posted on their bulletin board to remind them to practice J.O.Y.

### Questions

- Why is it difficult to put others' needs and feelings before our own?
- What makes people so self-centered?
- Why do you think following the idea J.O.Y.—Jesus, Others, You—works?

- Why is putting the needs of others first an important part of a good friendship?
- In what relationship are you willing to practice J.O.Y.?

### Bible Discovery

Read these Bible verses: Matthew 20:28; Mark 12:30-31; James 3:16.

### Bible Point

Good friendships are built when we put others' needs before our own. That's a sign of Christ in us, and it's a sign of love.

### Bottom Line

The best way to be a good friend is to put Jesus first and others second. That will lead to JOY.

# 2 How to Make Friends

***New Girl in Town***

Claire disgustedly threw down her books on the kitchen table with a loud *thunk.* Her mother, busy preparing dinner, looked up, startled. At the sight of Claire's dejected face, her mom put down the measuring cup and put her arm comfortingly around Claire's shoulders.

"What's the matter, honey? You look upset," her mom said gently.

"It's just, it's just that we've been here for nearly three months, and I don't have any friends," Claire said, bursting into tears. "I miss my old friends. I hate this place. Why did we have to move to this stupid town anyhow?"

Claire's mom handed her a tissue and waited until Claire had finished crying. The move had been hard on Claire. Although she seemed to be doing fine in school, she hadn't connected with any of the girls in her classes or at her church's youth group. It was time, Mom thought, for a heart-to-heart talk—and a little brainstorming.

Claire's mom took out a piece of paper and wrote in large letters across the top *C-IN.* Claire snuffled a bit, but her curiosity was piqued. She looked at her mom warily and asked, "What's that? What did you write that for?"

Her mom gave her a smile and began to explain, "Well, believe it or not, these three letters can help you begin to find some new friends."

Claire looked at her mom skeptically but said, "What do you mean?"

Mom continued. "Well, let's think about this for a moment. We *know* there are potential friends out there somewhere. It's simply a matter of finding them. By remembering these three letters, you'll be able to start 'looking' or 'seeing' around for friends. To find them, you need to start 'C-IN.'

"C stands for *close.* Right now, you may already be close to potential friends. Let's think of some places where you come in contact with kids your age," her mom encouraged. Together, they wrote down classes at school, the church youth group, choir, the neighborhood, and soccer practice.

"OK, that's quite a few places to begin looking for friends. Now let's move on to *I. I* stands for *interests.* Who are the kids you come in contact with that share your interests? Let's write down a few interests of yours to spark some ideas." Claire wrote down soccer, shooting hoops, singing, reading historical fiction books, collecting dolls and stuffed animals, listening to CDs. By the time she finished, she had assembled quite a list.

Then Mom pointed to the *N.* "This letter stands for *needs.* Who at school do you know needs a friend, like you do? Can you think of any other *new* kid at school or church or soccer practice?" Claire wrote down a few names, her face brightening at the prospect of knowing where to begin to find new friends.

Mom smiled at her daughter. "This is just a start, of course. But it is a good first step, don't you think?"

Claire smiled at her mother, grabbing her list and a couple of cookies as she headed out the door. "Yes, it is. I feel much better now. I'm going out to shoot some baskets. Who knows? I may see a kid who likes basketball and needs a new friend just like me!"

### Questions

- Where do you think Claire might be able to find some friends?
- Where would you go to find friends if you were new in town?
- What do you think it takes to be a good friend?

### Bible Discovery

Read these Bible verses: Proverbs 17:17; 18:24; Matthew 7:7; 1 Corinthians 13:4-7.

### Bible Point

Good friendships don't just happen. We have to make an effort to find friends and then build those relationships.

### Bottom Line

Seek friends and you will find them.

## *The Icebreaker*

Claire had been unusually quiet on the way to the store. Mom finally broke the silence and asked if anything was wrong. Claire shook her head and answered slowly, "No, nothing is really wrong. I just have this problem, and I don't know what to do about it. You see, there's this girl in a couple of my classes, and I would like to get to know her better. It's just that I don't know how to do it. By the time I think of something to say, she's already talking with someone else."

Mom smiled. "Well, that's the kind of problem I like to help solve. What you need is an icebreaker."

"An icebreaker? You mean something to crush up ice cubes? How's that going to help me get to know this girl?" Claire asked.

Mom laughed. "No, that's not what I mean. An icebreaker is something you say that helps start a conversation. Look for clues for something you and this girl have in common. For instance, you're both in the same English class, right? That's a good place to look for conversation starters. You might make a comment about last night's English assignment or the book you have to read for class."

"Oh, I think I get it. Like I could say to her, 'Miss Herold sure is giving us a lot of homework lately,' or 'That last chapter in our book was real exciting'," Claire said excitedly.

"Exactly," Mom replied. "That gets the conversation started."

Claire thought for a moment and then looked puzzled. "Well, what happens when you run out of stuff to talk about the English assignment? You can only talk about Miss Herold's assignments for so long, you know."

Mom nodded. "Yes, you're right. When you feel like the conversation is dragging a bit, move on to other topics. Try and find out what the other person is interested in. Ask this girl if she plays sports or enjoys reading books. If you want to get to know someone, it's important to find out what he or she is interested in. Get the idea?"

Claire nodded eagerly. "Yes, I do. I can't wait for class tomorrow, Mom! Next time I see this girl, I'm going to be ready!"

"That's the spirit, Claire," Mom replied. "Now let's see about getting these groceries for dinner."

### Questions

- What two icebreakers could you use to start a conversation with a new student?

- What other topics might also work as icebreakers?
- Why do you think it's important to find out about the *other* person's interests? Why not just share your own interests?

Bible Discovery

Read John 4: 7-14 to see how Jesus started a conversation with a very unlikely friend. Also look up Proverbs 18:2 and Philippians 2:4.

Bible Point

A true friend puts the interests and needs of the other person above his or her own.

Bottom Line

Build friendships on common interests.

## *The Name Game*

"I can't believe I just did that," Claire moaned. She sank into the armchair and covered her face with her hands. "I'll never be able to go back to school. How could I be so stupid? I can't believe I just did that."

"Hold on a minute," said Mom, wiping her hands on the dish towel. "What happened that has you so upset? Nothing can be as bad as you're making it out to be."

"Oh yes it can," Claire stated emphatically. "You don't know what a stupid thing I did today. I'll never be able to face that girl again. It was *so* embarrassing."

Mom waited patiently, and eventually Claire retold what happened at lunchtime. "You know that girl I told you about in my English class? Well, we've been talking and getting to know each other. But today I really blew it. I was in the lunchroom, and she came up to me and gave me a big hello."Claire stopped for a moment.

"Well, that sounds like that's a good thing," said Mom.

"It is if that were the end of it," Claire agreed sorrowfully. "But the awful thing was that I couldn't remember her name at all! I was so embarrassed all I could do was mumble a few words and get out of there as fast as I possibly could! Now she probably thinks I'm the biggest geek in the whole school. I'll never be able to go back to school."

Mom said sympathetically, "I know how embarrassing that can be. I wasn't very good at remembering people's names either, until I learned the R-A-W trick. Let me share it with you. Maybe it will help the next time you meet a new friend." Claire looked willing to listen, so Mom continued, "You see, Claire, our names are very important to us. We feel good when someone remembers our name—and we feel bad when they don't.

"The first step in remembering a person's name is to **R**epeat it. That's the *R.* Repeat it in your mind and then use the person's name in a conversation as soon as you can," Mom explained. "You might say, 'Oh, Judy, I have a cousin named Judy. How do you spell your name?' The key is to repeat the person's name aloud as soon as you can."

"OK," said Claire, "that makes sense, but what about the *A?* What does that stand for?"

Mom smiled. "Patience, patience! I was just getting to that. The *A* stands for **A**ssociate it. That means to use the person's name in your mind in a clever way or draw a mental picture. For example, if your friend's name is Sandy, you could picture a beach. Or if her name is Jill, you might picture a hill, which rhymes with the name. Get it?"

"Yeah," said Claire slowly. "The girl whose name I forgot is Jenny. I could associate her name with a penny! How about that?"

Her mom laughed. "That's the way. Now let's go on to the *W,* which stands for **W**rite it down. After you meet someone, write the name down somewhere. That will help you to remember the name, and in case you forget, you'll know where to find it again."

Claire jumped up from the chair. "Thanks Mom. That's a real help. But I've got to run."

"Hey, where are you going in such a hurry," Mom called after her.

Claire shouted back, "I've got to go upstairs to write down Jenny's name! Now that I've remembered it, I want to make sure I never forget it again!"

Questions

- Why do you think our names are so important to us? How do you feel when someone forgets your name? How about when someone remembers it?
- Think of two or three kids in your class at school whom you don't know very well. How can you associate their names?
- What do you think Claire should do the next time she sees Jenny?

Bible Discovery

Read these Bible verses: Genesis 32:27-29; Matthew 10:29-31; Luke 19:1-6.

Bible Point

Our name is very important to us and to God. God often gave people new names to reflect their changed lives. Be assured that God knows your name, too!

Bottom Line

Remembering a person's name shows that you care.

## *Rejected!*

Mom glanced up at the clock. Claire had only five minutes to get ready for the basketball game. Knowing what a slowpoke Claire could be, Mom shouted upstairs, "Claire, are you about ready? You're going to be late for the game."

Mom got a muffled grunt in reply. This was not a good sign. Sure enough, when Mom knocked on Claire's door and walked in, Claire was in her old sweatpants, her CD earphones plugged in her ears. Obviously, Claire was not going to the basketball game—an event she and her new friend, Jenny, had talked about all week.

"What's going on? I thought you and Jenny were going to the game tonight?" Mom asked.

"So did I," said Claire, "until Jenny told me at lunch that she had other plans for the evening. Then she ran off with this other girl who's real popular. I guess I don't rank very high on her friend list. You know, I really didn't like her anyway. She can be a real jerk!"

"Claire, I know you're disappointed and hurt by what happened. I would be, too, but we have to realize that despite our best efforts, at times we won't be successful in making new friends, and we will feel rejected," Mom said gently. "The important thing is to know how to handle rejection and keep on making new friends after being rejected. You don't need to give up or get even. You just need to know your *ABCDs*."

"Mom, what are you talking about? I already know my alphabet," Claire cried. But Mom had gotten her attention. Claire turned off the CD player and sat up. "OK, what do you mean by the *ABCDs*?"

Mom smiled. "I thought you might be interested in this. Let's see, *A* stands for Accept reality. We *all* face rejection at some point in our life. Not everybody is going to like us and want to be our friend. We need to accept the fact that rejection is part of life.

"That brings us to *B*—that stands for **B**ounce back. We need to shrug it off and get on with life. Don't let rejection stop you—you've got to keep going," her mother said. "*C* stands for **C**aution and **C**hange. Be careful *not* to try and win approval from another person by changing the way you are. Some kids will do almost anything to be liked by another person. But you must use caution. Plenty of other people will like you for who you are.

"And finally, *D*—**D**etermination. You've got to determine to keep trying! Don't let one experience keep you from trying to be someone's friend," Mom said.

Mom patted Claire on the knee. "I know this might be hard to think about right now, but if you concentrate on your *ABCD*s, you'll start to feel better. To help start the process, how about throwing on some jeans and going to get some ice cream?"

### Questions

- How did you feel when you were rejected or snubbed by a friend? Did you feel like getting back at that person or like shutting yourself up in a room?
- How well do you think you bounce back from rejection? What might you do the next time you run into that situation?
- What advice would you give a friend who has been rejected?

### Bible Discovery

Read Mark 6:1-6 to see how Jesus handled rejection. Also look at Exodus 5:1-3, Jeremiah 25:2-6, and Acts 5:15-21 to see how others handled rejection.

### Bible Point

Jesus faced rejection from his own family and neighbors, but he didn't let that stop him from continuing on and finding other people who would accept him.

### Bottom Line

Not everyone will be your friend.

## *Make Time for Friends*

Claire was in her room putting the finishing touches to her science project. She called Mom up to look at it. Proudly she displayed it, pointing out the various parts of her experiment. "This looks really good, Claire. I'm proud of how hard you worked on it. As a reward, why don't you call Leslie, and we can all go to the mall," Mom suggested.

"Boy, I'd really like to, Mom, but I've got to do some more work on these posters for the youth group's spaghetti dinner. You know we've got to earn money for our missions trip this summer," said Claire.

Before Mom left, she asked Claire, "When *was* the last time you and Leslie got together?"

Claire thought about it for a moment, "Well, it's been awhile. We've both been real busy with schoolwork and stuff. I don't really know when it was."

Mom came back into the room and sat down on the bed. "You know, Claire, unless you take time to *SMILE,* you could be in danger of losing your friends."

"Mom! What *are* you talking about? I smile all the time," Claire responded defensively. "Leslie is still my friend. I just haven't had much time to see her lately."

Mom held up her hands. "Hold on there! Don't get all upset. All I'm talking about is a trick for helping us cement the friendships we already have so they can grow and become stronger. Let me explain.

"*S* stands for Seeking your friends where they are. If you two have a lot of schoolwork and Leslie is spending a lot of time at the library, then go to the library together. Or Leslie can come help you at the youth group dinner. Go where your friends are," Mom said. "*M* is important—Make friends feel special to you. Maybe you can't spend as much time as you would like together, but a little note or a phone call may be all it takes to let Leslie know she's important to you.

"*I* stands for Invite your friends to activities you attend, like youth group or apple picking with our family. There are hundreds of ways to include your friends in your daily schedule. But that brings us to *L*—Leave time in your schedule for your friends. We all are very busy, but if we don't plan to include some time in our week to just hang out or have a Coke together, then we'll miss out on a very special gift God has given us—our friendships."

"OK, Mom, I think I get the picture. Maybe I haven't been such a good friend to Leslie after all. I think I will take you up on that offer to go to the mall. Let me call Leslie right now," Claire said, jumping up from the bed. Then she stopped a moment, "Hey, what about the *E.* There's an *E* in smile."

Mom smiled broadly. "Right you are. And that brings us to the most important thing—Enjoy your time together!"

### Questions

- What other things can Claire do to make her friend feel more special?
- How have you been able to balance your friendships with a busy schedule? What do you do to make time for your friends?
- Why do you think it is important to spend time with our friends? What could happen if we don't?

### Bible Discovery

Look up 1 Samuel 18:1-4 to see the type of friendship David and Jonathan shared. Also look up John 15:13-15 and Acts 9:23-30 to see other models of real friendship.

### Bible Point

Friendships require time and commitment. Like Jonathan and David's friendship, true friendships stand the test of time and stress and don't allow anything to come between them.

### Bottom Line

True friends find time for each other.

# 3 How to Help a Friend

## *Help!*

"The answer to that is . . . $n = 3$," Monica Marshall said, after looking over her homework page.

"So, what did you get for the second problem?" her best friend Lorraine Phillips asked.

"Thirty-two," answered Monica.

"Thanks, Mon," said Lorraine gratefully.

When Monica hung up the phone, she found herself facing the questioning gaze of her younger brother, Bernard. "You were *giving* her the answers?" he asked.

Monica planted her hands on her hips. "What're you doing listening in on my conversation?"

"As loud as you talk, who could help but hear?" Bernard retorted.

*Brothers! One of life's necessary evils?* Monica thought. Aloud she said, "Leave me alone, Rat Breath!"

"Fathead!" Bernard called back.

Monica suddenly heard a throat being cleared behind her. Their father stood there, staring at his two youngest children. "What's this all about?"

"Monica's giving Lorraine answers!" Bernard blurted out before Monica could say anything.

"Is that true, Monica?" Mr. Marshall looked at his daughter expectantly.

Monica looked down at her shoes. "I was just trying to help, Dad. She didn't understand how to do the math problems."

"Bernard, leave us alone. I want to talk to Monica," Dad said firmly and quietly.

"Aw, Dad, can't I hear you yell at her?" said Bernard.

Mr. Marshall gave Bernard a look that sent him scurrying out of the family room.

"And you think giving Lorraine the answers will help her understand the problems?" he asked Monica, after making sure that Bernard was really gone.

"Well, I explained how to do the problems," insisted Monica. "We were just talking over the answers we got."

"*We* got?" questioned Dad.

"OK, *I* got," admitted Monica.

"Honey, letting her come up with the answers herself is more helpful," said Dad.

"I was just doing it this once," said Monica. "Lorraine would do the same for me."

"This once?" Mr. Marshall looked skeptical. "Are you sure you haven't done this before?"

Monica couldn't look him in the eye. "Well . . . OK. I did it one other time."

"It's OK to *show* someone how to do something," Dad explained. "But when you actually *do* it for that person, you're just allowing her to use you. That's not wise. It's certainly not what God would want you to do. He wants you to use wisdom in everything you do. If you really want to help Lorraine, show her how to help herself. But don't do her work for her."

"OK," Monica answered. She started to walk away, but Mr. Marshall called her back.

"And don't do it because I caught you this time, either. Do it because it's the right thing to do, OK?" he added.

"OK," said Monica, and she really meant it.

Mr. Marshall put his arm around her shoulders. "That's my girl."

### Questions

- What are some needs your friends have?
- If a friend needed your help and that would involve doing something wrong, what would you do? Why?
- Where should someone draw the line in helping a friend?

### Bible Discovery

Read Proverbs 9:9; 14:23; 16:21; 21:3.

### Bible Point

Solomon's proverbs reveal God's thoughts on wisdom.

Wisdom helps us know the right way to help our friends. The right way never involves going against God's commands.

Bottom Line

Helping a friend means doing what's right.

## *A Friend in Need*

"Keith got in trouble as usual," Deena Gecewicz told her mother after school. "Today the teacher caught him wearing Dennis Michaels's fake fangs during math." She laughed at the memory.

"I worry about him sometimes," Mrs. Gecewicz said, shaking her head. "I know his mother does."

"Aw, Mom, you know how he is," said Deena. "He'll do anything to be funny."

"Deena, I don't see anything funny about getting into trouble." Mrs. Gecewicz paused to look seriously at Deena. "Are you really being Keith's friend if you encourage him to keep doing these things?" She looked disapproving.

"Mom, I didn't tell Keith to do that," Deena protested. "He did that on his own." Keith got a lot of attention because of his antics. As one of his best friends, Deena did too. And she wanted things to stay that way.

The next day, Keith wasn't in school. When he returned the following day, he seemed different, quieter. He didn't want to talk to any of his friends.

"Keith's being weird," Deena told her mother as soon as she arrived home. "He won't talk to anybody."

Mrs. Gecewicz put her magazine down. "I think I know why. I saw his mother at the grocery store. Keith's doctor just told her that Keith has ADD."

Deena looked at her. "What's that? Is that a disease?"

"Attention deficit disorder," explained Deena's mom. "One of the symptoms is that Keith has trouble paying attention in school. That's why he's been getting into trouble. He'll have to take Ritalin."

"Wow. . . . What's Riddlelin?" Deena asked.

"A medicine Keith will have to take every day," answered Mom.

"Oh. Is that what's making him weird?" asked Deena.

"Why would you think that?" Mrs. Gecewicz asked, turning to look straight at Deena. Then patting Deena's hand, she explained,

"No. His mother said the medicine will help him concentrate better. That means he won't be acting up as much in class. Maybe he seems different because he's afraid you'll treat him differently."

"Oh." Deena fell silent.

Mom continued. "Deena, right now, Keith's going to need a lot of help catching up on his schoolwork and adjusting to the medicine. He's going to need a friend who will stick by him, not because of what he is but because of who he is."

"Mom," Deena said, as if coming to a realization, "do you think we should pray for Keith?"

"Hey, Keith, wait up!" Deena ran to catch up with him in the alley where he was in-line skating the next day.

Keith stopped but looked as if he wanted to continue skating.

"I've been looking for you. I knew I'd find you here in the alley." Deena paused. "Mom told me you have to take medicine."

Keith scowled at her. "So what? It's no big deal."

"I didn't say it was!" Deena replied.

Keith skated around in circles. "You won't tell anyone, will you?"

"Not if you don't want me to," answered Deena. "Who knows? Maybe we'll all stop getting in trouble once you do." Deena grinned.

Keith smiled and seemed more like himself again. "Get your skates. I'll race you down the alley."

"You're on," yelled Deena. Suddenly she knew she would always like Keith, no matter what he did. After all, he was her friend. That was all that counted.

### Questions

- How did Deena prove to be a good friend to Keith?
- What do you appreciate most in a friend?
- What do your friends appreciate most about you?
- What do you think it takes to be a real friend?

### Bible Discovery

Read Proverbs 17:17 and 18:24.

### Bible Point

The Bible has a lot to say about friendship. Real friendship isn't shallow. It involves love and respect and being there when you're really needed.

Bottom Line

Real friends stick together during the tough times.

## *Support for a Friend*

"And I'm really nervous about being goalie today," Denise was telling her friend Brandon Tyler. "So, are you coming to my soccer game? It would help for me to see you there."

They both paused by the lockers in the hall. Brandon shrugged as he worked his combination. "I've got a lot to do myself today. I don't think I can make it. Sorry. Anyway, you guys always lose."

Denise looked stung. "Oh. Well, what about next Saturday? My team is playing Central Junior High."

"Aw, soccer's boring, Denise. Anyway, that's the day I have tryouts for the junior symphony. Look, I have to go. I'll see you." Brandon hurried off, thinking about all the things he had to do that day.

At home, Brandon collapsed in a heap at the kitchen table, where his father was putting together some homemade pizzas.

"Hard day at the office?" Mr. Tyler asked.

"Ha, ha, Dad. When's dinner?" answered Brandon.

"An hour. Grab a snack." Mr. Tyler nodded toward an overflowing bowl of fruit. "Oh, Denise called. She said to tell you her team stinks. She said she thought you'd understand."

"Oh, her team must've lost. They usually do. I told her that," explained Brandon. "She wanted me to go to the game. Now I'm glad I didn't."

"Not even to support your friend?" asked Brandon's dad.

"Dad, there's nothing I can do to help her team win. Only a miracle can do that." Brandon chuckled at that. "So, where's Mom? Working late?"

Mr. Tyler nodded. "How'd you guess?"

"Whenever Mom works late, you cook. That was easy," answered Brandon.

"I cook at other times. . . . And do you know why I do it?" asked Dad.

"Because . . . we wouldn't eat unless somebody does?" Brandon replied.

"My son is so smart," Mr. Tyler said. "No, really. Why do you think I cook?"

"Because . . . you're hungry?" answered Brandon.

"Because it takes the load off your mom," Dad explained. "I don't like to cook, but it's my way of supporting her. When she comes home, all she has to do is eat and relax. Mainly because you'll be doing the cleanup."

Brandon groaned while Mr. Tyler laughed.

"Good friends can do the same," he continued. "Being there when a friend is performing in a concert or playing in a soccer game—" he looked pointedly at Brandon—"is the best way to help a friend."

Brandon grabbed a banana and sat deep in thought. Finally, he got up and headed to the phone. "I think I'll call Denise back. Maybe I'll check out her next game."

### Questions

- How do you feel when your friends show up to cheer for you at an event?
- Why are loyalty and support important in a friendship?
- What things are your friends involved in?
- How can you show your support for them?

### Bible Discovery

Take a look at John 13:1-15 and see how Jesus loved and supported his friends.

### Bible Point

Jesus showed his love for his disciples by doing something we would consider gross—washing their grubby feet. He knew they needed that, so he humbled himself and did the dirty job. We can "wash our friends' feet" by doing something we might normally find unpleasant if it meets their need. All it takes is keeping our eyes off our own comfort and focusing on God.

### Bottom Line

Real friends support each other.

## *Being There*

"How do I look? Am I ugly? Tell me the truth!" Mona Thompson moaned. "My nose looks so huge."

"I like your new hairstyle. It's sooo seventh grade. What do you think of my new outfit?" Rachel Bartel twirled around, imagining that her blue-jean skirt billowed out.

Mona looked her over carefully and then gave her the OK sign. "I guess we're ready for seventh grade."

"We'd better be," answered Rachel.

Starting a new school had its ups and downs. Mona and Rachel wanted everything to be perfect and to fit in with a good crowd right away. Within days they could tell who was in and who was out. Two girls were quickly established as the most "in." They called themselves the "two Cs" because their names were Caitlin and Carolyn. Rachel and Mona wanted to be friends with them.

"The two Cs are having a pool party. They said to tell you to come. Do you want to go?" Rachel asked.

"Why didn't they call me?" asked Mona.

Rachel shrugged and then realized that Mona couldn't see a shrug over the phone. "I don't know," she answered. But she knew why. Mona could be gloomy at times.

"I don't think they like me," said Mona. "I was hoping you'd come over and help me make cookies or something."

Rachel really wanted to go to the pool party. A pool full of cool water was more inviting than a hot kitchen. "Why do you have to make cookies today? I want to go to the party."

"But I don't want to go," exclaimed Mona. "I look hideous in a swimsuit."

"Uh, I'll call you back," Rachel said.

Rachel was thoughtful as she hung up. Her older brother Michael entered the house at that moment. He was grimy from working on his car. "Hey, Munchkin," he called.

Rachel turned to him and asked, "Mike, suppose you had a friend who was always criticizing herself . . . uh, himself. What would you do?"

Mike shrugged. "OK, what's the problem? You only start that 'if you were' jazz when you have a problem."

Rachel quickly told him about Mona.

Mike shrugged again. "Oh, yeah, I should've guessed. She does talk a lot about her nose and stuff. I don't see anything wrong with it. The problem is, she doesn't like herself."

"What can I do?" asked Rachel.

"You need Dad on this one," Mike answered.

"But Dad's not here! Neither is Mom," Rachel replied.

Mike sat at the kitchen table. "Remember when I was fourteen? Man, I was convinced that I was ugly."

Rachel thought it her sisterly duty to inform her brother that he, indeed, had been ugly, but she knew it wasn't true.

Mike continued. "Dad kept telling me that God made me special and stuff like that. He helped me feel good about myself. Maybe you can do the same for your friend."

"But she doesn't want to go to the pool party," answered Rachel. "And if I don't go, the two Cs might not like *me.*"

Mike shrugged. "Well, you need to decide what's more important—going to the pool party or being there to help your friend."

Rachel shrugged. "Hot kitchen, here I come."

Questions

- What would you do to help a friend who feels bad about himself or herself?
- Why is it important for friends to build each other up?
- When did a good friend stand by you and help you feel better about yourself?

Bible Discovery

Read 1 Samuel 20:4-17.

Bible Point

David and Jonathan were best friends. When David had a problem, Jonathan was right there to help. Loyal friends willingly put aside their own desires in order to help each other.

Bottom Line

Real friends build each other up.

## *The Cover-Up*

"You won't tell anybody, will you?" Denny Adamson asked. He looked anxiously at Baxter.

Baxter Fields hung his head. "I said I wouldn't."

Denny looked relieved. "OK, see you."

Baxter slowly walked home from the arcade. He was sick of catching Denny stealing things. This time he had stolen a candy bar from a small store near the arcade. But Baxter couldn't tell anyone because he had promised.

That evening's dinner was quieter than normal. Baxter was usually the most talkative one at the table, followed closely by his younger brother, Phil. But that evening, he just picked at his food.

"I thought you liked meat loaf," Mrs. Fields commented.

"Huh?" Baxter said. His thoughts had been a million miles away.

"Something wrong?" Mr. Fields asked.

"Maybe he's in love," Phil suggested, a grin highlighting his milk mustache.

Baxter shot him a look. "No, doofus!"

"No name-calling, please," Mr. Fields said.

Baxter swallowed a few morsels of food. "It's good, Mom."

"Dad cooked today," she replied.

"Oh," mumbled Baxter.

"By the way, Baxter, I saw your friend Denny at the grocery store today," Mrs. Fields said.

Baxter's eyes shot up from his plate. He started to say something but decided not to. Instead, he excused himself and carried his plate to the sink.

Mr. Fields trailed Baxter to his room. "Is something wrong between you and Denny?" he asked.

Baxter shrugged. "I can't talk about it. I promised."

"Did Denny do something wrong? Is that it?" asked Dad.

"I said I can't talk about it," Baxter replied. "Remember you once told me that if I gave my word I should keep it?"

Mr. Fields nodded. "Yes, but it's also wrong to cover up something that's wrong."

Baxter struggled with his thoughts. Finally the whole story poured out. "And I don't know what to do!" he ended. "Denny keeps stealing!"

"You know stealing is wrong," stated Baxter's father.

"I know!" Baxter replied.

"Why is it wrong?" Dad asked.

That threw Baxter for a loop. "I don't know. Because it's against the law, I guess," he answered.

"Because it's against *God's* law, Son," replied Dad. "Denny has a problem. His parents need to be told."

"You're not going to tell them, are you?" Baxter implored. "Then he'd know I told on him."

"I didn't say I'd tell," Dad answered. "Denny needs to tell them. Son, this is serious. If he keeps on stealing, he'll get caught one day. He could go to jail at this rate. And not telling is the same as helping him."

Baxter looked stricken.

Dad continued. "I think you need to give Denny a choice: Either he tells his parents or you do. Either way, the truth must be told."

Baxter looked as if either choice was disagreeable.

"There comes a time when you need to speak the truth in love," continued Mr. Fields. "That means loving someone enough to tell that person the truth about himself or herself. The truth is, Denny has a problem. He needs to own up to it. It's wrong for him to make you a party to it."

"He'll probably hate me," blurted out Baxter.

"If he does, then he wasn't your friend to begin with," answered his dad.

### Questions

- When a friend does something wrong, what can you do to help him or her, instead of trying to cover up the wrongdoing?
- How does loving confrontation help a friend?
- What can you do to speak the truth in love to a friend?

### Bible Discovery

Read Proverbs 27:6; John 8:32; Ephesians 4:15.

### Bible Point

Often the truth hurts, especially if it reveals sin. A real friend speaks the truth to his or her friend, rather than trying to hide wrong.

### Bottom Line

When a friend is doing something wrong, you can help him or her best by speaking the truth in love.

# 4 How to Worship

## *More Than Just Music*

Doug Schmidt let the screen door bang extra hard as he entered the house. "What's with you?" Mrs. Schmidt asked from her perch on the living-room sofa. "Are you testing the doors?"

"Sorry," Doug muttered.

"Where's your father?"

"He's out talking to Mr. Reynolds next door."

"So, what did Pastor Mike want to talk to you about after the service?"

"They want me to lead the worship time in the youth group in a few weeks. Me!" Doug flopped onto his dad's favorite recliner. "Pastor Mike picks somebody to lead worship every third week. I'm supposed to help plan the order of service. But I don't know anything about worship!"

"Doug, you've been going to youth group since you were ten. You're thirteen now. You must know something of what goes on in worship. What happens?"

Doug thought hard. "Well, there's music. Pastor Mike plays lead guitar sometimes. Man, he can wail. I think he has a—"

"OK, so someone plays the guitar. I'm assuming your youth pastor isn't up there just playing a guitar."

"Well, we sing praise songs. Lots of them. Too many, if you ask me."

"Why do you sing praise songs?"

Doug shrugged. "To worship God, I guess."

"Well, seems to me you know a little something about worship."

Doug looked unconvinced. "It's different when you have to lead worship. That means I have to actually *do* it."

Mrs. Schmidt laughed. "You mean you weren't worshiping before?"

Doug shrugged. "I never thought about it before."

Mrs. Schmidt laughed again. "Ah. Well, I've got an idea. Why don't you go up and practice your guitar? That'll take your mind off this for a while."

Doug brightened immediately. "I won't play too loud, Mom, honest." He ran upstairs to his room and quickly plugged in his guitar. Within minutes, he felt relaxed as he sank into the music.

As the last chord died, he suddenly heard applause. Mrs. Schmidt stood in his doorway.

"You like playing the guitar," she said as more of a statement than a question.

"I *love* playing the guitar!" Doug corrected.

"You know, Doug, some people love to worship with their singing as much as you love playing the guitar."

Doug looked skeptical.

"When you're playing, what do you focus on?"

Doug looked blank for a second. "The music, I guess, and how much I love playing it."

"When people worship God, they focus on him and how much they love him." Mrs. Schmidt wrapped an arm around Doug's shoulders. "And we're people who love God, right?"

Doug grinned. "I guess. . . . Hey! Maybe I can play my guitar during worship."

"Well . . . you could . . . but do you think you'd be thinking about God while playing or about the music?"

Doug thought that over for a minute. "Well, maybe not. Maybe I'll just ask Pastor Mike to play. Or maybe . . . I should think about this worship thing some more before I decide anything."

"Good idea."

### Questions

- What do you think it means to worship God?
- Why is music used in worship services?
- In what ways can singing be a part of worshiping God?
- What can you do to help you focus on God when you sing?

### Bible Discovery

Check out Psalms 29:2; 96:1-2; 100.

Bible Point

In Bible times, people sang psalms in praise to God. The book of Psalms is really a hymnbook. Many of the psalms were written by David. They are reminders that God is great and worthy of praise. Worship begins with a heart that is focused on God.

Bottom Line

Worshiping God involves songs of praise.

## *Prayer Walk*

The wail of an electric guitar suddenly sliced through the conversations in the picnic area as Doug practiced his guitar riffs. "I'm sorry I let you bring that thing to the picnic," Mr. Schmidt said. "Please turn that amp down. Better still, unplug it."

"Sorry, Dad. I thought I was providing the entertainment," Doug said with a grin.

"Entertainment? Look around you." Mr. Schmidt waved his arm. The massive form of Stone Mountain loomed up behind him. "This is why we came to Georgia."

"I thought we came because of our family reunion," Doug said with a grin. He glanced over his father's shoulder. "Look out! Grandma's sneaking up behind you."

Grandma Schmidt wrapped her arms around her son's waist. "You weren't supposed to tell him!" she scolded her grandson.

"Sorry, Grandma." Doug set his guitar down and went to hug his grandmother. He towered over her by several inches.

"You boys want to take a prayer walk with me?" she asked.

"Prayer walk?" Doug asked.

Grandma Schmidt nodded. "I was trying to round up some of the family to take a stroll through the campground and offer up thanks to the Lord."

Doug looked puzzled.

"Your grandma always thinks of worship when we're near a mountain," Mr. Schmidt explained.

"Who can help but worship a God who created all of this beauty?" Grandma Schmidt said. "Makes me want to offer up a prayer of thanks."

"It's funny you should mention worship, Grandma," Doug said as they strolled through the picnic area. "In two weeks I'm supposed to lead worship during youth church."

Grandma linked her arm with his. "Leading worship is quite an honor. Have you prayed about what to do?"

Doug shook his head. "Hadn't thought about it, Grandma. I was thinking about playing something or asking Pastor Mike to play during the service."

"Prayer is part of worship too. It helps you join your heart to God's like music does."

"I like the music part. It's the praying-out-loud part I don't like."

No one spoke for a few minutes as they walked one of the park's nature trails. Every once in a while, Doug heard his grandmother mutter prayers of thanks to God.

"What do you think of all this, Doug?" she suddenly asked.

"All what, Grandma?" Doug swatted away a mosquito.

Grandma waved her arm to indicate the surrounding scenery set against the backdrop of Stone Mountain.

Doug shrugged. He walked a little ahead of them and began to pick up pebbles and fling them about.

Mr. Schmidt laughed. "Doug's seldom comfortable being *unplugged,*" he said.

"I like natural stuff," Doug said defensively.

"Seeing God's creation fills my heart with thanks," Grandma said, "especially being here with two of my favorites." She linked arms with Doug and his dad. "When I'm out in a park like this, I just want to tell the Lord how wonderful he is."

"OK, Grandma," Doug said. "I'll add prayer to the list."

"Add it to your daily list, too!" Grandma added.

### Questions

- How do you think prayer helps you to have a worshipful attitude?
- Why should prayer be part of worship?
- What do you think prayer adds to the worship service?

### Bible Discovery

Read Psalms 4:3; 5:1-3; 106:1.

### Bible Point

Prayer is how people communicate with God. David, who wrote many of the psalms, made prayer a part of his worship. He was a "man after God's own heart." We can be people after God's own heart by making prayer a priority in worship.

Bottom Line

Effective worship involves prayer.

## *Wonders of the Word*

"Did it come yet, Mom?" Doug asked as he threw his books down on the table.

"Put your books in your room," Mrs. Schmidt said over the roar of water swirling in the kitchen sink.

"Did it come yet?"

"Put your books in your room," Mrs. Schmidt repeated, emphasizing each word.

"OK, OK." Doug hurried to his room. There on his bed was what he had been looking for—the latest issue of *Guitar Player* magazine. "All right!" he yelled.

He quickly thumbed through it and then ran to show it to his mother.

"Look, Mom, this is the amp I was telling you about," he said, waving the magazine in front of his mother. "And look, here's a whole section on blues licks. Cool! Want to hear me try 'em, Mom?"

"Not right now, Doug."

Doug looked through the magazine once more. "Thanks for getting me a subscription to this magazine, Mom."

"You're welcome. Did you do your homework?"

"No."

"Don't you think you should get cracking?"

"I'd rather read this," Doug said with a grin.

"OK, I'll answer for you. Get cracking."

Doug sighed.

Mrs. Schmidt rubbed his head. "I'm glad you're excited about playing the guitar. I just don't want you to spend all your energy thinking only about the guitar."

"I think about other stuff, Mom. I've been thinking about having to lead worship in a week."

"I know you like to make lists. What have you got on it so far?"

Doug selected a piece of paper from among the many on the refrigerator door and quickly scanned it. "Let's see. Praise songs and prayer."

"Don't forget Bible reading. That's usually a part of the worship service—one of the most important parts."

"Sometimes, that's the most *boring* part," Doug said.

"Not really, Doug! It all depends on what you're interested in. Take your guitar magazine. Remember how excited you were to show me that magazine? You don't think that magazine's boring, do you? You know that it's full of interesting articles—stories that you wanted to share with me."

"Yeah. I especially like the section where they give playing tips."

"People who love the Bible get just as excited when God's Word is read. They know that it's full of interesting stories of God's acts and God's commands for our lives. It's full of tips too—tips to help us grow in Christ."

As Doug wrote "read Bible" on his list, Mom added, "You probably should choose verses that fit the theme of the worship service—you know, the emphasis of the songs and everything else."

"Wow, there's more to worship than I thought," exclaimed Doug as he wrote "theme" on the paper.

"Honey, there's a *lot* more to worship than any of us really think. Behind the music, the prayer, and the Bible reading is our whole, big God. Worship is more than just praising God. It's seeing God behind all of that. The Bible is our window to the Creator."

### Questions

- Why should the Bible be an important part of worship?
- Around what themes could worship services be centered?
- What Scripture passage could you read to emphasize God's love? his grace? his mercy? his forgiveness?
- How do music, prayer, and Bible reading fit together in your church's worship services?

### Bible Discovery

Read Micah 6:8 and Nehemiah 8:1-8.

### Bible Point

Nehemiah 8 tells about Ezra, the priest and scribe, reading the Law of Moses to the people. At that time, only priests and scribes had scrolls. The people were eager for the word to be read. Hearing God's words is an important part of worship.

### Bottom Line

Effective worship involves reading and hearing the Word of God.

## *Worshiping by Serving*

Doug glanced at the flyer hanging on the refrigerator door. "What's this about an auction at church, Dad?" he asked.

"Huh?" Mr. Schmidt looked up from the newspaper he was reading at the kitchen table. "Oh, that's to help raise money for some of the families who were burned out of their homes. You remember that fire over on Fourteenth Street?"

Doug nodded. Some of the kids in the youth group lived on that street. Their homes had been damaged by the fire.

"It says here that people are asked to donate services. What is that all about?"

"Well, instead of the usual things like old furniture and lamps, people are asked to donate an hour or two of their time to help someone learn a craft or play a musical instrument. For example, you know how your mother teaches violin?"

Doug nodded.

"Well, she's donating an hour's lesson to whoever comes up with the highest bid. The money raised will go to the families that need it."

"Mom's a good teacher. That should raise a lot of money. . . . Hey, maybe I could teach the electric guitar!"

Mr. Schmidt smiled. "Well, think about it; then talk to your mother. She's on the auction committee."

Doug smiled. "Mom's always doing stuff like that."

"It's one way that your mother worships the Lord."

Doug looked puzzled. "Worships?"

"Using one's gifts and talents for God's glory is an act of worship. Serving in God's name is an act of worship."

"Wow. I thought worship was just the Sunday service."

"Worship is a lifelong process, my boy. Anytime you use the gifts God gave you, it's like you're telling God 'Thanks' or 'Let this bring glory to you.' Sometimes we're tempted to focus on ourselves because we're good at certain things. But a true act of worship always brings glory to God. That's what your mother wants to do."

"Is my wonderful husband saying nice things about me?" Mrs. Schmidt said as she entered the kitchen. She placed her arms around her husband. He smiled at her.

"Uh-oh! Mush alert!" Doug said as he retreated to his room.

Later, Doug joined his parents in the family room. "Hey, Mom, I want to donate something to the auction," he announced.

"Still want to donate a guitar lesson?" Mr. Schmidt asked.

"No. I've changed my mind. I decided to mow somebody's lawn."

Mr. and Mrs. Schmidt both looked surprised. "What made you change your mind?" his father asked.

Doug looked embarrassed. "I thought about what you said, Dad . . . about worshiping God. I'm not sure I'd be doing that if I donated a guitar lesson. But if I do something I wouldn't volunteer to do, like cutting the grass, maybe that's the way I can worship God."

Mr. and Mrs. Schmidt exchanged glances. "I think that's a wonderful idea, Doug," Mrs. Schmidt said. "You know something?" she added after a pause.

"What?"

"I think you're beginning to see what worship is all about."

Questions

- In what ways are gifts and talents used in a worship service?
- How can a person use his or her gifts and talents to bring glory to God?
- In what ways is worship a "lifelong process"?
- What gifts has God given you?
- How do you think God wants you to use your gifts or talents in worship?

Bible Discovery

Read Psalm 95:1-2; 1 Corinthians 12:4-6; 2 Corinthians 9:6-8, 15.

Bible Point

God has provided everything: gifts, talents, and the resources of the earth. When believers use their gifts, talents, and resources to serve God, they praise and honor him with their lives.

Bottom Line

Worshiping God involves using our gifts, talents, and resources to serve him.

## *Giving Thanks*

Finally, the week that Doug had been dreading was over. He had led the worship at youth church and had lived to tell the story! The service had gone better than he had anticipated. His parents had attended and had expressed their enjoyment and appreciation. Pastor Mike, the youth pastor, had also been pleased. All that following week, Doug had celebrated the relief he felt at the conclusion of that service. Now he looked forward to hosting a sleepover with a couple of his friends at the end of that week.

"*This* is what I'd rather plan," he told his mom the evening before his friends were due to arrive.

"What's your plan for the evening?" Mrs. Schmidt asked while pouring herself a cup of coffee.

Doug looked at a list he had written. "Can we have pizza?"

"Sure. What else?"

"Uh . . . lots of snacks and soda!"

"OK, snacks and soda. What else?"

"Videos!"

"OK, we'll rent maybe two videos. You *could* use the ones we have, though. Then what?"

Doug shrugged. "I don't know yet, Mom. That's as far as I got with the list. Maybe we'll play Ping-Pong, too."

Mrs. Schmidt put down her coffee cup. "Well, in honor of this occasion, I already picked up some of your favorite snacks and . . ." Mrs. Schmidt pulled three slips of paper out of her pocket, which she handed to Doug.

Doug rewarded her with a broad grin. "Mini-golf passes! Cool! Thanks, Mom."

"Well, I know you want your friends to have a good time."

"I know we'll have a blast, Mom." Doug's face clouded. "Mom, . . . is it wrong to feel . . . I don't know . . . relieved that the worship service is over?"

Mrs. Schmidt shook her head. "Honey, I know you felt uncomfortable at the thought of leading the singing. There's nothing wrong with being relieved that that part's over. But the worship part hasn't ended."

Doug looked puzzled.

"When we think about who God is, we can't help but worship him. The ultimate act of worship is to give yourself to God—to worship him with all that you are each day." She smiled at him, a mischievous gleam in her eyes. "You can even worship God at your sleepover."

Doug looked worried. "Uh, Mom, we're not going to be singing and praying and stuff."

"Don't worry! I'm not suggesting that, although there's nothing wrong with singing praises to God. But thanking him for making good times like sleepovers possible is a way to worship him."

"That I don't mind doing!"

"I didn't think you would."

### Questions

- Why is it important to thank God for who he is?
- How can God's people show their gratitude to him in their daily lives?
- For what are you thankful?

### Bible Discovery

Read Psalm 103:1-5 and Hebrews 12:28-29.

### Bible Point

A believer's heart can be full of praise and worship. A thankful heart is the ultimate act of worship. David, the writer of Psalm 103, tells of some of the things God did and emphasizes the value of praising and thanking God. Knowing who God is provides enough of a reason for anyone to praise him.

### Bottom Line

Worshiping God involves giving God thanks.

# 5

# How to Solve a Problem

## *What's the Problem?*

Lisa hung up the phone and shook her head. She headed into the kitchen where her mom was preparing dinner. "Who have you been on the phone with for the past forty-five minutes?" her mom asked. "You know the family rule is no phone conversation longer than fifteen minutes."

"I'm sorry, Mom. I know I was on the phone longer than that, but you see, Anna really needed to talk. She's really going through a difficult time right now," Lisa explained.

"Oh, really," her mom replied. "What seems to be the problem?"

"Wow, that's the problem! Where do I start? I mean she's got a ton of problems. Her mom recently had a new baby, and that's causing a big stir in the household. Everything is crazy over there, and Anna is expected to do all the work. She's having a hard time getting her homework done. Right now she's just a basket case. And I feel so helpless. I don't know how to help her."

Mom came over to the kitchen table with a bowl of string beans. "Here, help me with the beans, and we can talk," Mom said. "One thing I think you can do for Anna is to help her see exactly what her problem *is*."

"I'm not sure I follow you. It sounds to me like *everything* in her life is a problem right now," Lisa answered.

Mom replied, "It certainly does sound like she's overwhelmed. But before Anna can even begin to think about solving her problems, she needs to learn how to pinpoint *her part* of the problem—the things she can change. Let me demonstrate."

Lisa's mom got up and grabbed a pad of paper and a pen that were by the telephone. "Let's start with an easy definition of a problem:

*A problem is a situation where you don't know what to do.* Now in every situation there are things we can't change—no matter what we do. Then there are things we can and *must* change. The tricky part comes in knowing which is which. Are you following me so far?"

Lisa nodded and watched as her mom made a box on the paper with three columns. She labeled the columns *Situation, Can't be changed,* and *Problem.* "This is a helpful way to break it down," her mother explained. "Now let's examine Anna's situation. How would you describe her situation?"

Lisa thought a moment. "Well, there's a new baby in the house, and Anna feels as though she has to do all the work," Lisa began.

"OK, let's write *new baby/overworked* in that column," her mother said. "Now what can't she change about this situation?"

Lisa had to smile. "Well, she sure can't ask her mom to take the baby back."

"Good answer." Mom smiled too. "So, let's put *new baby* in the *can't be changed* column. So what then is Anna's problem, really?"

Lisa looked at the paper again. Slowly she answered, "I guess Anna's problem is how to handle the workload so she can manage her homework."

Mom agreed. "Now that Anna's problem is pinpointed, she can turn her energies into coming up with solutions to that specific problem, rather than spend her time worrying about those things that can't be changed."

Lisa took the piece of paper. "After dinner, Mom, do you think I could give Anna a call? I think she might be interested in hearing this."

### Questions

- Think of a problem that you currently face. Use the columns *Situation, Can't be changed,* and *Problem* to help pinpoint your problem.
- Why does identifying the real problem help you solve it?
- Who can help you solve your problems?

### Bible Discovery

Read the following Bible verses: Psalm 17:7-8; 119:105; James 1:2-8.

### Bible Point

We need to ask God for wisdom. He will guide us, helping us understand and resolve our problems.

Bottom Line

The first step in solving a problem is to identify the *real* problem.

## Stop!

Sitting at the kitchen table with an empty pad of paper in front of her, Lisa stared into the air. Each time Mom walked through the kitchen, she noticed Lisa in the same position. Finally, she stopped to ask, "Are you planning to write anything on that pad or what?"

Lisa looked up, startled. "What? Oh, the pad. Yeah, eventually. I guess so."

Mom smiled at Lisa. "Looks like you've been deep in thought. Are you working on a term paper or something?"

Lisa shook her head. "I almost wish I were. No, I've got a real problem at school, and I'm trying to figure out what to do about it."

"Well, I know a good place to start. Remember that chart I suggested you use to help Anna with her problem—," Mom began, but before she could finish, Lisa interrupted.

"Yeah, I did that. You see, my situation is this: Play tryouts are on Tuesday immediately after school. I want to try out this year, but Mrs. Weldon is holding a mandatory meeting for the school newspaper. She said that anyone not attending this meeting can forget about being on the newspaper staff next year. I don't know what to do!"

"OK, let's take this one step at a time. We define a problem as a situation where you don't know what to do. Write down what your situation is," Mom advised.

Lisa wrote down *Two important events scheduled at the same time.*

"Now," Mom continued, "what can't be changed?"

Lisa thought a moment and then wrote *Physically can't be in two places at one time.*

"So far, so good," her mom encouraged her. "And that brings us to your problem."

After a minute, Lisa wrote *How can I manage to try out for drama and still attend the newspaper meeting?*

"Now that you've identified your problem, the first thing to do is STOP," her mom said.

Lisa looked up surprised. "Stop! What do you mean? How is that going to solve my problem?" she asked.

"What I mean," said Mom, "is now you need to stop and think about all your options. You have to believe that there is more than one solution to your problem. Go crazy with ideas. In other words, just make a long list of possible courses of action!"

Lisa took a deep breath. For the first time since she sat down with her pad of paper, she began scribbling furiously. After fifteen minutes, she put the pencil down and triumphantly announced, "OK—how's this for a start?" She held up the pad. It was filled with idea after idea.

"That looks great," said Mom. "Tell me a few of your ideas."

Lisa began reading:

"#1—Go to newspaper meeting and forget about trying out;
#2—Go to tryouts and drop newspaper;
#3—Ask Mrs. Weldon if she'll let me come late to newspaper;
#4—Ask drama teacher if I can come another time for tryouts;
#5—Videotape my tryout;
#6—Drop both the tryout and the newspaper and take up guitar;
#7—Ask Mrs. Weldon if she can reschedule the newspaper meeting;
#8—Have a friend dress up like me and go to the newspaper meeting in my place."

Mom laughed at that last "option." "I think you have gotten into the spirit of things! You've taken the first step toward solving your problem. Maybe you already have the solution written down on your pad. Maybe none of these will work out for you. But at least you have a place to begin thinking and looking for solutions. And look, you don't have a blank pad anymore!"

### Questions

- Why is it important to list potential solutions to a problem before making a decision?
- What problem are you facing right now? List as many potential solutions to the problem as you can.
- In Mark 2:1-12, what was the paralytic's friends' problem? How did they resolve it? Would you have considered that solution to the problem?

### Bible Discovery

Read the following Bible verses: Proverbs 2:6-9; 18:13, 15.

### Bible Point

Before deciding how to resolve a problem, consider all the

facts and be open to new ideas. Ask God for guidance in making the right choice.

Bottom Line

STOP and consider all your options before making a decision.

### *Look!*

Following the school newspaper meeting, Lisa walked out of school slowly. Her mom greeted her as she got in the car. "So how did it go? Was Mrs. Weldon pleased with the turnout? I've seen a number of your friends come out already."

Lisa grunted in reply.

"Well, what's the matter with you?" her mother said. "Were you given a really bad assignment?"

"No, actually, I was named editor," Lisa replied glumly.

"Why, that's great!" said her mom.

"Not so great," answered Lisa. "Right after I was named editor, my friend Joni came up and asked if she could be the sports-page editor. The only problem is that Joni doesn't know the first thing about sports! She just wants to meet boys. But if I don't make her sports editor, she'll get mad at me and probably won't be my friend. But if I do, then we'll have the worst sports page ever. I didn't think being editor was going to be this difficult."

"Now I'm beginning to understand," Mom answered. "Sometimes when we have a problem, we need to not only stop and consider all the options available to us but also LOOK at what's really important to us in a particular situation. Do you follow me?"

"I'm not sure," Lisa answered.

Her mom began to explain. "Let me put it another way. Before you can decide what to do about Joni and the newspaper, you need to consider what's most important to you in this situation. What are your values? Maybe it will help you to think of four different categories that you will frequently encounter: Family, Friends, Faith, Future. In each of these categories, what are some values to consider?"

"Well, when I think of family, I think about obeying my parents, helping others, showing respect, being good," Lisa said.

Her mom encouraged her. "That's great. Now think about friends. What's important there?"

"That's easy," Lisa answered, "having lots of friends, being a good friend, not hurting my friends, not lying to my friends . . ."

"How about faith? What's important in that area?" Mom asked.

Lisa replied, "Well, I guess the most important things would be doing what God wants, taking time for church activities, going to Bible study." She paused a moment. "But I'm not sure about the future."

"That just means what is important to you about what you want to be or become," Mom explained. "That might include getting good grades in school, going to college, marrying the right person, taking care of your health—those kinds of things. What you need to do is figure out, using these categories to help you, what is most important in this situation. Maybe you can give this some thought tonight."

Later that evening Lisa came downstairs with a piece of paper. She sat down next to Mom and said, "Here's what I've come up with about what's important to me: Not hurting my friends; doing the best job on the newspaper; possible career in journalism; getting the best people for each position; not letting Mrs. Weldon down; taking my job as editor seriously."

"That's an impressive list, Lisa," Mom said. "Did it give you any clues as to what your values are here?"

"Yes, I think it did," Lisa said. "It really is more important to me to do a good job on the paper and get the best people than to make sure my friend is happy. I'll just have to find a way to smooth things over with Joni."

### Questions

- Look is the second step, right after Stop. How should Lisa use Stop to help her solve this problem?
- In each of these four categories—Family, Friends, Faith, and Future—what two or three things are very important to you?
- How can knowing what is important to you help you solve a problem?
- How can choosing the wrong priorities lead to a wrong choice?

### Bible Discovery

Read the following Bible verses: Ecclesiastes 12:13-14; Micah 6:8; Matthew 16:26; Luke 12:34; Romans 12:1-2.

Bible Point

Before we decide what to do in any situation, we should remember that the most important values are the eternal values that God presents in his Word.

Bottom Line

In looking for the best solution to a problem, LOOK for what's important to you. Consider your values.

## *Listen!*

"So how did things go with Joni? Did you get it straightened out with the sports-editor position?" Mom asked after the newspaper meeting a week later.

"Oh, that went OK. She agreed to write some stories for us about the boys' soccer team instead of actually being the sports editor. I think she's going to do a good job for the paper. But I guess the real problem now is me," Lisa said.

Mom gave her a look that said "tell me more."

"Well, I just don't think I'm cut out to be an editor," answered Lisa. "In fact, I'm seriously considering resigning."

Mom considered this a moment. "Are you sure the problem is you, or is there something else going on?"

Lisa was quiet for a long moment. She answered slowly, "It's just that I'm the editor, and I'm supposed to make sure everybody's story is OK. But when I make suggestions to some of the staff, they get mad and accuse me of messing up their stories."

"Does everyone complain?" Mom continued to probe.

"Well, no, I guess not. It's this one girl, Amy. She doesn't like to be told anything. Earlier in the week I asked her to do an interview with the new gym teacher, and she turned in something completely different. On another assignment, when I made a small correction, she went ballistic. It's a personality conflict, and I think she's trying to get the rest of the staff against me."

"That's sounds pretty discouraging," said Mom. "Have you talked to anyone else about this?"

Lisa shook her head no. "I didn't want to say anything because I thought it would sound stupid," she said.

"You know, it's never stupid to ask for advice. In fact, when you're faced with a difficult situation, an important step in resolving the problem is asking for advice from someone with more experience or knowledge than you," Mom said. "This is the third step in solving problems. Remember, we had STOP and consider all the options and LOOK at what's important to you. This step is LISTEN to others' advice. Now let's start with the who—whom can you ask for advice? Usually people we would likely approach fall into three categories: family, friends, and other adults such as teachers, neighbors, or ministers. The key is that whomever you ask should be wiser or more experienced than you are in this area."

"Well, I suppose I could talk to Mrs. Weldon. And then there's Brenda. She was editor last year. She might have some advice," Lisa said. "Of course, there's always you, Mom!"

"Gee, thanks," Mom joked. "But seriously, now that you know *who*, you need to think about *how* you're going to ask for advice. There are some easy steps to remember. First, you need to explain your problem. Next, you describe your possible solutions. Then ask questions like What did you do? or What would you do? And finally ask, What should I do?

"Then it's time for the key question. Once they give you their advice on what you should do, ask why that's the *best* thing to do. By asking this question, you may discover new values to consider," Mom said. "The last thing to remember is to thank them for their advice. Don't argue if you don't agree. Just accept their advice and think it through."

"I guess it wouldn't hurt to talk to Mrs. Weldon and give Brenda a call," Lisa considered. "They might be able to help me find the best way to handle this situation with Amy. By the way, Mom, what would *you* do in this situation?"

### Questions

- Why is it helpful to get advice from others? Do your friends always provide the best advice? Why or why not?
- When you received advice, did you follow it? How did it help you think of ways to solve your problem?
- In a problem you are now facing, what three people could you ask for advice?

### Bible Discovery

Read the following Bible verses: Psalm 73:24; Proverbs 1:5; 11:14; 12:15.

### Bible Point

A wise person listens to the advice of those who are more experienced and knowledgeable.

Bottom Line

LISTEN and evaluate others' advice.

## *Just Do It!*

Lisa's mom glanced up at the clock. It was almost dinnertime, and Lisa and her friend Gwen were still holed up in Lisa's room. After coming home from school, the two girls had gone straight to Lisa's room and hadn't taken a break, even when Lisa's mom offered them a snack. It was time, Mom decided, to check it out.

Mom knocked on the door and walked in. She stopped in astonishment at the scene before her. Crumpled paper lay all over the floor. Yellow Post-it notes were stuck all around the room. In the middle of the room sat Gwen and Lisa, poring over a well-scribbled notepad. "What's going on in here? It looks like a war room!" Lisa's mom exclaimed.

"Oh, Mom, we'll clean up, I promise. It's just that I've been helping Gwen work through a problem, you know, using all those steps like you told me, and I think we're getting somewhere!" Lisa said excitedly. "Come on, Gwen; let's show her."

The girls flipped back a few pages of the notepad. "You see, Mom, Gwen has this problem. Mrs. Bradstreet asked her to help out with the three-year-olds at church starting this Sunday. That's a good thing, but her soccer coach holds some practices on Sunday mornings," Lisa began.

Gwen jumped in to finish. "The practices aren't mandatory, but Coach Potter made it pretty clear that those who don't attend this Sunday's practice won't be able to play in the big game next Saturday. It's our final game, and I really want to play."

"So what did you decide your problem is?" Mom asked.

"Well, since Gwen can't change either of the times, she has to choose which one to attend," Lisa said. "So her problem is which activity to choose."

Gwen handed Lisa's mom the paper. "Here are some of my options for the STOP step," she said.

On the paper she had written:

#1—Help at Sunday school;
#2—Go to soccer practice;
#3—Ask Mr. Potter if I can make up the practice;
#4—Ask Mrs. Bradstreet if I can help another Sunday;

#5—Find a sub to work with Mrs. Bradstreet;
#6—Quit soccer;
#7—Don't do either.

Next on the paper was a list of things that were important to Gwen—the LOOK step: Playing soccer; playing in the final game; pleasing God by going to church; obeying her parents' rule that church comes first; being loyal to her team; keeping her commitment to the team; helping out her team; learning to be a teaching assistant at Sunday school.

"Did you talk to anyone about this—you know, the LISTEN step?" Lisa's mom asked.

Gwen nodded. "Yes. I talked to my soccer coach and Mrs. Bradstreet. I also talked to my older cousin, who plays a lot of sports and is involved in church activities."

"I'm impressed. It sounds as though you've done just about everything you can to make a wise decision, Gwen," Lisa's mom said. "So what have you been doing these past few hours?"

"We've been going over everything and narrowing down Gwen's options," Lisa said. "You see, Gwen thinks she should go help out at Sunday school and take her chances about playing in the game, but I think she should get a sub this one Sunday and go to practice. What do you think?"

"I think it's time, Gwen, for you to make up your own mind," answered Lisa's mom. "You've done your homework, and you've listened carefully to others' advice. But when it comes right down to it, *you* have to choose a solution and go do it. After you stop, look, and listen, you have to GO!"

"You're right, Mrs. G. It's decision time! And I think I'm ready!" Gwen said.

"Good for you, Gwen. But before you make that decision, how about you girls cleaning up the room for me?"

### Questions

- What is most difficult about making a final decision?
- Think of a problem you are currently experiencing. What do you need in order to make a wise decision?
- Why is it important for you to make your own decision?

### Bible Discovery

Consider the decisions of the Bible characters in the following Scripture passages: Ruth 1:16-18; Nehemiah 4:10-15; Daniel 1:8.

### Bible Point

After you have considered all the options, analyzed your values, and have listened carefully to wise advice, make the decision—step out in faith and act with determination.

### Bottom Line

Make a decision, and go with it!

# 6

# How to Understand the Bible

***Who's There?***

The junior high Sunday school class was finally settling down.

"So you're the new youth pastor?" Bill asked.

"That's right," the newcomer replied. "I'm Dan Foster." Addressing the whole group, he asked, "Why don't you each introduce yourself and say what you expect out of this class."

Bill ventured, "I'm Bill. I just expect to not have to be in the boring church service." The other kids laughed.

"My name is Tina," said a petite eighth grader. "I don't know what to expect. I guess I figured you'd tell us what's in the Bible since you just went to seminary."

"Yeah, that's what I figured. It's pretty hard to understand. Oh, I'm Roger, by the way," added a boy at the end of the row.

The rest of the class—Kevin, Erica, and Carolyn—introduced themselves.

"I'm glad to meet you all," replied Dan. I have bad news and good news for you. The bad news is that I'm not here to give you the answers, so you'll have to do some work."

Roger smiled and said, "Are we going to read the whole Bible this year, Dan? There must be two hundred books there!"

"Actually, there are sixty-six books," answered Dan, "and reading the whole Bible straight through would take too long. Also, if we read the Bible with just the goal of getting done, of reading it through as quickly as possible, we would miss many of the important teachings in there. Actually, the Bible is a big collection of stories, and we're going to read one story at a time."

"How about baby Moses in the bulrushes?" asked Tina. "That's my favorite story."

"Sorry, not this time," replied Dan. "That is a good story, however, and it brings us to the first step of our Bible study method—people. We'll read a story in the Bible and ask, Who are the people involved?" On the chalkboard Dan drew a simple staircase with five steps. On the first step he wrote *PEOPLE.*

"Turn to the second Gospel, the one written by Mark. Kevin, please read verses 1-4 of the first chapter."

Kevin read the passage.

Dan then asked, "Now, who are the people in the story?"

"Jesus, of course," said Bill.

"John the Baptist," added Kevin. "Oh, and Isaiah."

Carolyn and Erica pointed out God and the people who heard John speak. "And there's mention of 'everyone,' whoever they are," said Tina. The group was quiet.

"There's one more," said Dan. No one said anything. Finally Dan spoke. "Don't forget Mark, the writer. Notice that it's fairly easy to find the people in a story, but we shouldn't forget the people 'offstage,' like the audience and the author. Besides being an easy first step, why do you think it's important to identify the people in a Bible story?"

After a few kids spoke, Dan summarized their answers. "You see, you and I are people too, so we can begin to see ourselves in the story. As we read, we can think of which people we would be like if we were living at that time and in that story. We can also think about who those Bible characters would be today if the story were happening here in our town."

Dan continued. "Now, here's an assignment. This week I want you to read the Bible for about five minutes every day—any book of the Bible—although Mark would be good. Each time after you read, ask yourself, Who are the people in the story? Make a list. Next Sunday you will tell everyone about one story you read and the people you found."

### Questions

- Why did Dan say that the Bible is a big collection of stories?
- Why did Dan put *people* as the first step of the staircase?
- What people are "offstage"?
- How can identifying the people in a story help us understand the Bible?

Bible Discovery

Read Mark 1:16-20 and list the people in the story.

Bible Point

God cares about people. He also cares that we understand his ways, so he guided the writers of Scripture to include lots of stories. A story wouldn't be a story without people; Jesus calling the first disciples is no exception.

Bottom Line

To understand the Bible, first identify the people in the story.

## *The Plot Thickens*

"Then, you'll never guess where he hid the key to the secret compartment. He put it right next to—"

"Stop, Roger!" Carolyn yelled. "Don't tell me what happens. I really want to see that movie." She looked toward the door. "Oh, hi, Dan."

"Branching out to movie reviews, Rog?" Dan joked. "Actually, that's a perfect setup to our next step on the Bible study staircase. We'll get to that in a few minutes. First, however, let's review last week and see how you did on your assignment." He then had them all explain the story they chose and the people they identified.

After complimenting everyone on their fine work, Dan went to the board and drew the staircase diagram. He wrote *PEOPLE* on the first step, and on the second step he wrote *PLOT*. "Today we'll talk about how to find the plot of a story," he explained. "Last week we looked at the people, so we asked the question *who?* Now we'll also ask *where?* and *what?* In other words, What is happening in the story? and Where is it happening?

"Turn in your Bibles to the Gospel of Mark again. Carolyn, please read verses 9-11 in the first chapter; then take us through the first step and point out the people in the story."

Carolyn read the story of Jesus' baptism and then answered, "There was Jesus, John the Baptist, God, and Mark."

"That's great. Where did this take place?" Dan asked the class.

"In the Jordan River," said Bill.

"That's right, and that answers *where,*" said Dan. "Now let's look for *what*—what happened there?"

Kevin started. "Well, it says here that in those days Jesus came from Nazareth—"

Dan interrupted. "Kevin, could you say it in your own words, concentrating on the action?"

Kevin frowned and then started over. "Jesus went—I assume he walked—to the Jordan River where John was. John baptized him in the river. Jesus saw the heavens open. God's Spirit came down on him like a dove. Then a voice said that Jesus was his beloved Son and that he was very pleased with him."

"Great work, Kevin," said Dan. Turning to the whole group, he added, "You see—Bible study isn't really that difficult. Already in two weeks, you have learned the first two steps: PEOPLE and PLOT. The plot of a story is simply a summary of the action—what happened and where. Sometimes it helps to look for the *conflict* in the story. Most stories feature some kind of tension or conflict. In this story the tension involved Jesus, the sinless Son of God, approaching John and asking to be baptized. Let's talk about that for a few minutes."

Dan explained the background of the story. Then the class looked at a couple of other stories and identified the people and plot in each. Concluding the lesson, Dan said, "You'll have the same assignment this week. Every day, read the Bible for about five minutes. Continuing in Mark would be good. After you read a story, ask these questions: Who were the people involved?, Where did it happen?, and What happened? See you next week!"

### Questions

- Why is it important to know where a story took place?
- What can help you determine the plot of a story?
- Why did Dan stop Kevin from rereading the passage?
- What do you think the third step in understanding the Bible will be?

### Bible Discovery

Read Mark 2:1-12. Answer the WHO, WHAT, and WHERE questions.

### Bible Point

Sometimes we can overlook the most basic elements of a Bible story, especially if it is a familiar one. To understand the Bible, it is important to identify the conflict in a story and determine the plot.

### Bottom Line

To understand the Bible, identify the plot in each story.

## *Get the Point?*

Class began with Dan reviewing the assignment from last week. Some kids had followed through very well, while some hadn't done much. Everyone was a little restless, especially those who hadn't done the assignment. But everyone became quite attentive when Dan wrote three titles on the chalkboard: *"The Tortoise and the Hare," "The Boy Who Cried Wolf,"* and *"The Grasshopper and the Ants."*

"Does anyone recognize these?" he asked.

"Sure," said Tina. "They're fables."

"Oh, yeah," added Roger. "I've seen them on TV! They're called Aesop's Fables."

Dan laughed and said, "Roger, I'll never say another word about your TV-viewing habits. You're absolutely right. Does anyone remember how these fables always end?"

Roger couldn't hold back the answer. "There's always a little lesson. The narrator says, 'And the moral of the story is . . .' Like for the first one, the moral would be 'Slow and steady wins the race.'"

"Right you are," said Dan. "Now, how do you think knowing the 'moral of the story' can help us understand the Bible?"

After taking a few suggestions, Dan turned to the chalkboard, drew the staircase diagram, and asked what should go on the first two stairs. Everyone called out "people" and "plot," which he wrote on the stairs. After explaining that all the words begin with *P,* he wrote *POINT* on the third stair and said, "Today we'll look at the point of a Bible story. This is the *why* question—why the author wrote it and the lesson God wanted the people in the past to learn. It's like finding the moral of the story."

At Dan's direction, the class turned to Mark 3:1-6. Tina read the story aloud and quickly identified the PEOPLE: Jesus, the man with a deformed hand, the Pharisees (Jesus' enemies), the congregation in the synagogue, the Herodians, the disciples, and Mark.

Then Bill identified the PLOT, telling in his own words about Jesus' activities in the synagogue, healing the man, and the reactions that followed. It was pretty easy to spot the conflict in this story.

"Now we come to POINT. Remember, we want to discover the meaning for the people in the story—what God wanted his people to learn back then," explained Dan. "To do this, we need to ask and answer one of two questions: What is God like? or What should people be like? In other words, every Bible story will reveal something about God or about how people should act. Some stories concern both questions, but for now we'll just look at one per story. So, does today's story tell us what God is like or what people should be like?"

Kevin looked at the story and replied, "I think it tells both." A few of the others nodded.

"I agree," said Dan. "Let's focus on the question What should people be like? What do you think Jesus wanted the Pharisees, Herodians, disciples, and the crowd to know about how people should act? How would you answer that in one sentence?"

After about a minute, Kevin said, "I think it's saying that people should have pity on those in need and try to help them."

"Wow!" Dan shouted. "You got the point!"

The class discussed why this was a controversial situation at that time and why the point was important for each group to learn. After going though this step with another story, Dan concluded by giving another assignment. "This week, I want you to continue reading and go through all three steps. I hope you will use a notebook and record your answers. And this week, let's all do the assignment. In fact, I will have a special treat for those who do the assignment and bring their notebook to class."

### Questions

- Why does every Bible story have a point?
- Why is it important to get the point of a story?
- What makes it difficult to get the point of a story? What makes it easier?

### Bible Discovery

Read Mark 3:31-35 and answer the *who, what, where,* and *why* questions (PEOPLE, PLOT, and POINT).

### Bible Point

The writers of Scripture did not set out to write nice stories to entertain readers. God directed that each story give a lesson, a moral. In the story of Jesus describing his true family, the lesson is a hard one when we answer the question What should people be like? The point: Those who want to follow God will put devotion to him above all earthly family loyalties.

### Bottom Line

To understand the Bible, identify the point in the story.

### *Present and Accounted For*

After all the class members had sat down, Dan asked how everyone had done on the assignment from the previous week. He was pleasantly surprised to find that everyone had brought a "notebook," although for some that just meant scribbling on scratch paper. As promised, Dan gave everyone a treat—a small candy bar—for completing the assignment, and he spent time hearing the points everyone had discovered.

Then Kevin asked, "Well, Dan, what *P*-word do you have for us today? How about pretzels? I could go for a snack about now."

"Nice idea, but wrong *P*-word. Besides, I just gave you a candy bar!" Dan had Kevin draw the staircase on the board. Next he had other students write the key word on each of the first three steps *(PEOPLE, PLOT,* and *POINT)*. Dan wrote the word *PRESENT* on the fourth step.

"Today we'll be looking at the POINT—which we learned about last week—and bringing it into the PRESENT. In other words, we will answer the question What does the Bible story say to us today?"

The students looked around at each other. Finally, Roger asked, "You mean this Bible story is supposed to mean something for junior high kids a couple thousand years after it was written?"

"Shocking, isn't it?" replied Dan. "To find out how the moral of the story relates to us, we'll ask how it applies to our *family,* our *friends,* our *faith,* or our *future.*" He wrote the four words under the word *PRESENT* on the staircase.

"Today we'll look at a story that includes a twelve-year-old girl—"

"Hey, I'm twelve!" Erica interrupted. "Can I read it?"

"Sure," Dan replied. "There's another story stuck in the middle of the one we'll look at. So please read Mark 5:21-24, then skip ahead and read verses 35-43."

Erica read the story. The group quickly answered the PEOPLE and PLOT questions. Dan said, "Our next step is to determine the POINT. Remember, to do this, we should ask if it tells us what God is like or what people should be like. I think it tells us both. Bill, what do you think the point is?"

Bill considered his options, then said, "The point is this: We should bring any problem to Christ, no matter how big it might seem, because he can handle it."

"Well done," said Dan. "Now for the PRESENT. How does the point apply to your family, friends, faith, or future? Anybody want to share your thoughts?"

Carolyn was the first to speak. "I have a friend at school. Her parents are getting divorced, and it's a big mess. I haven't known how to help her, but now I'm thinking that, because we can bring any problem to Christ, I should pray and talk to God about my friend and her family."

"You've really brought the point into the present," commented Dan. Then he took ideas from other group members. Some of the answers to PRESENT were pretty personal; kids shared struggles they were having that they could take to Christ. To conclude the study, the group spent time praying for each other—actually taking the problems to Christ.

Wrapping up their time together, Dan announced, "OK, group, great job today. We're sure learning a lot from God's Word, aren't we? And thanks for being so honest today. By now you can guess your assignment for this week. That's right, work through the four steps on a Bible story each day. I'll bring treats again for those who complete the assignment."

### Questions

- Why does the present step help a person understand the Bible?
- What four categories help us bring a point into the present?
- How might the point of the story of the twelve-year-old girl be brought to the present using the subject of faith instead of friends?

### Bible Discovery

Read Mark 6:1-6 and answer the *who, what, where,* and *why* questions. Then bring the POINT to the PRESENT, applying it to family, friends, faith, or future.

### Bible Point

The Gospels provide a wonderful account of Jesus' life. More than merely history, they are meant to teach people today. An important step in understanding the Bible is to bring its lessons into contemporary life. Rather than shake our heads at the foolishness of the people of Nazareth when Jesus returned to his hometown, we can consider how they *should* have received him and do that in our own life.

Bottom Line

To understand the Bible, bring the point of a Bible story into the present.

## *Gotta Have a Plan*

"Welcome back," said Dan to the junior high class. After checking on everyone's assignment and passing out the treats, he drew the familiar staircase on the chalkboard.

"Today we'll take the last step toward understanding the Bible. Does anyone remember the first four?"

"I do," said Tina. "PEOPLE, PLOT, POINT, and PRESENT." She wrote the words on the steps. Then she added, "There were four things under the last step, but I can't remember those."

Kevin remembered. "You bring the point to the present by seeing how it applies to your family, friends, faith, or future."

"Fantastic!" exclaimed Dan as he wrote those categories under PRESENT. Then he asked, "Can anyone guess what the last *P*-word is?"

Several humorous and a few serious suggestions later, Dan said, "Actually, the last word is PLAN—that's the last step in understanding the Bible. This means deciding what specific steps we can take—right away, this week—to carry out what we decided under PRESENT." He wrote *PLAN* on the last step; under it, he then jotted *Pray, Look,* and *Do.* "This step means putting what we learn into practice.

"A plan is always important. It's easy to say that we will do something, but if we don't have a plan, we probably won't do it. If you have ever been on a diet, you know what I mean. You need a plan to make it work, to actually change your eating habits. The same is true with Bible study and application. *Pray* just means deciding what you can pray about. *Look* means deciding what you should look for and *do* means deciding what you can and should do.

"Let's take the story from last week, the healing of Jairus's daughter." After the class summarized the first three steps, Dan continued. "Remember how Carolyn brought the point to the present. She told us about her friend whose parents are divorcing. Then she said, 'Because we can bring any problem to Christ,

I should pray and talk to God about my friend and her family.' Now here's the PLAN: Carolyn should decide what to *pray* about, what she should *look* for, and what she can and should *do.*"

Carolyn spoke up. "Well, I guess I've taken care of the *pray* part of the plan. I'm going to *look* for ways to reach out to my friend, like listening when she needs to talk instead of just trying to cheer her up. And for *do,* I'm going to encourage my friend and suggest that she talk with God too."

Dan took another application from last week's story and worked it through with the class. They seemed to understand *pray* pretty well, but struggled a bit with *look* and *do.* So Dan gave a few more examples, and pretty soon everyone was *doing* very well.

The class time was almost over, so Dan concluded, "That's all for today. Keep up your personal study of Mark during the week. Starting next Sunday, we're going to take a look at another book of the Bible. The steps aren't just for Mark anymore!"

### Questions

- How can *pray, look,* and *do* help to accomplish the PLAN step?
- What other PLAN would you suggest to Carolyn?
- Which is the most difficult step for you?
- Which Bible stories are you interested in using the steps to understand?

### Bible Discovery

Reread Mark 6:1-6. Take the answers to yesterday's PRESENT step and develop a PLAN (Pray, Look, Do).

### Bible Point

The final step in understanding the Bible is to design and carry out a plan of action. If we bring the point of a Bible story into our life today but never act on it, we might as well randomly read the telephone book. The negative example of the people of Nazareth can point us to positive action in our relationship with Christ.

### Bottom Line

To understand the Bible, design and carry out a specific action plan.

# 7

# How to Ask for What You Want

### *What Are You Saying?*

Daniel had gone out to eat with friends last week so he didn't have enough money left over to purchase his favorite group's new CD coming out this week. What was he going to do? He decided he would ask his parents for the money. That night, while Mom was cleaning up the kitchen, he made his move.

"Hey, Mom!" he shouted from his room down the hall as he stared at a handheld computer game called Turbospace that he was playing. It even looked like he was about to finally win! "Can you come here?" he shouted.

His mother wiped her hands on a towel and waited for Daniel to join her in the kitchen. *"Mom!"* he yelled even louder.

"Daniel, *you* come here to me. I'm busy right now," she said in a firm tone.

Frustrated, Daniel rolled off his bed, game still in hand, and tromped down the hall into the kitchen. Without taking his eyes off the game's tiny screen, he mindlessly mumbled, "Hey. That CD is out . . . and I need some money." Suddenly his Turbospace vehicle almost bit the dust. "Oh no!" he shouted excitedly. "I'm almost there!" He furiously worked the computer game, oblivious to his mother.

Suddenly Mom's hand appeared over the screen. "What? Hey, what'd you do that for?" Daniel objected.

"Listen, Son," she said, "the next time you want to ask for something that's important to you, act like it's important. First, come into the room where I am. Second, don't yell down the hall. Third, put down your game and give your full attention to your request. Then I'll listen."

Speechless, Daniel gave a shocked look to his older sister who was sitting nearby. "It's all part of learning how to get what you want, little brother," she said knowingly. "With adults, what you say without any words sometimes speaks the loudest! It's called nonverbal communication. Listen to Mom. She gave you some great tips for setting up your question next time!"

"What do you mean?" Daniel asked.

"OK," answered his sister, "I'm going to repeat this one time, but that's it. After that, you're on your own. Mom said, 'Go into the same room. Don't yell down the hall. And give your full attention to your request.' Do you get it?"

"Yeah, I guess so," Daniel answered.

### Questions

- What is nonverbal communication?
- What were some of Daniel's nonverbal communication moves?
- What did these actions communicate to his mom?
- What great nonverbal communication tips did Daniel's mom give to Daniel?
- Why are these important for getting what we need?

### Bible Discovery

Read these Bible verses: Exodus 20:12; Leviticus 19:3; 1 Peter 2:17.

### Bible Point

God expects us to treat others with respect. This means giving them our full attention when we talk with them.

### Bottom Line

Getting what you need begins with nonverbal communication.

## *Pretty Please?*

The big eighth-grade banquet was almost here. Carrie was so excited about the evening's plans that she could hardly wait. For weeks she had thought about what she was going to wear and how she would look. She had a fabulous dress, knockout shoes, and a terrific new hairstyle that she had seen in a magazine. There was only one problem—a coat. It was still cool outside and not one of her school coats was appropriate for such a dressy occasion. But her older sister,

Dawn's, coat was perfect. All week long, Carrie worried about how she would ask Dawn if she could borrow the coat. If there was something her sister was tight about, it was letting Carrie borrow clothes.

Earlier in the week, Carrie even went to her mom and asked for her advice on how to approach Dawn. Her mom had given her some really good ideas on how to best bring up the subject. "Be polite, number one," her mom told her. "Be sure you ask her in a polite voice without being demanding. It's her coat, and she can say no if she wants to. But I think please, thank you, and some extra good manners will go a long way."

Carrie thought for a long time about what her mother had said, and finally she decided to go ahead and ask Dawn. When she approached her sister like her mom had advised, Carrie was surprised at how easy it was. Dawn was a little hesitant, but Carrie's polite behavior won her over. Carrie was going to look great in the coat for the banquet!

Later Carrie told her mom, "I couldn't believe how nice Dawn was. She said I could wear the coat as long as I took good care of it. She even said that she would like to take a picture of me all dressed up."

"That's great," replied Mom. "I'm always amazed at how far a little politeness will go. That's a very important lesson to learn in getting what you need. Ask in a nice and respectful way—be polite."

### Questions

- What does it mean to be polite?
- Why does being polite help you get what you need?
- What were some specific examples of Mother's advice to Carrie?
- How could Carrie have asked to borrow the coat in ways that would *not* have been polite?
- In what ways can you be more polite when communicating with your family?

### Bible Discovery

Read these Bible verses: Proverbs 11:17; 1 Thessalonians 5:13; Titus 3:2.

### Bible Point

Being polite with others shows respect and consideration for them. The Bible teaches that those who are kind and considerate to others will be blessed.

Bottom Line

Being polite helps you get what you want.

## *The Curfew*

Compared to the other parents he knew, David thought his parents were pretty strict on their house rules. Curfew was a prime example. When all his friends were having fun at a party, David was usually outside waiting for his mom or dad to pick him up in time for his curfew. Despite the fact that he wished he could stay out a little later, David was careful to obey his parents' wishes. He rarely kept them waiting, and even when he did, it was only for five minutes or so while he told everyone good-bye.

The day for which he had been waiting finally arrived—his sixteenth birthday. He could drive, and he could date. David was excited beyond words. There was still one item up for discussion, however—his curfew. David had thought about how to approach the subject with his parents. He would be direct and adult about it, he decided. The worst thing they could say was no. David decided it was worth the risk.

One night after supper, David brought up the subject of curfews. Just as he was about to launch into his prepared speech, his father interrupted him. "Son, your mother and I have been talking lately. You haven't always agreed with the rules we've set for you, but you've always obeyed them. Whenever we increased your independence here and there, you always did very well with what you had been given."

At that point, David's mom jumped into the conversation. "It's easy to give you the freedoms and growing independence you need now that you're older because of the trust you've built in the past. Let this be a lesson to you. Your actions communicate what you're capable of handling. Because you've been trustworthy in these other areas, we have no doubt that you can handle a curfew extension responsibly."

David couldn't believe his ears. His mom and dad were actually going to give him the curfew extension he wanted, and he didn't even have to ask!

Questions

- What was David's attitude toward his parents' rules?
- What did David's obedience communicate to his parents?

- What do your actions communicate to your parents about your potential to be trusted?
- How does a track record of being trustworthy help you get what you need?

Bible Discovery

Read these Bible verses: Deuteronomy 28:1-2; Psalm 19:7, 11; John 14:23.

Bible Point

Those who have proven to be trustworthy in the past are likely to be trusted in the future.

Bottom Line

Trust is essential to getting what you want.

## *The What and the Why of It*

Michael was hoping to have the best weekend of his life starting this Friday. There was a terrific band in town who would be in concert. All of his buddies were going to the concert together, and they were going to spend the night at a friend's house afterward. It would be a terrific weekend, no doubt! But first Michael had to make sure it was all right with his parents.

When his mother picked him up after basketball practice at school, he launched right into a ninety-mile-an-hour speech on the weekend plans. He talked so fast it hardly made any sense. "Mom, you won't believe it. This is the *best!* They're the greatest group, and I can't believe they're going to be here Friday. And then we're going to spend the night out. It is going to be so much fun. So, can I go?"

"Wait a minute. Wait a minute. Hold on!" his mother interrupted. "I don't know what you're talking about, but I can't deal with that right now. I've got to get you over to the east side of town to get your hair cut. We're already late!"

Michael was disappointed that his mom had cut him off. He decided to wait until another time to ask her again.

Later that evening, Michael's father knocked on his door. "Come in," called Michael.

Dad entered and sat on the edge of the bed where Michael was sitting and reading. "Son, I hear you're talking about going somewhere this weekend with your friends?" he began. "Your mother told me something about a concert, but everything was pretty fuzzy. Here's some advice for the next time you want to ask our permission for something. We parents basically want to know two things—*what* you're asking and *why* you're asking. In other words, we want to know exactly what you want. But we also want to know why—the reasons. Practice answering these two things in a slow and brief way; then come to me and we'll sit down and talk about it. Oh, I'm also supposed to tell you that freshly baked chocolate chip cookies are now available in the kitchen." Then Dad got up and left the room.

Although Michael could smell the cookies, he thought about what his father had said. He knew his dad was right. So before going down to the kitchen, he practiced answering the what and why questions about the concert and the night with his friends. A few minutes later, he was sitting across from his parents at the kitchen table and discussing Friday night's plans.

### Questions

- Why did Michael's mom have a hard time granting him permission?
- Why is it important to answer the what and why questions?
- Do you think Michael's parents gave their permission for the concert and night out? Why?
- For what activity do you need to ask your parents' permission?
- How would you answer the what and why questions concerning that activity?
- Why does it help to practice what you want to say ahead of time?

### Bible Discovery

Read these Bible verses: Psalm 20:5; Matthew 7:7; Philippians 4:6.

### Bible Point

An important part of getting is asking. When we ask, we need to be clear about what we want and why we want it.

### Bottom Line

To get what you need, be sure to explain what you want and why.

## *Give and Take*

Brent was on the school baseball team. A few weeks after the season ended, the coach passed out information about a baseball camp in July. The camp was expensive, but Brent figured if he started saving now, by July he would have enough money to pay for everything. He was excited about the possibility of attending camp with some fantastic professional athletes scheduled to appear. And he would improve his skills as well.

Of course, he had to talk to his parents and get their permission before he could go. So one evening after dinner when everything had quieted down for the night, Brent saw his chance. *This will be a perfect time to ask,* he thought to himself. *They're bound to be as excited about it as I am.* Giving his request his full attention, he went to his parents and politely and respectfully explained all about the camp and why he wanted to go. He even shared his plan for saving the money. His parents thanked Brent for the way he had stated his request and said they would discuss it together and give him an answer in the morning.

The next day Brent asked if they had had time to talk yet. His mother replied, "Yes, we talked it over, and I'm afraid we'll have to say no. The dates of the camp are the same dates we've scheduled our family vacation. I'm sorry, Son."

Brent was deeply disappointed and upset. If this had happened a few months ago, he probably would have said something back in anger or stomped off to his room. This time, however, instead of pouting or rebelling, Brent remembered a lesson from a recent church youth group meeting—the art of compromise. Marianne, the youth director, had taught about the importance of being willing to give if we're willing to take.

A few minutes later, Brent asked his mom if they would consider allowing him to go if he could find another camp with different dates. His mom said that sounded like a great idea and that they would be willing to check into the possibility together.

Questions

- What did Brent do right when he asked his parents about the camp?
- Why did they say no?
- What do you think would have happened if Brent had responded to his mom's answer with anger or pouting?
- How was Brent willing to compromise?

- How can compromise help you get what you want?
- How do you usually respond when your request is answered with a "no"?

### Bible Discovery

Read these Bible verses: Leviticus 19:3; Proverbs 13:13; Matthew 15:4.

### Bible Point

The Bible tells children to respond to their parents' decisions with respect. Being willing to compromise is a respectful response.

### Bottom Line

Willingness to compromise can help you get what you need.

# 8 How to Look Good

## *Put On a Smile*

Jackie stood in front of her closet with one hand on her hip and a bad attitude in her heart. What was she supposed to wear to this dinner anyway? It was for her parents and their friends. Why did she have to go?

What she really wanted to do was play video games with Uncle Dan. Now *that* would be fun. But even Uncle Dan was putting on a suit to go with them. Finally Jackie picked out the red dress her mom had bought her last month for a piano recital. Her mom had been so cool that day. Too bad she wasn't being cool tonight. Did that noodle-brained dog drag her other shoe off somewhere?

Finally Jackie brushed her hair and said to herself in the mirror, "Well, I guess that's as good as it's going to get."

Uncle Dan and Jackie's father were sitting in the kitchen talking about a golf game when Jackie walked in. She rolled her eyes and sat down at the kitchen table with a sigh. Uncle Dan looked over at her and said, "When are you going to finish getting ready?"

"What do you mean?" Jackie asked. She looked down to make sure her socks matched.

"You go back upstairs and look for yourself." Uncle Dan almost seemed irritated with her.

When she looked in the mirror back in her room, she began to get irritated. She *was* ready. What did he know anyway?

Back down to the kitchen she flew. Her voice was a little louder than she meant it to be when she said, "What are you talking about Uncle Dan? I'm as ready as you are!"

"Oh no," he said. "You march right back up those stairs and don't come down again until you are completely ready to go."

Her dad just sat there as if he agreed! They must be losing their minds! Halfway up the stairs she heard them start laughing. Wait a minute! Was this some kind of joke? Uncle Dan walked toward her and said, "Jackie, you don't really need to go back upstairs. You can find what you're missing right down here." He pointed to the big mirror hanging in the living room.

When Jackie stood in front of the mirror, he put his face next to hers. "This is the test, Jackie. I'm ready to go, but you're not. Look in the mirror and see what I've got that you're missing." When Jackie looked into that mirror, her Uncle Dan broke out in the biggest, silliest smile she had ever seen. Even though she was irritated and tired and dreading the dinner, she had to smile too.

"There! You found it!" Uncle Dan called out.

"What?" Jackie called back, laughing for the first time that afternoon.

"Jackie, there's one thing you need to learn. The first step to getting ready and looking good is putting on a smile. You're definitely not going to have any fun without it."

Jackie grinned up at her uncle. Maybe if she worked at it, this evening wouldn't be so bad after all. Looking at her family, she said, "Well, are you all ready to go yet? My smile and I have been waiting forever!"

### Questions

- How does it feel to get dressed up when you don't want to?
- What kinds of things can we be happy about, even when we have to dress up?
- Does God care whether we smile or not?
- Why does smiling improve a person's appearance?

### Bible Discovery

Read these Bible verses: Psalm 68:3; Proverbs 17:22; Ecclesiastes 11:9; Matthew 5:16.

### Bible Point

Life is never perfect. We know, however, that no matter what happens, God is with us, and he has given us good things in life. If we go around with unhappiness on our face, we look worse, and we send the message that we don't have anything to be happy about. If we let God's goodness make us joyful, we feel better, look better, and help others feel better too.

Bottom Line

The first step to looking good is putting a smile on your face.

### *Do Everyone a Favor . . . Clean Up!*

Brian Moore's littlest sister, Kelly, was at the stage where she repeated *everything* anyone around her said. On a regular day, Brian found this annoying, but on *this* day, it was downright unbearable.

When Brian's mom, Mrs. Moore, picked up Brian and his friend Jeff from school, Kelly was strapped into her car seat in the backseat. While Mrs. Moore chatted for a minute with a teacher, Brian and Jeff discussed the day's events.

"The absolute worst," Brian said, "was when Miss Lucas moved my seat to behind Robbie Reiner. Man does he stink!"

"Oh yeah," said Jeff, "I sat by him in algebra last year. I wanted to tell him to hit the showers. What a pig!"

Just as Mrs. Moore sat back in the car, Kelly chirped up from her car seat, "What-a-pig, what-a-pig!"

Mrs. Moore turned to Jeff and Brian with that look that means "What's the story?"

"We were talking about a kid I had to sit by in class," Brian said. Then he held his nose to show his mom the problem.

Mrs. Moore didn't say a lot as she drove the guys to ball practice. Jeff's mom picked them up afterward and dropped Brian off at his house. Brian walked in to good news.

"How long till you can be ready to go out for pizza?" his mom asked.

"About as long as it takes me to put away my books and practice gear," Brian called back.

"Oh no," said Mrs. Moore. "Kelly and I are not riding with you smelling like that. I'm surprised that Jeff's mom didn't make you ride in the trunk."

"Oh, Mom, I'll take a shower in the morning. We won't see anybody we know. It'll just be family. I'll just put my stuff away."

Brian headed to his room without realizing that his mom was right behind him. "Brian," she said, "why did you talk the way you did in the car about your classmate? Did he hurt you?"

"No, Mom. He just wasn't clean," Brian answered.

"Did he look bad?" she asked.

"Who knows? I was too busy holding my nose . . ." Brian heard his own words and knew he had been caught. Even before he looked over at his mom, he knew that she was standing there holding her nose and laughing at him.

"Brian, an important part of looking good *and* being kind to others is to clean up so they won't smell you coming before they see you. People won't know how handsome you are if their first impression is that you need a shower. I know we're just family, but—"

"I know, Mom, I know. I'll take a quick shower so we can go to the pizza place and smell only the pizza."

Brian's mom smiled again. "Thanks. Now can you teach your sister something to say besides "What-a-pig?"

### Questions

- Do you think Robbie Reiner knew that he smelled bad?
- Why wasn't it as important to Brian to clean up for his family as for his friends?
- What makes someone smell clean as well as look clean?
- How can cleaning up improve a person's appearance?

### Bible Discovery

Read these Bible verses: Genesis 41:14; Ruth 3:3; 2 Samuel 12:20.

### Bible Point

In Bible times, like today, part of getting ready to meet someone was to wash up and put on clean clothes. This told other people that you cared about yourself. It also told them that they were important to you. When we clean up, we look better and show kindness to the people around us.

### Bottom Line

It doesn't matter how good you think you look if everyone else is wishing you'd take a shower.

## *Personal Best*

Jared lived in a house with his big brother, Justin; his little sister, Christy; and his dad. Jared's mom had died a long time ago.

Jared loved to go into Justin's room and try on his leather jacket. It smelled great and felt good. Of course, he only did this when Justin wasn't around, or he might have gotten into trouble. But each time Jared did it, he thought, *I hope one day this is a hand-me-down that I get to wear.*

Even though Jared was careful to not get caught, one day it happened. Justin walked in just as Jared had put on the jacket and was looking in the mirror.

"What are you doing?" Justin asked, but he didn't seem angry.

Jared quickly started taking off the jacket. "I was just thinking about how this will look when I finally get to wear it."

"Jared, why would you want to wear that old thing?" Justin asked.

"Because it smells great and feels great. Don't you like it anymore?"

Justin lay down across his bed as he said, "Sure, I like it. But it goes with *my* style. It doesn't look right at all with your clothes."

"But my clothes all used to be your clothes!" Jared shot back.

"No, they didn't," Justin answered. "Dad knows the difference between the things you like and the things I like. He buys you those loafers and khakis because that's what you like and look good in. He buys me a leather jacket and high-tops because that is my style."

Jared hadn't thought a lot about it, but for once, Justin was right. That night he asked his dad about it.

"Well, once you started choosing your own clothes," Dad said, "I could tell that you had different preferences than Justin. That's fine with me. What's important is that you find *your* personal best. I want you to know how to put on clothes that show you care about yourself and want to do your best. If that means jeans and sneakers, that's OK, as long as they are clean. If it means khakis and loafers, that's OK too, as long as they are cared for. What a person wears needs to fit who that person is and how he or she lives. If you try to be something you aren't, you won't look good, no matter how much you try. And I know it is important to you to look good, at least when you want to."

This was Jared's first conversation like this with his dad—you know, where his dad really sat and talked with him like he would with a friend. Jared liked it and didn't want it to be over too soon.

"What's your style, Dad?" he asked.

"I like to wear a sports jacket and shoes that are in between dress shoes and casual shoes. That way, if I have an appointment at work I can straighten my tie and look dressier, or I can take off my jacket and not look so dressed up. As you grow up, you'll find your own style."

After that, Jared didn't try on the leather jacket quite as much, just every now and then. And he started polishing his loafers himself. When his dad took him clothes shopping, he tried to think more about what *he* liked than what Justin wore.

Questions

- Why do you think Justin and Jared liked different kinds of clothes?
- What kinds of clothes do you like to wear?
- What kinds of clothes make you feel uncomfortable?
- How can finding your personal style help you look your best?

Bible Discovery

Read these Bible verses: Genesis 27:15; Numbers 18:29; Ecclesiastes 3:11.

Bible Point

Each person has his or her own style, no matter how flashy or calm. Esau had a distinctly different style than Jacob did. What is important to God is that you treat yourself with respect by finding your personal best and sticking with it.

Bottom Line

Don't try to be like everyone else. You're not in a competition. Be the best *you* there is.

## *Faddish!*

Jen always wanted the "in" thing. If there was a new fashion, she wanted it. If there was a new fad, she *had* to have it. If there was a new brand name, she wanted to be the first to wear it.

So? What was the problem? The problem was that Jen wasn't old enough to work. That means she depended on her parents to buy all her clothes. They didn't always have the money to buy her the latest fashions, and, to be honest, they didn't always want to.

They didn't want her to dye her hair a funny color or wear expensive makeup or play in tennis shoes that cost so much money. Now don't get the wrong idea. Jen's parents bought her nice stuff. They just bought it on sale or bought it even if it wasn't the most recognizable brand.

One day, Jen had had *enough.* She went to her mom to talk it out. "Mom, you always say that you want me to look good and to fit in with my friends at school. But you won't buy me the clothes I want, and that's making it really hard."

Mom didn't seem surprised at all by Jen's comments. It was almost as if she had been waiting for them. "Jenny—" only her mom called her that—"I think you need to learn the difference between *fashion* and *fad.* I think that if it were up to you, you would have every new thing that came out. We would be buying new clothes and accessories all the time. And, as you know, you aren't the only one in this family. All our money can't go to you and your outfits. I want you to have well-made clothes that are fashionable, but we can't throw out all your clothes every season for the new color or style."

Later that day, Mom asked Jen to come to the den. They sat back on the couch, and Mom pulled out her old yearbooks from high school. "Jenny, I think this will be a good way to show you what we were talking about earlier. Let's look through these books and see if we can pick out what styles were fads then and what were good fashion."

Jen and her mom looked through the books for almost an hour. By the end they were laughing and pointing and almost falling off the couch. Some of the clothes styles and hairstyles Mom and her friends wore in high school were hilarious—now. There were other styles that Jen saw, however, that were just as pretty now as they had been then. "That's the difference between fashion and fad, Jenny," said Mom. "It's OK for us to spend *some* of the money we work hard for on a few fun things for you to wear that you'll only like now. But we need to spend *most* of our money on things that you can feel good about when you look back at your yearbooks with your daughter."

The next time Jen and Mom went shopping, Jen tried to remember to look for stuff that would look good for a long time. And she thanked her mom for the money she got to spend.

### Questions

- What is a fad?
- Why do we get tired of some clothes after just a little while?
- Why does choosing "good fashion" over "fad" help a person look his or her best?
- When kids want one thing and parents want another, how can they work it out?

### Bible Discovery

Read these Bible verses: Ecclesiastes 8:1; Colossians 3:20; 1 Peter 3:8.

Bible Point

God asks us to be wise in everything. Sometimes the latest fashion seems like the thing we've just got to have. But remember to depend on your parents' wisdom and your own closet to help you make wise clothing and accessory purchases. Don't let some fad dictate how you will spend your money.

Bottom Line

Build your wardrobe on basic clothes that will look good for a long time.

## *Confidence*

Tim worried a lot more than anybody thought. He worried about whether people liked him. He worried about his looks (he didn't think he was very good looking). He worried about whether girls would go out with him when he was *finally* old enough to ask them out. He worried about his parents because they were always fighting. He worried about his grandfather because he was getting old.

Tim worried so much that when he went to school, he forgot to talk to people sometimes. He would rush from one class to another trying to do his homework on the way.

Tim needed some confidence. He needed confidence that he was a nice person and that people liked him. He needed confidence in his parents, that they could handle their own problems. He needed confidence in God, that God could handle the problems he and his parents couldn't.

You might think that Tim's classmates at school would have known he was worried, but they didn't. To them he was an OK-looking guy who made good grades. They just thought that *he* didn't like *them!*

That's what happens sometimes when a person is shy or scared. The person clams up and doesn't tell anybody about it. Everyone else thinks that he or she is a snob.

Tim found this out one day when he got a new lab partner, Rita. They were putting away the Bunsen burners when Rita asked, "Tim, why don't you like anybody here?"

Tim looked at Rita for a second and realized the mistake he had made. He answered, "I like *everyone* here. I'm just afraid they won't like me."

Rita rolled her eyes. "Get into the real world, Tim. You've got to let people know what you're thinking, or you'll never know if they like you or not."

On the way home, Tim decided he needed to start doing things a little differently. Even though he was still worried, he decided to start talking to more kids at school. He even prayed about it, asking God to give him the confidence to make more friends. By the end of that semester, he had quite a few friends and was feeling a lot better about everything.

At the beginning of the next term, Tim got another new lab partner, Diane. He had heard that she was a stuck-up snob, so he dreaded meeting her. But before he entered class, he thought, *Maybe Diane is just worried too. Instead of thinking that she might not like me, maybe I should just think about letting her know that I'll be her friend.*

It doesn't always work this way, but when Tim made an effort to be friends with Diane, he discovered that she wasn't stuck-up at all. Her parents had just split up, and she was a little nervous about a new school.

The more confidence Tim developed, the better his life became. When he looked in the mirror, he thought he looked much better now that he had gained some confidence. But the way he looked hadn't changed. He just changed the way he looked at himself by trusting God, believing in himself, and helping other people to do the same thing.

### Questions

- Was Tim the best-looking guy in the class?
- Why did Tim look better to himself when he had more confidence?
- How does having confidence help a person look good?
- What causes you to lose confidence?
- What can you do to be a more confident person?

### Bible Discovery

Read these Bible verses: 1 Peter 3:3-4; 2 Timothy 1:7; Hebrews 13:5-6.

### Bible Point

An important part of looking good has nothing to do with what's on your body and everything to do with how you feel about yourself. Trust God that you are just like he wants you to be and believe in yourself! Trust him to take care of you. Try to help other people instead of worrying about what they say about you. If you make a mistake, that's OK; everyone does sometimes. God is on your side, and you should be too.

### Bottom Line

The finishing touch to every outfit is your confidence and kindness in addition to what you're wearing. Confidence can help you look good.

# 9

# How to Feel Good

### *You Are What You Eat*

The alarm rang—right in Lindsay's ear. She hit the snooze button, pulled the pillow over her head, and went right back to sleep. Ten minutes later the alarm jangled again. Lindsay opened one eye and peeked at the clock. "Ten more minutes," she mumbled and whacked the snooze button once more. All too soon, Lindsay was pulled out of dreamland by the alarm and Mom calling.

By the time Lindsay got to the kitchen, she had exactly seven minutes to eat breakfast and get to the bus. She grabbed two pieces of white toast, slapped on some jelly, and washed them down with a glass of apple juice. As Lindsay ran out the door, she yelled, "Bye, Mom. I'll be home late. Got a volleyball game after school."

About ten o'clock Lindsay's stomach started rumbling and grumbling. She sure hoped no one else could hear the noise. It sounded like a growling monster that wanted to be fed. Then Lindsay remembered that she had bought a candy bar yesterday and had stuck it in her jacket pocket.

"This is great," Lindsay said as she munched on the candy bar between classes.

"I don't know," said Jane. "I think my apple is better for me."

Lindsay thought about that and answered, "You sound like my mom. At least I won't starve before lunch!"

Lindsay's stomach did stop growling, but it sure was hard to pay attention to the math assignment. She just couldn't concentrate on percentages, decimals, and fractions. Her mind seemed to be stuck in low gear, and she felt as though she was going to fall asleep right at her desk. Fortunately, she was saved by the bell, and she hurried off to lunch.

Most of the time, Lindsay brought a sack lunch, but today she had money to buy her food. Lindsay quickly chose a hot dog with everything on it, a small bag of chips, some apple juice, and a big chocolate chip cookie. When she joined her friends at the table, all the girls were talking about the volleyball game. Lindsay was a starter, and she was feeling excited and nervous at the same time. "That other team is really good. We will have to play our super best to win," she said.

Later, as the team was getting ready for the game, Lindsay flopped down on the floor to tie her shoes and sighed.

Coach Reynolds came over. "Something wrong?" she asked.

"No, I'm just tired and my head's starting to hurt. I sort of feel like I have jelly legs. You know—no muscles, just jelly," answered Lindsay.

"Hmmm! What did you eat today?" the coach asked. Lindsay ran through her food intake for the day.

"Not much energy-building food in that diet, Lindsay. You need healthy food to feel good and do your best," said Coach Reynolds. "Drink a carton of milk and eat some fruit before the game. That should help put some muscle back in your jelly legs."

### Questions

- Why was Lindsay feeling the way she did?
- How could Lindsay have improved her eating habits?
- In what ways do healthy foods help you feel and do your best?
- How can you improve your diet?

### Bible Discovery

Read these verses: Daniel 1:8, 12-15; 1 Corinthians 10:31.

### Bible Point

When considering food, remember these two words: *quantity* and *quality*. Quantity means the amount. Eating too much or too little are both bad, affecting a person's weight and energy. Quality means eating a variety of healthy foods. God didn't make the human body to run on garbage. Unless the right quality of food is there, the body won't work as well as it was meant to.

### Bottom Line

Eat for your health.

## *Choose Life*

Bryan was not happy. In fact he was boiling mad and frustrated. Worst of all, he couldn't really do anything about the situation. Well, maybe he could write a letter to the school board. But, no, that wouldn't change anything. Bryan had liked Wentworth Junior High. It was close to home, and he had lots of friends there. Why did the school board decide it was too crowded and switch some of the students to Central? And why had he been one of the kids who had to switch? It just didn't seem fair.

After two months here at Central, Bryan still felt like an outsider. He was doing OK in his classes and he liked most of the teachers, but he felt lonely. He missed his old friends at his old school.

Bryan knew who the most popular boys at Central were. Everyone knew them—Jesse, Mike, Pat, Doug, and Matt always seemed to do everything together. They came to school together, ate lunch together, hung around together in the halls, and went home together. They usually had a crowd around them telling jokes, laughing, and having a good time.

Jesse sat next to Bryan in English class. They had only talked to each other a few times when Jesse didn't understand what Ms. Julian was saying. So Bryan was quite surprised when Jesse stopped him after class one day. "Know many kids yet?" he asked Bryan.

"No, not really," mumbled Bryan.

Jesse thought a minute and then said, "Tell you what. Meet me in the park across the street after school. I'll introduce you to some of the guys."

Bryan could hardly believe his ears. "Sure," he blurted out. "See you at three."

After school he headed to the park. *Maybe school is going to be more interesting,* he thought. If he became friends with Jesse and the others, things were sure to improve.

Bryan crossed the street and there they were—standing around, laughing and joking. "Hey, Bry!" Jesse yelled. "Glad you came. Meet some new friends."

Bryan smiled and hurried toward them. Then the smile faded and he froze in his tracks. Every boy had a cigarette in his fingers or in his mouth. "We saved one for you, Bry," Jesse said as he held the pack toward Bryan.

Bryan remembered an article he had read in a magazine. It had talked about how harmful things like cigarettes, drugs, and alcohol were "power stealers." They stole power and energy from the body and should always be avoided.

Bryan shook his head and pushed away the cigarettes. "I don't smoke. Cigarettes can kill me," said Bryan as he turned and walked away.

Bryan could hear Jesse and his friends making fun of him and calling him names as he recrossed the street. *Those kinds of friends I don't need,* he thought as he headed home. Suddenly Bryan began to feel more sure of himself and happier than he had in months.

### Questions

- Why did Bryan want to be one of Jesse's friends?
- Why do you think Jesse invited Bryan to meet his friends?
- How does smoking stop people from feeling good?
- What are some other harmful things people may want you to try?
- How can you keep from getting involved with those things?

### Bible Discovery

Read these verses: Deuteronomy 30:19; 1 Corinthians 6:19-20.

### Bible Point

Harmful activities such as drinking, smoking, and using drugs are "power stealers." They take away our power for living and hurt us. We need to make a choice. We can choose to get involved with these power stealers or we can say no to them and feel good about ourselves.

### Bottom Line

Stay away from harmful activities.

## *Use It or Lose It!*

Mr. Riley taught health at Washington School. He believed his students remembered important information better when they saw it as well as heard it. So the classroom was plastered with large, colorful posters—one or two covering every topic. Mr. Riley used the posters to emphasize what he was talking about. The poster for exercise and fitness was one of his favorites. The illustration showed two kids—an energetic exerciser and a couch potato. USE IT OR LOSE IT! was written across the top in huge fluorescent letters.

"Your bodies need to exercise every day," Mr. Riley explained. "Use those muscles or they will become flabby, and you will feel sort of droopy and listless."

Mr. Riley asked, "Are you a user or a loser? How do you spend each day from the time school's out until bedtime? Do you use those muscles, or are they turning to mush?" The students wiggled in their seats and looked out the window, but no one said anything.

Mr. Riley gave them an assignment. During the next two weeks they were to exercise more each day. Then they would report back with the results. Samantha, Jamal, and Matt were among the students in Mr. Riley's health class. They each needed to improve their daily exercise habits.

Samantha always had lots of homework. She sat in her room studying most evenings. Once in a while she watched a favorite TV show. She decided to get more exercise by walking home from school each day instead of riding. Samantha also decided on a fifteen-minute break every hour while she studied. She did exercises to music, rode her bike, or walked the dog during the breaks. These activities made her feel more energetic and helped her concentrate on her homework.

Every day Jamal went home to an empty house. Usually he found something to eat and then watched TV or played computer games until Dad came home. He did his homework after dinner. Jamal decided he definitely needed to use his muscles for more than eating and sitting. So he eliminated afterschool TV and computer games from his daily schedule. Instead, Jamal and some friends met at the park each day after school. They played basketball, football, soccer or some other active sport until dinnertime. Jamal soon found he had more energy and stamina. His muscles grew stronger, and he was in better shape.

Matt's exercise habits were like a roller coaster. Some days he would plop in a chair and read or listen to music in his room. On other days he would ride his bike, jog with his dad, or do his jobs around the house.Matt decided to even out his exercise habits. So every day, even if he was reading or listening to music, he did something active for at least thirty to forty-five minutes. The everyday use of his muscles gave them more firmness and strength.

Questions

- What does "use it or lose it" mean to you?
- In what ways are you like Samantha, Jamal, or Matt?

- What do you do after school?
- How can you get more exercise into each day?

Bible Discovery

Read these Bible verses: Proverbs 6:6-8; 1 Corinthians 9:24-27.

Bible Point

God made our bodies to move and be active. An important part of feeling good and doing our best is exercise. The phrase "use it or lose it" is true when it comes to muscles. If we don't exercise our muscles regularly, we become listless and may put on weight.

Bottom Line

To feel good, exercise your body every day.

## *Recharging*

Hurry, hurry, hurry! Go here! Go there! Do this! Do that!

These words seemed to bounce around in Sonia's brain like an annoying song as she went through her busy day. *How am I going to make it from soccer practice to choir and still have time to eat dinner?* she wondered as she grabbed her shoes from her locker and headed to the soccer field. Sonia always seemed to be going somewhere, and she always seemed to be in a hurry.

Sonia liked being involved in lots of different activities. She was on a soccer team, took art classes, and sang in the youth choir at church. Sometimes she also baby-sat for Mrs. Wilson, her next-door neighbor. On top of it all, there were family chores and homework to do each day.

At the end of a particularly hectic week, Sonia dragged herself into the lunchroom. She plopped down on a bench next to her friend Megan and stared out into space. Megan started talking to Sonia about a book she had just read. There was no response from her. "Yoo-hoo! Earth to Sonia," said Megan. "You haven't heard a word I said. Hey, you don't look so good. Are you sick?"

"Not really," sighed Sonia. "I'm just *so* tired. I'll probably fall asleep at choir practice or paint my hand instead of the paper in art class. I still have to write a book report for tomorrow too. I wish I hadn't waited until the last minute to do it. I'll never get it all done!"

"Maybe you need to quit doing so many things and relax a bit," suggested Megan.

"But I like everything I do," said Sonia. "I wouldn't know which activity to cut out. Maybe I could quit doing my homework; then I'd have more time."

Megan laughed. "Good try, Sonia, but you know that won't work. Come on, think. What else can you do so you won't be so wiped out?" she asked.

Sonia thought about it between yawns. "Well, I *could* go to bed earlier—maybe at nine-thirty instead of ten. I feel like I have a bad case of 'brain drain' by that time anyway," Sonia answered.

"Sounds like a good plan to me," Megan said. "Now let's finish lunch so we can have a break before math class."

"You just gave me another idea," Sonia told her friend. "I can take little breaks when I'm working. That will help too. Thanks, Meg!"

"Don't mention it! Just call me Megan, Doctor of Rest," said Megan in a deep, dignified voice.

Questions

- What was Sonia's problem?
- What suggestions would you make to Sonia?
- When do you feel like Sonia? Why?
- In what ways do you need to improve your sleep and rest habits?
- How will you do it?

Bible Discovery

Read these Bible verses: Genesis 2:1-3; Exodus 20:9-11.

Bible Point

God created us with a need for rest and sleep. If we go without enough sleep for long periods of time, we can have real problems. We will feel lethargic, grumpy, and unable to think very clearly. We also need to relax and take breaks when we are working or feeling stressed out. Taking a walk, daydreaming, or just being alone for a while can help recharge us.

Bottom Line

To feel good, get enough rest and sleep to "recharge."

## *Attitude Check*

Josh and Manuel lived in the same neighborhood, went to the same school, and played on the same baseball team. They were alike in some ways. Both boys were about the same size, and they both did well in school. But Josh and Manuel were completely different in how they regarded people and events in their lives.

Manuel saw the bright side of situations—he had an optimistic attitude. Josh always seemed to think of everything that was bad about something. Josh complained and grumped about lots of things.

One Monday Mr. Grimes, the history teacher, announced, "I want each of you to write a two-page report about a famous person. The person can be living or dead, but you need to tell how his or her life influenced others. Reports are due next Monday."

Josh grumbled and moaned to anyone within earshot about how tough the assignment was. Thursday when he walked to school with Manuel, Josh complained, "I have no idea who to write about. We don't have enough time to do this. And it's too long; who can write that much?"

Manuel said, "I went to the library and found rows of books about famous people. I'm reporting on Francis Scott Key, the writer of the 'Star Spangled Banner,' It was really interesting reading about him. I learned a lot of neat stuff."

The favorite afterschool activity for the neighborhood boys was a pickup game of basketball in the park. Jim, who worked for the Park Recreation League, supervised the games to keep order. He took a real interest in the boys who played and often watched their games.

Each day they would choose up sides and go at it. Sometimes it got a little rough, but no one was hurt and everyone had a good time. Well, almost everyone.

Josh used his mouth as much as his hands and feet. "Pass the ball to me; I never get to shoot. That was a foul. I should shoot a free throw," he'd complain.

One day before the game started, Jim said, "You're a pretty good player, Josh."

"None of the guys think so. I'm always the last one chosen for a team," Josh replied.

"Well, Josh," said Jim, "maybe you need to have a better attitude. People like being around someone who's cheerful and optimistic rather than negative and complaining. There are a lot of things you're stuck with, like your size and eye color. But you can *choose* the kind of attitude you want to have."

Josh thought about what Jim said while he waited, with a smile, to see which team got him.

### Questions

- What's the difference between Josh's and Manuel's attitudes?
- Which boy would you choose for a friend? Why?
- Do you tend to be more like Josh or Manuel?
- Why is it important to have a positive attitude?
- How can your attitude affect others?

### Bible Discovery

Read these Bible verses: Proverbs 15:13; Philippians 4:11-12.

### Bible Point

There's an old saying: "Honey attracts more flies than vinegar." The same can be said about a person's attitude. A complaining, pessimistic attitude chases people away. People enjoy being around those who have a positive attitude. An optimistic attitude makes us feel good and look good. A smile is always more attractive than a frown.

### Bottom Line

To feel good, develop a positive attitude.

# How to Do Your Best

## *Nothing to Cheer About*

"We are the Hawks, the mighty, mighty Hawks!"

For the seventh time that evening, Lauren and Charmaine practiced the cheer that they were certain would land them spots on the cheerleading squad. It was late Saturday evening, and Lauren was staying overnight at Charmaine's.

Charmaine's dad knocked on her bedroom door. "OK, girls. It's bedtime. That was your last cheer."

"But Dad," Charmaine replied. "tryouts are Monday after school. We've *got to* make the squad."

"Well, right now you've *got to* get ready for bed. Good night."

The girls turned to what they would wear for the tryouts. It was nearly 1 A.M. when they finally turned out the light. The next morning Lauren and Charmaine had to be called several times to get up.

"Girls, we're leaving for church in twenty-five minutes," Charmaine's mom shouted. "You don't want to be late for your first time helping with Sunday school."

Lauren looked at Charmaine. "Yikes! We forgot to prepare the Bible lesson for the kids!"

"Oh no," Charmaine moaned. "We were supposed to do that last night. I guess we got carried away with practicing cheers. I hate to let the kids down."

When the girls rushed to the breakfast table, it was obvious that they were upset. "What's wrong now?" Dad asked.

Charmaine spilled out all the details—how they had volunteered to help in the third-grade Sunday school class but had forgotten, so they weren't prepared.

"Look," interjected Dad, "I know we don't have time for a lecture right now. It was obvious to everyone in the house last night that the cheerleading tryouts are very important to you girls—more important than sleep and, now we learn, more important even than your other commitments. That's too bad. I'll help you put a lesson together for the class, but I hope you've learned *your* lesson. To do your best, do what's most important first, and that begins with your relationship with God."

Lauren nodded sadly and said, "You're right, Mr. Davis. Our promises to God are more important than cheerleading."

### Questions

- Why do you suppose Lauren and Charmaine agreed to help with Sunday school?
- How did they let this commitment slip their minds?
- Why was cheerleading so important?
- When would have been a better time to practice?
- What happens to your closeness to God when other activities take over?
- What can you do to guard against this?

### Bible Discovery

Read these Bible verses: Joshua 23:6-8; Matthew 6:33-34; Colossians 2:5-7.

### Bible Point

Only God is worth a person's complete attention and devotion. Other activities and goals have their place, but sometimes they get in the way of a relationship to God. Just as Joshua and Paul encouraged believers to keep their promises to God, the Lord urges us to keep our commitments to him and obey his Word.

### Bottom Line

To do your best, do what's important first and stay close to God.

## *The Real Deal*

Grace stared at the lunchroom bulletin board. It was filled with flyers announcing next week's tryouts for the varsity chorus, informational meetings for the fall sports, and the first get-togethers of every club imaginable. To Grace's eyes, it soon became a blur.

"Isn't it great?" exclaimed a voice next to her. "What are you going to try for?" Grace hadn't even noticed that her good friend Becky had walked up.

"Oh, I don't know," mumbled Grace. "My dad keeps bugging me to join the chess club. Says he's sure I could be the star since I had such a great teacher—him. My mom wants me to go for the lead in the musical this year."

Just then Coach Larson walked up—he was a favorite at school. Besides coaching track, he was also a school counselor. "My advice," he said with a smile and a short laugh, "would be to go out for track. We'll run, run, run in the sun, sun, sun and have fun, fun, fun!"

"Grace's problem, Coach," began Becky, "is that she is good at so many things that she doesn't know which activities to choose!"

"Right!" said Grace sarcastically. "That's not even close. Actually, Coach, my problem is that a lot of people are giving me advice about what I should do, and I'm not sure what to choose."

Coach Larson thought for a moment. "But what do *you* want to do, Grace?" he asked.

"Huh? Well, I guess . . ." Grace looked down as she searched for an answer. Then she looked up and replied, "Honestly, I don't really know. My brother says, 'Don't try for something if you can't be number one.' But then, he's used to seeing his name in the paper."

"Well your brother certainly was an outstanding student, in many areas," replied Coach Larson, "but you're a different person. You are outstanding too, but in *your* way, not his. Think about what *you* would enjoy doing." Glancing at the clock, he exclaimed, "Oops, I'm supposed to be at a meeting!" He rushed off.

"He's right," said Becky. She turned again to the bulletin board. "Which of these things looks fun to you?"

Grace reread some of the notices. She thought about the times she had gone to plays and dreamed not of capturing the limelight but of painting realistic scenery. Art class was at least something she enjoyed.

"The drama club could be interesting," she finally said. "Maybe I could work backstage on the musical."

Becky smiled. "That's more like it. That sounds more like *you.*"

Questions

- How might Grace answer her family's expectations?
- Why is it good to choose activities that you enjoy?

- What do you think interests have to do with abilities?
- Who or what can help people discover their gifts?

### Bible Discovery

Read these Bible verses: Exodus 4:1-17; Acts 18:1-3, 24-26; Ephesians 4:11-13; 1 Peter 4:10-11.

### Bible Point

God made each person with a unique combination of interests and abilities. The early church needed the well-known Paul, but it also needed the quiet, home-based ministry of Priscilla and Aquila. What we enjoy provides a big clue to the area in which we will do well. Beware of being pressured toward a certain arena.

### Bottom Line

To do your best, get to know the real you and do what you enjoy.

## *When the Shoe Doesn't Fit*

"Hey, are you *Kevin* Seeley's little brother?" the gym teacher asked.

Mark smiled politely and for the umpteenth time that week replied, "Yes, I am." Then to himself, he continued, *Yes, I am the little, puny, sixth-grade brother of the greatest basketball player to ever walk onto a court in this or any other town.*

"Boy, those are pretty big shoes to fill. Think you'll be as good as he is?" asked the teacher.

Mark shrugged his shoulders and hurried away. *Why did Kevin have to be so great anyway?* he thought. Kevin had been a star at Mark's school, and now, four years later, he was the starting center for the high school varsity team and leading the league in scoring.

At lunch, Mark told his friend Tom about the latest tribute-to-Kevin experience. "You know, some days I never even want to hear the word *basketball* again," he exclaimed. Mark ate a few more bites of his sandwich and then continued. "But the crazy thing is, I really like the game. I've even thought about trying out for the team next year."

"But what if you're not as good as Kevin?" Tom asked.

"That's a good question," Mark answered. "And that's what worries me."

After school, Mark walked home with Tom. After shooting baskets in the driveway for a while, they went inside for a drink. Just then, Tom's older brother, Trent, walked in the door. He was attending a local junior college, and he helped with the junior high youth group at church. He and Mark had hit it off pretty well.

"Hey, Trent," Mark began, "let me ask you something."

"Shoot!" answered Trent. Then Mark explained his frustration at being compared to his older brother and his question about trying out for basketball himself.

Trent listened carefully and said, "Actually, Mark, you may never be as good as Kevin—let's face it, he's great! But that's OK. Remember the pastor's sermon last Sunday? He emphasized doing *our* best in life. So don't worry if you're not as good as someone else, even your brother; just do *your* best instead of trying to be a Kevin clone."

"Thanks, Trent," said Mark. "That helps a lot. Maybe I'll go to a basketball camp this summer and work on *my* game."

### Questions

- When have you felt like Mark at the beginning of the story?
- What do you think God expects of Mark?
- What was good about Trent's advice?
- How can we keep the reputations of others in perspective?
- What do you think of Mark's plan?

### Bible Discovery

Read these Bible verses: 1 Timothy 4:11-16; 2 Timothy 2:15; Hebrews 11:32-38.

### Bible Point

God does not have one set of shoes for everyone to fill. Just as God's Word commends the boldness of Paul and the relative quietness of Timothy, it commends our attempts to do the best *we* can. In the "faith hall of fame" found in Hebrews 11, the common denominator is not achievements but each individual's faithfulness to God and commitment to do what he required of them.

### Bottom Line

To do your best, be *yourself* and don't try to be anyone else.

### *Excuses, Excuses*

Homework time. Sue went over to her desk, sat down, and opened her assignment notebook.

"A chapter to read in history," she said aloud, "and start researching my project for the science fair. Oh, and that math test tomorrow. Well, nothing to worry about there."

Sue had been sailing along in math for the last month. The subject had always come easily to her. *Why study for the test?* she reasoned. *I'd rather go to the library and get a jump on the science-fair competition.*

It was a wobbly version of Sue who made her way to her locker the next afternoon. The math test had been a killer. She was still in shock. She knew that she would be lucky to get a C on it.

Her math teacher, Mr. Collins, happened to walk by just then. "Oh, Sue. Glad to catch you. I glanced at the tests and, I must say, I expected better from you. Didn't you study for this?"

"Uh . . . yeah, sure I did. I mean, a little. But it's really my parents' fault. They're putting a lot of pressure on me to win the science fair, and I had to work on that last night."

She could hardly look at Mr. Collins. "Oh, really?" he asked, voicing his concern. "That's a tough situation. Are you sure they made you bomb this test? I could talk with them, if you like."

Sue looked up with panic in her eyes. "No! Don't do that. I'll take care of it."

Sue was one of Mr. Collins's favorite students. He knew she could do much better, so he said, "Sue, from your reaction to my suggestion, my guess is that what you said about your parents was just an excuse. As a teacher, I hear a lot of excuses. I've even heard the old my-dog-ate-it excuse for not turning in a homework assignment. Believe me, I'd much rather hear the truth than excuses. And we'd both be better off."

"The truth is—" Sue took a deep breath and then continued—"the truth is that I thought I didn't need to study. I guess I learned my lesson."

Questions

- In what school subjects or other activities do you feel the most confident?
- Why did Sue try to blame her problem on her parents?
- Why do people make excuses?

- What do you suppose God thinks when we try to pass the blame?

Bible Discovery

Read these Bible verses: Genesis 3:8-13; 2 Samuel 11:1-5; 12:1-14; James 1:12-16.

Bible Point

One of the oldest human tricks in the book is to make excuses. Adam tried to pass the blame for his sin onto Eve; Eve then blamed the serpent. Ever since, people have in various ways tried to avoid owning up to their mistakes and sins. God wants us to own up to our mistakes and be responsible. If we fail, we should admit it, take the consequences, and learn from the experience.

Bottom Line

To do your best, don't make excuses.

## *Try, Try, Try*

It was Wednesday, the day of the county orchestra tryouts. Mike was there, cello in hand.

*OK, OK, stay calm,* he told himself. He remembered what his mom had said at dinner the night before: "The worst that can happen is that you might not make the orchestra. I doubt that will happen, but it might. Even if that happens, it won't be fatal. We'll still love you and support you. But at least you will have given it your best shot!"

By thinking about his family's support, Mike was able to stay fairly calm and do his best.

That evening he got a phone call from the conductor. "Mike? This is Mr. Peters from the county orchestra. You did a fine job in tryouts, but I'm afraid you didn't make the orchestra. As you know, the competition was brutal, especially with all the older students who tried out. I hope you'll try again next year; you have a nice technique."

"Oh, all right, uh, thanks, Mr. Peters. Good-bye." Mike banged down the phone, stomped off to his room, and slammed the door. His mom gave him a few minutes to himself and then knocked on his door.

"C'mon in, if you want to talk with a loser," Mike almost yelled.

When Mom walked in, he continued. "Thanks for having me make a fool of myself, Mom. I'm going to quit cello—I'm no good at it."

His mom took a deep breath and let it out slowly. "What exactly did Mr. Peters say?" she asked.

Mike told her.

"Mike, that doesn't sound like encouragement to quit playing," she said. "You just weren't ready for this, and you heard what he said about the level of competition. There's always next year."

"But I'm a failure, Mom," Mike groaned. He lay back on his bed.

"A failure?" Mom exclaimed. "No, not yet. A failure would drop the cello. A failure would not consider trying out next year." Mike sat up and looked at his mother. She was looking right at him and speaking intently. "God has given you the gift of music and the opportunity to enjoy it. Don't throw those away."

Mike looked down, back up at his mom, and then over at his cello case. "You're right, Mom. I enjoy playing too much to give it up."

### Questions

- Should Mike have expected God to give him a place in the county orchestra?
- When have you faced a disappointment like Mike's?
- Why did Mike feel like quitting?
- What do you think of his mother's definition of failure?
- What will be your reaction the next time you feel like quitting after a setback?

### Bible Discovery

Read these Bible verses: Mark 14:66-72; Acts 2:1, 37-41; 2 Timothy 4:9-11.

### Bible Point

At some point, everyone suffers setbacks, makes mistakes, and commits a sin. These do not take God by surprise and do not signal the end of his confidence in people. Peter went so far as to deny Jesus, but shortly after Jesus' resurrection, he had become an effective leader of the young church. When we fall down, we should get up and try again.

### Bottom Line

To do your best, try again after setbacks or failures.

# 11

# How to Do Well in School

### *The Balancing Act*

The first week of junior high school was just about over. Liz was excited—the weekend! Her first plan was to sleep over at her friend Barb's on Friday night and sleep in on Saturday before taking a much needed trip to the mall. She had heard rumors of a party on Saturday night too.

The first part of the weekend went just about as expected. At church on Sunday morning, she heard about a roller-skating get-together that afternoon. She asked her parents if she could go.

"What about homework?" asked her mom.

"Oh, I don't have much," Liz replied. "And I'll be home in plenty of time this afternoon to get it done." The truth was that Liz could hardly remember what assignments she had.

Liz didn't get home until about four o'clock and was exhausted. When she got to her room, her bed looked incredibly inviting. I'll just rest my eyes a bit, and then I'll hit the books, she told herself.

The next thing Liz knew, her older sister, Gretchen, was knocking on her door, calling her to the dinner table. "Uh, come in," Liz said. "What time is it?"

"It's six-fifteen, Slumber Girl. I see you've made great progress on your homework."

"Oh, wow!" Liz exclaimed. "Well, maybe I don't have too much." She reached for her still-unopened backpack. When she pulled out the large social studies and math textbooks, her assignments came back to her. "Gretchen, what am I going to do? There's a lot due tomorrow. And I promised Barb that we'd have a long phone conference tonight on how she can get Stephen to notice her."

Gretchen shook her head and smiled. "You remind me of someone else a few years ago."

"Who?" Liz wondered.

"Me. I got all overloaded with the social scene and by the third week of school, I was way behind in three classes. There's so much more to choose from now. I'll bet you plan to go to some club meetings this week and try out for the chorus, right?"

Liz nodded unhappily.

Gretchen hugged her and said, "You have to keep everything in balance. If you pile up responsibilities and obligations in any one area, the other areas will go out of whack. God gave you a great personality and lots of friends, but he also gave you a good mind. And he put you in a good school where you can learn a lot."

Liz smiled and said, "Thanks, Sis. I think I'll call Barb after dinner and tell her the consultation will have to wait until lunchtime tomorrow. I've got work to do tonight."

### Questions

- When have you felt like Liz did when she opened her backpack?
- Why do kids put off doing their homework?
- Why do people function best when things are in balance?
- What other steps could Liz take this week?

### Bible Discovery

Read these Bible verses: Psalm 90:12; Ecclesiastes 3:1-13.

### Bible Point

God made us to enjoy all kinds of things and to have many experiences—social, academic, spiritual. There is a time for everything in life. Life goes best when we keep responsibilities and activities in balance.

### Bottom Line

To do well in school, keep your life in balance.

## *Keep the Focus*

Liz finished her last slice of apple and took her final swallow of milk. OK, she told herself, afterschool snack time is over. Time to hit the homework!

She grabbed her backpack and headed to her room. When she got to her desk, she opened her backpack and took out her Spanish textbook. *Vocabulary words—that'll be easy,* she thought. So she found the right page and started down the list of words.

She got about halfway through the words when she remembered the math problem set was due the next day also. She pulled out the text and her notebook. *I'd better do these before I forget the tips Mrs. Nielsen gave us this morning,* she thought. Then the phone rang. It was Barb.

"What pages are we supposed to read in social studies?" Barb asked.

"Just a minute. Let me see." Liz dug around in her backpack. "Barb, I can't believe it. I forgot to bring the book home. I'll be right over—I know I'll remember when I see the book."

Liz went over to Barb's, where they took turns reading the chapter aloud. They had read about two-thirds of the assignment before Barb's mom called her for dinner. Liz went home and arrived just as her family was sitting down to dinner.

"Hi, Liz," her mom greeted her. "Thanks for leaving the note that you went to Barb's. I assume your homework was done before you left?"

"Actually, Mom, I was studying social studies with Barb. But we didn't quite finish." Liz paused and thought about the math and Spanish homework awaiting her. And who knew what else lurked in that backpack. But now it was time for supper; it had been awhile since those apple slices, so Liz was hungry.

Her older sister, Gretchen, passed Liz the salad and said, "So how's the student today?"

"Oh, great. Just great. I did nothing but homework after school, but I didn't finish anything. I started my Spanish vocabulary words; then I remembered a tricky thing about the math assignment. Then Barb called, and I realized that I had forgotten my social studies textbook."

"I know how that goes," Gretchen said sympathetically. "Do you still have that calendar book Mom bought with your school supplies? It's a good idea to write down each day's assignments."

"I do that sometimes. Guess I'd better not trust my memory so much."

Liz's mom added, "When you get home from school, you could check the calendar and see what needs your attention first. Then stick with that assignment until it's done. That will help you feel more in control, by staying organized and focusing on one thing at a time. Anything we can do to help you?"

"There's one thing," Liz answered. "After dinner, could you help me find that calendar?"

### Questions

- Why did Liz have trouble getting anything done?
- How hard or easy is it for you to focus on one task?
- What's wrong with working on different assignments at once?
- What tools do you have to stay organized with your school assignments?

### Bible Discovery

Read these Bible verses: Genesis 6:11-22; Luke 15:8-10; Philippians 3:12-14.

### Bible Point

The Bible records the accomplishments of many of God's people who had seemingly impossible tasks to do. They were able to do great—and small but important—things because they were clear about the job and then stuck with it until it was done.

### Bottom Line

To do well in school, be organized and focus on one task at a time.

## *Friend Trend*

"Hey, Liz, want to come over to my house after school?"

Liz closed her locker and looked into the smiling face of Louise. "Sure, thanks. We could quiz each other on Spanish."

"Maybe," said Louise. "But I bought some amazing CDs over the weekend that you must hear."

The girls went to Louise's house and soon were listening to the music. "This is terrific," Liz finally said, "but shouldn't we get busy on homework?"

"Later. Come over to the window. See that house down the block, the one with the green awnings? Guess who lives there." But before Liz could reply, Louise said, "Tim Hansen!"

"You're kidding!" said Liz. "He is really cute. Today at lunch I heard that . . ."

Soon it was time for Liz to go home. In the days that followed, she spent more and more time with Louise, especially after school and on weekends.

One evening after dinner, Liz's mom asked how things were going in school. Liz shrugged. "I asked because I got a call from your homeroom teacher today. She says you haven't been getting your assignments in on time. Any special reason?"

Liz shrugged again. Her mom continued, "I haven't seen Barb around lately. You two seemed to be good study buddies."

"Mom, how babyish. Barb's fine, but I'm really enjoying my new friend, Louise."

"And how are Louise's grades?" Mom asked.

"Well, she's not really into studying right now," answered Liz. "But she knows so much about music, it's amazing!"

Liz's mom took a deep breath. "Honey, friends can help you, or they can bring you down. Choose friends who will help you stick with your priorities."

"You can't tell me who to like!" yelled Liz. "You don't want me to have any friends!"

"I'm not telling you that you can't see Louise. But I think you've made a trade-off without even realizing it. You've neglected both Barb and your grades."

Liz was silent for nearly a minute. "I'll think about it," she said.

Questions

- What do you think of Liz's choices?
- How can Liz spend time with both Barb and Louise?
- What can friends do for us?
- Who are your friends and how do they help you?

Bible Discovery

Read these Bible verses: Nehemiah 2:16–3:5; Matthew 4:18-22; Acts 16:1-3; 18:1-18.

Bible Point

The Bible is about friendships as well as history and theology. Nehemiah, Jesus, and Paul chose friends and partners who would help them accomplish their goals.

Bottom Line

To do well in school, choose friends who will help you keep your priorities straight.

## *Help!*

Liz stared at the long rows of shelves in the reference section. She had always felt at ease and at home in a library, but today she felt like an alien.

Her first big term paper was due in three weeks, and she was determined to do a good job on it. She was reasonably interested in her topic, but she was baffled by the organization of the school library. She had missed the orientation tour during the first week of school. Now she was embarrassed to admit that she was having trouble finding the sources she needed.

That evening in her room she found herself staring again—this time at her notebook. Her older sister, Gretchen, stopped by and asked, "How's the junior high scene these days?"

"Pretty good, except for this stupid term paper," answered Liz.

"Oh? What's the problem?" Gretchen asked.

Liz frowned, then seemed near tears. "Actually, it's not the term paper that's stupid—it's me. I can't even figure out the library! How dumb is that?"

Gretchen smiled. "Hey, give yourself a break. You're not dumb. Have you ever done a paper this size?"

"Well, no," Liz answered.

"First, is there a handout or something that describes this project?" asked Gretchen. Liz pulled out a piece of paper from her notebook and handed it to her. Gretchen continued. "Always be sure you're clear about the assignment. Then swallow."

Liz looked up at her sister suddenly.

"Swallow your pride," Gretchen explained. "Admit that you don't understand it and need some help. Take the library, for instance. Explain your problem to one of the librarians—those people live for this stuff. And if you're still having trouble with the project, talk with your teacher. Soon."

Liz finally smiled. "I suppose it's better than waiting till the last minute to ask for help or turning it in late."

"You bet it is, Sis," said Gretchen. "You just have to know when to ask for help."

### Questions

- If you were the school librarian or the teacher who gave the term-paper assignment, what would you think of Liz's request for assistance now?
- Why can asking for help improve a student's performance in school?
- How hard is it for you to admit that you need help in school?
- How important is understanding the assignment?
- What other advice might you give Liz?

Bible Discovery

Read these Bible verses: Nehemiah 2:1-8; 2 Timothy 4:9-21.

Bible Point

Asking for help is not a sign of weakness or failure. It takes wisdom to recognize one's need and who can meet it. From Nehemiah's contemplating the rebuilding of the wall of Jerusalem to Paul's admitting that he needed his friends and a few provisions, God's people have done best when they were honest with themselves and with others.

Bottom Line

To do well in school, ask for help when you need it.

## *Body Language*

"No, you may not go to Janet's party this Saturday."

"But, Mom," Liz complained, "this is really important. All my friends will be there. Please let me go."

"I know it's important to you. I'm not trying to be mean," her mom replied.

"Yes, you are!" exclaimed Liz. "You don't want me to have any fun."

"That's not true," answered Mom. "I was just going to say that I think Janet's a great kid. I'm saying no because I care about your health."

Liz rolled her eyes. "Muh-ther. Honestly, I'm not a child."

"You may not be a *small* child," her mom countered, "but you're still my daughter. You were home sick two days this week. You seem to catch every cold bug that comes within three miles of this town. There are dark circles around your eyes—"

"What?" Liz ran to the mirror and took a long look. She had to admit that a tired and drained face stared back at her.

Mom continued. "Liz, our bodies were made by God to do wonderful things. You *are* doing wonderful things in school. But we need to take care of our bodies, and that means all the good old-fashioned stuff like not letting yourself get run down, getting enough sleep, having a decent breakfast, and following good medical advice. Your getting sick and those dark circles are your body's way of saying, 'Hey, take better care of me!'"

Liz looked at her mom and said quietly, "But I really want to go to that party."

Her mom walked over to her and gave her a hug. "It's very disappointing. I appreciate that. But you know there will be other parties. And we've got to get you healthy."

### Questions

- What warning signs tell people to take better care of their health?
- What signs does your body typically show when you're under stress or overtired?
- Describe a time when you didn't listen to your body's message about needing better care.
- What else could Liz do to stay healthy?

### Bible Discovery

Read these Bible verses: Genesis 2:1-3; 1 Kings 19:1-9; 1 Corinthians 3:16-17; 6:17-20.

### Bible Point

God rested after the work of creation was done; his people function best when they follow his example. The prophet Elijah became disoriented and depressed; food and sleep were what he needed at the time. We need to take good care of the body that God has given us.

### Bottom Line

To do well in school, take good care of your health.

# 12
# How to Know the Truth

### *How about Some Hearsay?*

Felecia Barnes stormed into the house, slamming the door. "I will never, ever speak to Ramish Gupta again as long as I live!"

Her stepmother had been in the middle of feeding the family cat, Barnabas. She looked at Felecia in surprise. "Isn't he your best friend?" she asked. "What did he do?"

"I heard from Ramona, who heard from Howard, who heard from Sheila that Ramish said my new haircut is ugly!" Felecia tried to blink back angry tears.

Mrs. Barnes glanced at Felecia's short red hair. "Did you hear Ramish say that?" she said.

Felecia answered, "No. I heard it from Ramona, who—"

"Did you ask Ramish about it?" asked Mrs. Barnes.

"Well, no. I tried to ignore him this afternoon at school," answered Felecia. "He kept trying to get my attention, but I—"

The ringing telephone cut her off. "If it's Ramish, I'm not here!" she called.

"You know I'm not going to lie for you." Mrs. Barnes picked up the cordless phone. "Hello?" Her face took on an amused expression. "Felecia, it's for you. It's Ramish."

"I don't want to talk to him!" Felecia yelled.

"Felecia, take this phone." Mrs. Barnes handed it to her.

Felecia threw her stepmother a tragic look before taking the receiver. "I'm not talking to you, Ramish," she said.

"Chantel told me what Ramona told you," said Ramish. "I didn't say that! Honest!"

"You didn't?" Felecia sounded unconvinced.

"You know I wouldn't say something like that," Ramish said. Felecia thought he sounded hurt.

"Then why did Ramona say you did?" Felecia asked.

"Ramona's a big fat liar!" exclaimed Ramish. "She's mad at me because I wouldn't give her the answers to the algebra test. Remember when she spread that rumor about Todd Franklin? I can't believe you'd believe anything she said!"

Felecia suddenly felt foolish. "I'm sorry, Ramish. I should've checked with you first."

Felecia hung up soon after that and went looking for her stepmother. She found her in the kitchen petting Barnabas.

"Everything all straightened out?" Mrs. Barnes asked.

"I feel silly, Mom. I should've known Ramish wouldn't say something like that. I should've checked with him first, instead of getting mad at him."

"Instead of being quick to believe hearsay, be quick to seek the truth," replied Mrs. Barnes. "Check out the character of the person talked about. Also consider the source. Is the person trustworthy? If not, don't believe what you hear."

"I guess I just wanted to believe the worst." Felecia fingered her hair.

"Is that because . . . you're not that crazy about your new haircut yourself?" Mrs. Barnes asked quietly.

Felecia hesitated before nodding.

"A real friend wouldn't talk about you behind your back. Ramish has always proven to be trustworthy, hasn't he?" asked Mrs. Barnes.

Felecia nodded.

"And this other person, Ramona, was it?" continued Mrs. Barnes. "How trustworthy is she?"

"Not very," Felecia answered quietly.

"Next time, consider the source and find out the truth," said Mrs. Barnes.

### Questions

- When has someone told you something that you believed at first but later found out was untrue? What did you do?
- Why should you consider the source of a statement before believing it?
- When are you most tempted to listen to gossip?
- When are you most tempted to spread gossip? Why?

### Bible Discovery

Read Proverbs 16:28; 20:19; Ephesians 4:29-32.

Bible Point

Instead of spreading gossip and hearsay, we are to speak what is "good and helpful" and "an encouragement" (Ephesians 4:29). Gossip does little to better a friendship. It's pretty good at tearing one apart, however.

Bottom Line

Gossip and hearsay can separate you from a good friend and the truth.

## *I Doubt It*

Katrina Richmond slowly walked home from school, thinking about what her science teacher had talked about that morning. He had been full of enthusiasm as he talked about the big bang theory. She knew that her teacher believed this theory—that the universe had been created out of a great cosmic explosion. But she believed that God had created the universe. Or did she? Lately she had been having doubts about whether she believed in God. She felt guilty for doubting.

"Watch it, Katrina!" A voice called her back to reality. She had almost bumped into her pastor as she stepped around the side of her house.

"Sorry!" she said. "I didn't see you."

"I can see that." Pastor Bob smiled. "I just stopped by to see your folks. What're you so deep in thought about?"

"Something at school." Katrina shrugged indifferently.

"Wish I could get my own daughters so engrossed in their schoolwork," Pastor Bob said with a grin.

"It's not that I'm interested," Katrina said, then blushed. "I was just thinking about something my teacher said."

"Something bad?" replied the pastor.

"He was talking about how the universe was formed," Katrina answered.

"So what did he say?" asked Pastor Bob.

"That the universe was formed by a big explosion," answered Katrina.

"Ahh. The big bang theory," said Pastor Bob.

"You've heard of it?" asked Katrina.

Pastor Bob laughed. "That's not a new theory. When I studied astronomy in college, I heard a lot about it."

Katrina's eyes grew wide. "Really? So, what's the truth?"

Pastor Bob's eyes grew wide then. "What's the truth about what? About that theory? Or about how the universe was formed? What do you think is the truth?"

Katrina's gaze shifted to her feet. She hesitated, fearing he would put her down for voicing her doubts. Finally she said, "Well, I know I'm supposed to believe in God . . . and I do. . . . It's just that . . . well . . ."

"Well, you're at that age where you want to know the truth for yourself, really know what's true, right?" Pastor Bob asked gently.

Katrina nodded. *How does he know?* she wondered. *That's just how I feel.*

"There's nothing wrong with questioning what you've been told—about scientific theories and about God," Pastor Bob explained. "God never imposes belief on anyone. He does, however, want people to know the truth and not blindly accept everything they hear."

"Do you think God is mad because . . . well, because sometimes I have doubts?" Katrina asked.

"God is never thrown for a loop by the doubts we have," answered her pastor. "The best thing to do with doubts is to talk to someone you trust about them. If you ever have questions about the Bible or just want to talk about the big bang theory or otherwise, don't hesitate to talk to me—after talking with your parents first."

Katrina looked relieved. "OK. Thanks, Pastor Bob." She felt better, knowing that she could voice her doubts without being put down.

### Questions

- What do your doubts center around?
- Why is it important to look for answers to questions and doubts?
- Who can you talk to about your doubts?
- Do you think God cares about you, even when you doubt? Why or why not?

### Bible Discovery

Read John 20:24-31.

### Bible Point

Thomas had lived closely with Jesus for three years, yet he had doubts about Jesus' resurrection. When Jesus appeared to the disciples, he didn't criticize Thomas for having doubts. He just wanted Thomas to know the truth—he was alive! He wants us to know the truth too. We should admit our doubts and look for answers.

Bottom Line

You can deal with doubts by talking about them with someone you trust.

## *The Trial*

Ashley Piedmont felt as if she were on trial as she waited outside the principal's office. Her mother was due any minute to talk with the principal.

When Mrs. Piedmont arrived, she didn't look happy. She looked at Ashley, then they both went into the office.

"What is my daughter accused of?" Mrs. Piedmont asked.

Ashley noticed that the principal, Ms. Anderson, bristled at her mother's words. Ashley felt sure that Ms. Anderson believed her to be guilty.

"Your daughter has a known history of starting fights with other students," Ms. Anderson said, reading from a file in front of her. "She was seen pushing another girl in the lunchroom."

"That's because she had a big hunk of my hair in her hand!" Ashley declared. "I was just trying to get her to let go!" She felt tears forming in her eyes and swallowed to keep from shedding them.

Ms. Anderson still looked skeptical.

"Ashley," Mrs. Piedmont said quietly, "look at me."

Ashley looked into her mother's eyes.

"Did you start this fight?" her mother asked.

"No," Ashley said promptly.

Mrs. Piedmont looked at her daughter for a few moments and then turned her gaze on the principal. "I believe that my daughter's telling the truth. Why didn't you ask this other girl to come to your office too?" she asked.

Ms. Anderson replied, "I can understand that you want to defend your daughter, but the fact remains—"

"If my daughter did something wrong, I wouldn't defend her action," Mrs. Piedmont said coolly. "But if she is accused of something that I know she didn't do, that's a different story."

"But how do you know she's telling the truth?" asked the principal.

Mrs. Piedmont smiled suddenly. "Because I know my daughter."

Ms. Anderson was silent.

Ashley's knees still shook with relief, even after she returned home later that afternoon. "Thanks for believing me, Mom," she said. "I felt like I was on trial!"

"Well, you were," answered Mrs. Piedmont. "Only your principal had already decided that you weren't telling the truth. I'm glad that girl finally admitted what really happened."

"It helped to have Mrs. Carver, the lunchroom monitor, back me up," Ashley added. "She saw the whole thing."

"I'm glad she didn't try to lie about it," Ashley's mom said. "People do, sometimes."

"Then how does anyone know the truth?" Ashley asked.

"Knowing a person's character helps you know whether or not that person is telling the truth," answered Mom. "If you're accused of doing something that's out of character for you, then I wonder whether the person accusing you really knows what's true."

"How did you know I wasn't lying?" Ashley asked.

Mrs. Piedmont smiled. "I know you. Whenever you lied in the past, and I'm thankful you didn't try that often, there was one thing you did each time that let me know you were lying."

"And what's that?" Ashley asked.

Mrs. Piedmont smiled. "I think I'll keep that to myself."

Questions

- What do you look for to know whether someone is telling the truth or not?
- Why is knowing the truth important?
- What situations tempt you to not tell the truth?

Bible Discovery

Read Matthew 26:59-66; John 14:6; 18:19-24, 33-38.

Bible Point

Jesus was put on trial before the chief priests and the Sanhedrin, the Jewish ruling council. But he had already been judged and found guilty, even though he was innocent. He didn't just speak the truth. He *was* the truth. But the chief priests weren't interested in Jesus; they didn't care to know the truth.

Bottom Line

Knowing a person's character helps you know the truth.

## *The Final Authority*

"Hey, Mom, how do you spell *pulchritudinous?"* Alex Chen asked.

Mrs. Chen glanced up from the potatoes she was peeling at the kitchen sink. "Look it up in the dictionary," she replied.

"Mom, how can I look it up if I can't spell it?" Alex asked.

"How do you think it's spelled?" replied Mrs. Chen.

"I don't know," answered Alex.

"Sound it out," offered his mother.

Alex reluctantly grabbed a dictionary and found the word.

"Why do you need to know how to spell that word?" Mrs. Chen asked.

"'Cause I just read it in this paragraph." Alex held up the work sheet he had been looking at.

Mrs. Chen stopped peeling the potatoes to stare at Alex. "If it's written down, why do you need a dictionary?"

"I just wanted to know if it's right," answered Alex. Mrs. Chen had a look on her face that made Alex laugh. "I'm not crazy, Mom," he said.

"You're sure about that?" Mrs. Chen looked doubtful.

"This is part of my homework assignment," replied Alex. "See the underlined words? Some are supposed to be misspelled. We're supposed to find out which ones."

"Oh. Now you're making sense," said his mother. "So why ask me how to spell that word? You were supposed to look it up for yourself."

"I did," answered Alex.

"Uh-huh." Mrs. Chen muffed Alex's hair. "You know, Alex, looking up things for yourself is a good way to know the truth about something."

Alex sensed that his mother was leading up to something. He tried to think of a way to escape to his room.

"Take the Bible, for instance," Mrs. Chen said before he could make a break. "If you want to know the truth about something, see what God says about it in his Word."

"You mean I can't just ask you?" Alex asked with a grin.

"There are some things you can take my word for," Mom answered. "But some things you can't. Like your spelling words. The dictionary is the final authority for that. It won't leave you guessing about how to spell a word. It tells you the spelling. The Bible is our final authority on what's true and what's not true."

"Hey, Mom, how do you spell *acrimony*?" asked Alex.

Mrs. Chen sighed. "Look it up."

Questions

- What methods have you tried in order to seek the truth?

- Which of the following authorities have you recently explored in order to know the truth about something:
  - a dictionary
  - an encyclopedia
  - an almanac
  - the Bible
- Why did you choose that source?
- When is it better to look something up for yourself rather than rely on someone's opinion?

Bible Discovery

Read John 8:31-32 and 17:17.

Bible Point

Jesus repeatedly talked about the truth and how to know it. God's Word, Jesus said, is truth.

Bottom Line

God's Word is the final authority for all truth.

### *Finding the Truth*

"Are you going to get that game?" Dexter Morgan asked. "Buck's Computer Barn has the lowest prices in town for CD-ROM games."

Sherman Phillips shrugged. "How do we know that's true? We haven't been anyplace else."

"But I always get my stuff from here," replied Dexter. "Joey Cantello's the one who told me about this place."

Sherman knew that Joey Cantello was one of the coolest kids in school. That almost settled the matter for him. "What about that new store—Computer Closet on Oak Street?" he asked.

"That dump? They hardly have anything there," said Dexter. "You should get the game here at Buck's."

What Dexter said made sense, so Sherman bought the game. Half an hour later, he met his older brother Cal at one of the mall entrances.

"I want to stop at Computer Closet before we go home," Cal said. "There's some stuff I need."

"Dexter says they don't have a lot of stuff," Sherman said.

"Have you ever been inside?" asked Cal.

"Nope," answered Sherman.

Cal just shook his head. Soon he had pulled up in front of a large store. Sherman's eyes opened wide when he first saw the place. They grew even wider when they went inside. "Wow! They've got twice the stuff Buck's Computer Barn has," he exclaimed.

"That's why I asked if you'd been in here," said Cal. "I knew you hadn't if you thought that Buck's had more stuff."

They split up; Cal went off toward the modems while Sherman checked on the game prices. When they met fifteen minutes later, Sherman's expression was downcast. "The game I wanted is $15 cheaper here than at Buck's," he said. "I wonder why Joey Cantello didn't talk about this place."

"Joey Cantello?" Cal suddenly laughed. "That's Rick Cantello's younger brother, right?"

"Yeah, so?" said Sherman.

Cal replied, "Their uncle is Buck, the owner of Buck's Computer Barn!"

Cal continued laughing about that even after they arrived home.

"What's the joke?" Mr. Phillips asked.

Cal quickly told his dad the whole story.

"You know you can return that game, Sherm," Mr. Phillips said.

"We already did," Cal said. "Sherm didn't want to at first, even though he saved $15. He was afraid his friends would see him."

Cal went off, still chuckling. Mr. Phillips turned to Sherman. "So it pays to do some investigating yourself, huh?"

"I guess," answered Sherman. "I wondered about Buck's prices earlier. I had asked Dexter how he knew Buck's had the lowest prices."

"Son, you have to find out for yourself what's true," said Mr. Phillips. "Now, there are some things you don't have to investigate in order to know the truth about them. For example, you don't have to take drugs if you're wondering whether it's true that drugs are harmful. There are enough reports on that to help you know the effects. But there are other matters that you can explore for yourself in order to know the truth."

### Questions

- What do you need to know the truth about?
- Why is it important to try to find the truth, rather than merely taking someone's word for it?
- What are some things you don't have to investigate in order to know the truth?

### Bible Discovery

Read Psalms 25:5; 119:30-32; Matthew 7:7.

### Bible Point

According to a popular TV show, "The truth is out there." The wise person seeks to know the truth and keeps seeking it until he or she finds it. The best way to start on any truth hunt is in prayer to your heavenly Father. After all, he *is* the truth.

### Bottom Line

Investigate the truth for yourself rather than rely only on someone's word.

# 13

# How to Get Along with the Opposite Sex

***Recognize the Difference***

"I just don't like boys very much," Stacey said to her dad. "All the boys at school tease us and pick on us girls. What is that all about?"

"Would you like the boys better if they just left you alone?" Dad asked.

"Well, it wouldn't be much fun if they didn't talk to us at all," Stacey said with a very small grin, "but why do they have to be so irritating?"

"They are irritating, my dear, because they are different from you. They think differently. They talk differently. They even listen differently," answered Dad.

"But we're all people, Dad. Why aren't we more alike?" asked Stacey.

"Well, I guess only God knows the answer to that. He made us to be different. Even when he made the first man and woman, he *made* them differently. He made Adam from the earth. He made Eve from Adam's rib. Maybe the differences started there. But Stacey, differences aren't all bad, you know," explained her father.

"No, they aren't," agreed Stacey, "but they sure take some getting used to. Mom always called me a tomboy and I'm a good athlete, so I thought it would be easy to get along with boys. But they just try to be as gross as possible. They laugh at stuff I don't even understand. And they never like it when I win."

"Some of those things, Stacey, you'll probably never understand," Dad responded. "That's part of being different. But as you grow up, you'll figure a lot of it out, and before it's over, you'll probably find a guy or two that you really like. The important thing to remember is that you don't have to completely understand someone to enjoy being with him."

Stacey's dad went out to walk their dog, Spike. Stacey watched them out the window and thought, *There aren't any guys like my dad left.*

When Stacey's mom walked in the room, Stacey said, "Mom, I don't know any guys my age that are great like Dad."

Stacey's mom laughed and laughed. "Stacey," she said, "when your dad was your age, he was just like those boys. He liked to be gross, and he acted goofy around girls. Remember, I knew him then, and I wondered sometimes if he had a brain!"

"Mom! You did not!" Stacey howled.

"You have to remember, hon," her mom continued, "that there is a lot of growing up for you to do and for the guys in your class too. They will always be different from you, but eventually they won't be quite so annoying. By the way, a guy named Rod called with some questions about homework. I told him to call back this evening."

Stacey was a little excited to hear that Rod had called. Maybe what Dad said was true. Maybe even if she didn't understand Rod, she could still have a good time talking to him.

### Questions

- What does it mean to be a tomboy?
- What things are often different about girls and guys?
- Why do you think God made girls and guys different?

### Bible Discovery

Read these verses: Genesis 2:20-23; Mark 10:6.

### Bible Point

God used a different method to create the first woman than he used to create the first man. He created the man and the woman to *be* different. He made them with different strengths and abilities. Guys and girls today have those same differences. Sometimes being different can make it difficult to get along. If we work at it, however, our differences can be a wonderful thing.

### Bottom Line

Realize there are differences between guys and girls and respect those differences.

## *When in Doubt, Be Courteous*

Today Jay was going to ask Rachel to go with him to a concert on Friday night. His mom would have to drive and go with them, but that was all right. Last night he had talked to his dad about it."Dad, I'm really nervous, and I'm afraid I'm going to say something stupid."

"Well, Son, you'll just have to think it out beforehand and try to stay calm," Dad advised. "Just remember, if you run out of things to say, go for nice, not sarcastic."

So all afternoon Jay had been thinking it out. He'd say, "Hi, this is Jay." She'd say, "Hi, Jay, what's up?" He'd say, "I was wondering if you wanted to go to the concert Friday with my mom and me." She'd say . . . what would she say? From there on out the conversation was one black hole. Was it even worth it? For some reason, he thought it was. So at four o'clock Jay dialed Rachel's number.

"Hello?" answered Rachel.

"Hi. This is Jay." That was all Jay could get out before he took a breath.

"Hi, Jay," was all she said. No "What's up?" No question to respond to. *Go for nice, go for nice,* Jay thought.

"How has your day been, Rachel?"

"Oh, just horrible. My dad forgot to pick me up at practice, so I missed my orthodontist appointment, and now I have a headache with two tests to study for tomorrow."

Obviously this was *not* the best time to ask her to the concert, but Jay couldn't think of another excuse for calling. *Go for nice.* "Well, Rachel, you know about the concert Friday at the community college. It's the guy we talked about last week at school. My mom and I are going, and I wondered if you'd like to come too." Whew! There, he said it.

"Jay, could you hold on a minute?"

"Sure, OK," Jay said, but what he thought was *Oh no! What is this? I took the risk, and now she's going to leave me hanging?*

"I had to let my dog in. Sorry. The concert sounds great. I'll check with my mom to be sure, and I'll let you know tomorrow if there's any problem. Thanks for asking."

The one thing Jay hadn't thought about was how to say goodbye. He wanted to make some kind of joke, but all he could hear was his father saying, "Go for nice." Finally he just said, "Listen, have a good night, and I'll talk to you tomorrow."

Jay walked into the next room after turning off the phone. Dad looked up and asked, "How did it go?"

"Well, she said yes, so I guess it went well. I think she could tell how nervous I was."

"You might be surprised, Jay. I bet you came off better than you think." Dad smiled reassuringly.

At Rachel's house, Rachel was telling her mom about the call. "You know, Mom, Jay always seems to know the right thing to say. I bet he's talked to girls on the phone a lot more than I've talked to boys. I'm really lucky to be going to a concert with such a nice guy, aren't I?"

### Questions

- How would you describe Jay's feelings just before he made the call?
- Why does fear mess up the things we say sometimes?
- How can trusting God help us when we are nervous about talking to someone?
- Why is it important to "go for nice" with the opposite sex?

### Bible Discovery

Read these verses: Genesis 18:15; Luke 8:37; 1 John 4:18-19.

### Bible Point

Fear makes us react to people differently. Usually it makes us more uptight and less kind. When girls interact with guys and guys interact with girls, sometimes they both get nervous, which is a kind of fear—fear of doing or saying the wrong thing or fear of not being accepted. We have to remember that even in guy/girl relationships God is there to help us. And even in guy/girl relationships we are commanded to be kind to each other.

### Bottom Line

If you feel nervous and don't know what to do, be polite, be kind—go for nice.

## *Be Yourself*

Anna loved to laugh and have fun. Her family had big family parties where they played games and teased each other and had a big time of it. When Anna was around other people, however, she tried to be quiet and reserved. She thought they'd like her better.

Anna met Robb when she was a volunteer in the family life center at her church. She and Robb checked out equipment from six o'clock until nine o'clock every Thursday while their dads played basketball in the men's league. Anna always tried to be her quietest around Robb. He was a little distant, and Anna was afraid that if she was too friendly, she would scare him off.

All the time Anna was quiet around Robb, he was wondering what was wrong with her. Robb knew some of her family members, and they were so friendly and fun. He thought she must really dislike him to be this quiet around him, so he kept his distance. He didn't want to make her dislike him any more than it seemed she already did.

Volunteers in the family life center were expected to work in their position for three months; then they could stop or volunteer for a different position. Anna and Robb had only one more week to go. The family life coordinator, Todd, came by one evening with his clipboard and schedules.

Todd asked Robb and Anna if they enjoyed their positions and what they thought could make their jobs easier. Then he said, "I've got to be honest with you both. I think you are great kids, and I'd love for you to do this again. But I'm just not sure you guys ever relax and just be yourselves in here. It's like you're both trying to be something you're not. Although you give out the equipment very well, you don't seem to enjoy doing it."

Anna swallowed hard, trying to think of what to say. Robb looked down at his shoes and cleared his throat. Todd just waited.

Finally, Robb said quietly, "This is sort of a small room, and I just thought I'd stay out of Anna's way."

Anna was shocked. Who said she wanted him to stay out of her way? She blurted out, "Well, I didn't want to get on Robb's nerves, so I was trying to be quiet and just do my job."

"So what you're saying," Todd said, "is that neither one of you just relaxed and had fun because you were worried about what the other one would think. Is that right?"

They both smiled and said, "Yes."

"I'll tell you what," Todd said; "why don't you two get to know each other a little better and then decide if you'd like to commit to another three months of volunteering. Talk to you later!"

After Todd left, Robb said, "I guess I've been so uptight because I thought you didn't like me."

Anna replied, "Didn't like you! I've been trying so hard to be quiet because I thought *you* didn't like *me!* I'd love to volunteer another three months and this time get to really know each other."

"Me, too," said Robb. "It's funny how you don't get to know somebody else because you're not being yourself, huh?"

### Questions

- Why didn't Robb and Anna get to know each other?
- Why is it scary to be yourself around someone of the opposite sex?
- Why do people try to be something they aren't?
- How does being yourself help you get along with others?

### Bible Discovery

Read these verses: Proverbs 13:7; Romans 15:7; 1 Corinthians 13:4; 1 Peter 3:8.

### Bible Point

God teaches us to accept and care for one another, and he wants us to be honest. Sometimes, however, we protect ourselves by pretending to be different than we are because we think someone will like us better. It doesn't work that way. We have to be true to ourselves and let other people do the same.

### Bottom Line

Don't try to impress people by being something you're not. Be brave enough to be yourself.

## *Listen Hear!*

Paul was staying with his grandma for the week, and he was glad. She had a cool old house, and she talked to him just like he was a grown-up. Paul was particularly glad because he was having a problem that he wanted to talk to her about. He had been trying to get to know a girl named Bethany at school. She was in band with Paul, but something went wrong each time he tried to have a conversation with her.

"Grandma, there is a girl in band that I would really like to get to know, but something isn't working. Can you help me?"

"What do you talk about?" asked Grandma.

"Well, we talk about our instruments and music and stuff. And because I want her to like me, I try to tell her about the good grades I make and the awards I'm getting in Scouts."

Grandma smiled and asked, "What does she tell you about herself?"

"She doesn't tell me anything! She doesn't talk much at all, so I just keep talking because I don't want her to leave."

"Let me make a suggestion, Paul. Get a list in your mind of things you'd like to know about this girl. The next time you talk, ask about one of the items on your list. After you ask, wait until she answers and don't start talking until she's finished. Most girls want to be listened to and understood. It sounds like your friend may be a little shy, which you are not. So slow down and give her the chance to open up."

Paul thought of his list and even prayed about it before he went to bed. He asked God to give him the patience to listen to Bethany instead of talking the whole time. He wondered if God minded his praying about a girl, but he figured if it was worrying him, God would be glad to hear about it.

The next afternoon, Paul had good news. "It worked, Grandma!" he blurted out. "While we were putting up our instruments, I asked Bethany how she liked Mr. Mahoney's class. She just said a few things at first, but I listened as hard as I could. Then I felt like telling her what I thought, but I waited. I looked her in the eye like you said, and she talked more than ever. Then she said her favorite teacher was Mrs. Greene. I wanted to tell her all about Mrs. Greene, but I didn't. I said, 'Oh, really?' And she talked even more. We spent more time together than ever. I like her even more than I did, and I think maybe she likes me too."

"I'm sure she does, Paul," commented his grandmother. Grandma knew how hard it is for girls and guys to get to know each other. She knew Paul would do fine as long as he learned to be a good listener.

### Questions

- Is it easier for you to talk or listen?
- Why do people seem to want to just talk about themselves?
- Why do you think Bethany liked Paul more after he listened to her?
- What keeps people from listening to each other?

### Bible Discovery

Read these verses: Proverbs 12:15; 18:13; Luke 6:31; James 1:19.

### Bible Point

Everybody wants to be listened to. The Bible teaches us to listen for several reasons: (1) You'll probably learn something; (2) you'll probably help somebody; (3) you'll probably communicate better. Getting along with the opposite sex is not about saying stuff to impress them. It's about listening to what they say and being impressed.

### Bottom Line

If you want to make friends with the opposite sex, look them in the eye and listen to them when they talk.

## *No Leading On*

Amy's parents heard her sobbing in her room. "Can we come in?" they asked. Amy nodded, but she didn't stop crying.

Amy's mom spoke first. "Amy, honey, I'm afraid you're going to make yourself sick. Take a big breath and let it out slowly. Now see if you can tell us what happened, from beginning to end, just like a story."

Amy did what her mother asked, and it really did help her calm down. The story was that there was a guy named Eric from school whom Amy really liked. She and Eric got paired for a project in social studies. They spent a lot of time getting the project together and worked so much on Eric's part of the project when they were together that Amy ended up doing a lot of her part alone at home. She didn't mind, however. Eric acted like he really liked getting to know her, and she began to think that maybe after the project was over they might stay close.

Amy and Eric had turned in their project last week. Ever since then, except for saying hi in the lunchroom, Eric hadn't talked to Amy at all. They got their grades back today, and they got a good grade. After class, Amy overheard Eric talking to some of his friends. He said, "I guess it was worth spending all that time with Amy. She did my work and hers too, and I got an A out of it. That's a pretty good deal."

Amy was hurt, and she had spent that afternoon crying in her room. When Amy finished, her dad went downstairs to get them something to drink, while her mother helped Amy wash her face and clean up.

When Dad returned, he said, "Amy, I want you to know how

sorry I am about what happened with Eric. I am angry at Eric for hurting you."

"Are you angry at me for being foolish?" Amy asked.

"No, Amy. I don't think you were foolish. You were helpful and kind to someone who was special to you. That's not foolish. That's natural. It's not your fault that Eric took advantage of your good heart.

"But I do want you to know that you will face other situations like this. What Eric did was lead you on. He led you to believe that he was feeling a certain way about you so that he could get you to do things for him. Then when he didn't need you anymore, he stopped acting.

"When I was young, there were times when girls led me on so that I would help them with their homework or give them rides. Leading someone on is lying with your actions and your emotions. And it really hurts."

"I don't ever want to lead anybody on if it feels like this," Amy said.

"The important thing, Amy, is for you to be the honest, loving person that God wants you to be. Don't let that change because somebody let you down."

### Questions

- Why did Eric stop being nice to Amy?
- Do you think Amy should have done anything differently?
- Why do some girls and guys pretend to like others and lead them on?
- Have you ever seen anyone act like Eric did?

### Bible Discovery

Read these Bible verses: Leviticus 19:11; 25:17; Ephesians 4:25; 1 Thessalonians 4:7-8.

### Bible Point

Sometimes we can make a promise we won't keep just by the way we treat someone. We act like the person is going to be our best friend when he or she isn't. We act like we really like the person when we don't. God tells us not to lie, and that includes lying with our actions and emotions.

### Bottom Line

Be honest with the opposite sex, even if it hurts them or hurts you.

# 14

# How to Deal with Disappointment and Pain

### *Golden Opportunities*

Leslie was confident this was the year she was going to make the school's basketball team. Today she would find out if all her hard work and efforts were going to pay off. All fall she had spent countless hours dribbling up and down her driveway, shooting hoops. She had attended a basketball camp this summer and improved her ball-handling skills dramatically. Leslie felt she did well at her tryout, although she probably didn't shoot as well as she could have. But that was yesterday. Today, the list of girls who had made the team would be posted. And Leslie just knew her name would be up there.

Word spread quickly through the halls that the list had been posted. As soon as Leslie's eighth-period class had ended, she hurried to the gym. There was a group of girls crowded around the list. Peering over their heads, Leslie scanned the list for her name. She looked a second time. Then a third. A dull ache began in the pit of her stomach. Her name was not on the list. *There must be some mistake,* Leslie thought.

She ran into the locker room; Coach Beth was sitting in her office. Timidly, Leslie knocked on the door. Coach looked up and motioned her in. "Coach," Leslie began, "I know there has to be some mistake here. I worked really hard over the summer and this fall. I just had to make the team."

But there wasn't a mistake. The coach told her gently that the other girls had worked just as hard and had more experience than Leslie. "I'm sorry, Leslie. Not everyone makes the team," she said.

Leslie's friends tried to comfort her after school, but Leslie would not listen. She was too dejected, too disappointed. Besides, she thought bitterly, they made the team. How could they understand how she felt? When she got home she immediately went to her room, slammed the door, and flung herself on the bed and cried. She didn't hear her mom enter the room, but when she felt a comforting hand on her shoulder, Leslie threw herself into her mother's arms. "Oh, Mom, it's not fair. I worked so hard this time. I can't believe I didn't make it," she cried. Mom held her until Leslie had stopped crying.

"Leslie, I know you worked very hard. And I know how disappointed you must feel. It's tough to accept when we work hard for something and fail. I know you feel awful right now. But sometimes when a door is closed to us, it means that God is opening another door somewhere else," Mom said.

Leslie looked up. "What do you mean?" she asked.

"Well, one way to handle your disappointment is not to concentrate on your failure but to see this disappointment as an opportunity to grow," Mom answered. "You may not be on the basketball team, but there might be something else that will open up to you that you hadn't expected. Things might not always work out the way we expect, but God does work things out for us. Keep praying and looking for those opportunities."

A few weeks later, Leslie ran excitedly into the house. "Mom, guess what, guess what?" she shouted. "Mr. Davis at church asked me to be a student leader at youth group this year. It's going to mean a lot of Saturday morning meetings and getting there early on Sunday, but he said he asked me because I'm good at organizing things and I'm reliable. Isn't that great?"

Mom smiled at her daughter. "Remember our conversation after the basketball team tryouts? If you had made the team, you probably couldn't have fit all this into your schedule. I think God has given you a wonderful opportunity to use your gifts. That *is* great."

### Questions

- How did you react when you worked hard for something but didn't succeed?
- When have you found yourself with other opportunities that you didn't expect?

- How can viewing our disappointments as opportunities help us cope with trials?
- How does knowing that God will work things for our best help when we face disappointments?
- What else do you think Leslie learned from this situation?
- What have you learned from disappointments you've experienced?

Bible Discovery

Read the following Bible verses: John 16:33; Romans 8:28; Philippians 1:12-14; James 1:2-4.

Bible Point

Jesus said that his followers would face trials and disappointments. We can take heart that God is working things out for our good, according to his purpose. When trials come, we should view them as opportunities to grow and trust God's plan for our life.

Bottom Line

See your disappointments as opportunities to grow.

## *Be Positive*

Ben stared glumly at his leg as it lay useless, wrapped securely in a plaster cast. He had broken it in two places in a recent car accident. Now he would be laid up for at least eight weeks this summer, possibly longer if the leg didn't heal as it should.

Immediately following the accident, Ben had a flurry of visits from his friends. But as the days went on, the number of visits decreased dramatically. Ben understood. *Sure,* he thought bitterly, *they have better things to do than visit me. They get to play baseball and go swimming. Me—all I get to do is sit here and watch the reruns. What a great vacation.*

With each passing day, Ben grew more and more depressed. Even when the doctor told him he could move around on crutches, Ben didn't want to leave the house. "It's too much trouble," he told his mom. "Besides, I don't want people staring at me and offering to help me. It's bad enough to have this stupid cast on my leg. I don't want people to feel sorry for me."

Finally, Mom decided to call Mr. Davis, Ben's youth group leader at church. Ben had gotten to know Mr. Davis well over the past year and enjoyed a close relationship with him. If anyone could get Ben out of his funk, Mr. Davis probably could. Ben might just listen to him.

Mr. Davis entered Ben's room with a cheery hello. "How's it going, champ?" he called out.

Ben grunted in reply. "How's it going? How do you think it's going? I'm stuck in this bed with a broken leg for the entire summer. I can't go swimming. I can't play baseball. Nobody comes to visit me. You want to know how it's going—rotten, that's how it's going."

Mr. Davis ignored Ben's reply and said, "We've missed you at youth group. Your mom said you are able to get out if you want. Why don't you come next Sunday?"

"What for?" Ben snorted. "So you all can stare at me and feel sorry for me? No way. No thank you."

"It seems to me there's only one person feeling sorry for you—and that's you, Ben," Mr. Davis answered gently. "The way I see it, you have a choice. You can either sit here the rest of the summer feeling sorry for yourself, or you can choose to be positive."

Ben looked at Mr. Davis in disbelief. "Be positive about what?" he exclaimed. "Can't you see I can't walk or move my leg? What's there to be positive about?"

"Well, I see a young man who can still join in a discussion and read Bible stories to younger children at VBS, who will be up and about in less than two months and won't always need crutches to get around, and who can be thankful that he isn't more seriously injured," Mr. Davis began. "That's a whole lot to be thankful for in my book."

Ben turned away from Mr. Davis. "Well, I guess I have to go now," Mr. Davis said quietly. "I sure hope you'll think about what I said, Ben. And remember, we *do* really miss you and would love to have you come back to class this Sunday."

That Sunday Mr. Davis had already begun the lesson when he heard a commotion at the door. It was obvious that someone was struggling with the door. "Hey, Adam, could you please see who's at the door?" Mr. Davis asked.

The class was stunned to discover Ben on the other side of the door, trying to balance himself with his crutches and a big box of doughnuts.

"Hi, everybody. I thought you could use some doughnuts. I know how hungry you guys always are about this time," Ben said, hobbling into the room. He took his usual place in the class, and Mr. Davis began the lesson again.

After class, all the kids made their way over to say hello to Ben as they left. Then Mr. Davis walked over. "I'm really glad to see you here—and you can tell your friends were glad to see you also," he said.

"Well, I had a lot of time to think about what you said," Ben replied with a big grin. "And I decided there was something better to do than have a one-person pity party. Besides, I thought you might suggest a good Bible study that I could work on in my free time."

Mr. Davis grinned back. "Yeah, I think I can. How about one on patience?"

Questions

- Why did Ben feel so sorry for himself?
- When did you have a one-person pity party?
- What are some ways to combat feeling sorry for yourself?
- What else could Ben do to break out of his depression?
- What would you say to Ben to help him?
- Where do we need to focus to avoid feeling self-pity? How can you do that?

Bible Discovery

Read the following Bible verses: Psalm 46:1; Proverbs 15:13; 17:22; Lamentations 3:21-26; Habakkuk 3:17-19.

Bible Point

A positive attitude helps us focus on what is truly important: that God is always with us despite our hurt and pain. He will not disappoint us but will strengthen and protect us during our trials.

Bottom Line

Avoid pity parties; look for the positives.

### *Pain Control*

Mr. Davis was surprised to see Brad walk into the church office. It already was close to 6 P.M. Mr. Davis had a meeting later and had decided to catch up with some paperwork here at the church. "Hey,

Brad, what are doing here? Want a head start on the Sunday school lesson?" he joked.

Brad shook his head no. "Actually, I wanted to see you," he said.

Brad's response surprised Mr. Davis because Brad was one of the most popular students in the youth group. Brad was an excellent athlete, an honor student, and very involved participant in the youth group's service projects. Everyone liked Brad, and he was friendly to everyone. Now, standing in Mr. Davis's doorway, he appeared dejected, confused, and upset. *What could possibly be wrong?* Mr. Davis wondered. "Well, now is as good a time as any. Are you sure, though, that your parents aren't going to be looking for you?" Mr. Davis asked as he pulled a chair around for Brad to sit down.

"Nah. They think I'm at Gary's house. But that's part of the problem," Brad began. Gary was Brad's closest friend, but Mr. Davis had noticed that the two of them seemed to be drifting apart lately. Brad sat down and said bluntly, "I'm in big trouble, Mr. Davis. My parents *think* I'm at Gary's, but I really was going over to Stewart's house."

Again, Mr. Davis was surprised at this, although he said nothing. Stewart ran with a crowd of boys at the middle school that were always in trouble. Stewart and his friends were recently suspended for drinking under the bleachers at the football games, and they were known around the school for the wild parties they hosted.

"So what were you going to do at Stewart's house?" Mr. Davis asked.

Brad answered bluntly, "Drink. We were going to drink."

Mr. Davis didn't say anything for what seemed like a long time. Then almost gently, he asked, "Want to talk about it?"

That was all the invitation Brad needed. "I've been having trouble with my classes. I'm in over my head in math and science; a couple weeks ago both teachers told me I was going to flunk their class if I didn't start working hard. If I flunk, I get kicked off the football team. My parents would have an absolute fit if that happened. I don't know why, Mr. Davis, but after one of the games, Stewart invited me over to his house for a party. I got really drunk and got sick. But I keep going back. It just makes me forget about all these other things."

Mr. Davis didn't respond at first. Then he said, "You know, sometimes we can allow our disappointments to lead to bigger problems—ones that aren't quite as easy to resolve. Drinking to forget about your troubles in school could lead to being kicked not only off the football team but also out of school. And that's not to mention all the other problems that *could* happen while you are drinking."

"I know that," Brad said miserably. "But I don't know how to deal with everything else. How can I tell my parents about my schoolwork? They're going to flip."

"We all face setbacks and struggles, Brad. That's part of life while we are on this planet. Jesus told us that we all *will* face struggles. It's *how* we handle these struggles that's important. Let me show you a three-step plan I use for dealing with setbacks," Mr. Davis said. "Just remember ADD, and it will all add up. First, *accept* it. Don't spend your time feeling sorry for yourself. Accept your situation in school. Remember that God knows your situation and wants to help you accept it, deal with it, and then move on.

"Next, *decide* you are going to do your best. That doesn't mean you'll become an A student again overnight. But decide to take a first step toward that—maybe scheduling some before-school help sessions. And third, *don't give up*. You might not get A's this marking period, but if you hang in there, your work will pay off. Never lose hope."

By the time Mr. Davis finished talking, Brad had brightened considerably. "It might be worth a try, Mr. Davis. And I *know* it has to be better than drinking. I think I need to have a long talk with my mom and dad. Speaking of that, can I make a call on your office phone? I think I need to tell them where I am."

### Questions

- How can a person's disappointments lead to bigger problems?
- What other problems did Brad have to face because of his choices?
- How can you prevent setbacks from developing into major problems?
- What are some positive ways to deal with disappointments and setbacks?

### Bible Discovery

Read Genesis 39:19-23 to see how Joseph dealt with a major setback.

### Bible Point

Joseph's life was filled with setbacks. At any point he could have turned to bitterness, revenge, or hopelessness. Yet, Joseph accepted each situation, looked for ways to do his best, and never gave up.

### Bottom Line

Don't allow life's setbacks to lead to bigger problems.

## *Back to the Basics*

Nicole knew something was up when her father called a family meeting. Never could Nicole remember having a family meeting for *anything,* including the time Mom and Dad had decided to give away the dog because of her brother's allergies. Now this. It couldn't be anything good, thought Nicole. What Nicole didn't expect, though, was how *bad* it was going to be.

After she and her brothers had gathered around the table, her father announced with great enthusiasm, "I got a really big promotion. It's a great job—something I've worked very hard for my entire career." At that, they all cheered for their dad, who they knew had been putting in lots of late nights.

"Does this mean you'll have more time at home?" her older brother asked.

"Well, actually, what it means is that we are going to be moving," Dad answered. There was a stunned silence.

Nicole and her brother Luke looked at each other. "You have to be kidding," Luke said. "We can't move now. I want to try out for baseball this spring—I know I have a good chance of making it."

"Luke, there will be baseball teams in our new city—you can count on it. Plus, the weather's nicer there, so you can play year-round," Mom said. "This is going to be a good opportunity for everyone."

Nicole wasn't too sure about that. In fact, as she got ready for bed, she wasn't too sure about anything. Their family had never moved before. She had lived in this same house ever since she was a baby. Lots of her friends had moved over the years, and each time it had been difficult saying good-bye. She never heard from some of her friends after they moved. Only a few still wrote to her. Would her friends forget about her? Would she leave here and never see this place again? Would she make new friends in her new town? Where would they live? Where would they go to church?

Endless questions raced through her mind. She tossed and turned and tried to concentrate on other matters, but her thoughts kept coming back to the move. Finally, she decided to get up and get a drink of water.

Nicole stumbled into her mom in the hallway. "What's the matter, Nicole, can't you sleep?" Mom asked. "Come on downstairs and I'll fix us a snack."

As they sat at the table eating warm muffins, Nicole began, "I don't know, Mom. I feel so confused. There are so many questions I have. I don't know how to deal with this."

"Well, one thing you can do is go back to the basics," Mom said, smiling at Nicole's puzzled expression. "When life seems overwhelming, we have to remember one basic fact: Who's in charge."

Nicole smiled a bit. "You mean besides you? I guess you mean God, right?"

Mom laughed. "Right on the second count. God is in control, and he promises to be with us if we're here or in California. The same God who protects us and cares for us here will also care for us as we make this move. We may have lots of questions that won't be answered right away, but we can be sure of this: God is with us and will guide us. Does that help you at all?"

Nicole finished her muffin, stood up, and gave her mom a hug. "Thanks, it does, Mom. I guess I need to wait and see how God plans to work out all these issues. But I think I'll get some sleep first."

"Good idea. I think I'll join you," her mom said.

### Questions

- Which promise of God helps you when you are going through a difficult time?
- How did knowing God is in control help Nicole? How does it help you?
- In what situation did you have more questions than answers? What happened? How did God work in that particular situation?

### Bible Discovery

Read the following Bible verses: Psalm 34:1-9; Jeremiah 29:11-13; Hebrews 13:5-6.

### Bible Point

Regardless of the circumstances or situation, God is in control of the future and will guide those who follow him.

Bottom Line

When life gets hard, go back to the basics.

## *Tomorrow's Trouble*

Since his parents' divorce, Trent had been spending a lot of time hanging out at Mr. Davis's office at church. Mr. Davis had an open-door policy, and Trent had used it quite liberally. Mr. Davis didn't mind. Trent was always willing to lend a hand when necessary, but mostly he just wanted a place to come and talk. Sometimes they would talk about the divorce; sometimes they would discuss the latest football games.

Despite the upheaval in Trent's life, with his dad moving out and his mom working full-time now, he seemed to be coping well. His friends and the youth group continued to pray for him and encourage him, and Trent had grown in his faith through this experience. But lately, Mr. Davis had noticed that Trent seem preoccupied. Something was bothering him, and it was not like Trent to keep it to himself.

Today when Trent stopped by, Mr. Davis noticed that he looked very tired. "Trent, have you been getting enough sleep? You look wiped out," Mr. Davis observed.

Trent looked at the floor. "Actually, I haven't been sleeping much at all lately," he replied.

"What's up, Trent? Is something wrong at home?" Mr. Davis asked.

At first, Trent seemed reluctant to talk. But after a few hesitating starts, he explained, "It's Christmas."

"Christmas?" Mr. Davis repeated, surprised. "But that's two months away. Are you worried about not having money to buy gifts?"

"No," Trent answered with a small smile. "This will be the first Christmas since my parents' divorce. I just can't imagine what it's going to be like. Usually, my dad and I get the tree and put the lights on. Who is going to do that now? And where will we spend Christmas? I don't want to go to my dad's little apartment in the city. I want my parents to come to church with me, but I know they won't sit together. So what do I do? Go to one service with one and then the other service with the other? I just can't stop thinking about it."

"Trent, let me ask you a question," said Mr. Davis. "If you were going on a train trip next spring for vacation, would you expect me to give you your ticket today?"

Trent looked at Mr. Davis as if he had lost his mind. "No, of course not. But what does that have to do with anything?"

Mr. Davis continued. "You're right. You wouldn't need the ticket until you were ready for your trip. God's grace and power are just like that. He promises to provide us with what we need for each day—not for tomorrow, not for two days from now or two months from now. But for today.

"Jesus taught that we should not worry about tomorrow because today's troubles are more than enough for us to handle. Worrying about the future or what might happen down the road is more harmful than helpful. It hampers our efforts for today, keeps us from being productive, damages our health, and undermines our faith," Mr. Davis said. "The only way to combat being consumed by worry is to tackle one day at a time—the day that God has given to you to live.

"Give your worries to Jesus and trust that he will work out the details of your life. When Christmas comes, trust that Jesus will give you the grace and the power to cope with whatever the circumstances are. Until then, however, remember that our God, who cares for the lilies of the fields and the birds in the sky, cares for you even more," Mr. Davis concluded.

Trent looked at Mr. Davis a bit sheepishly. "Thanks, Mr. Davis. I'm glad we had this talk. I guess I did get a little carried away, letting my imagination run a bit too wild," he said. "I think I'll wait for my ticket until I need it, right?"

### Questions

- What are some things you worry about?
- Why does worrying not help the situation?
- How can Trent keep from worrying? How can you keep from worrying?
- How can knowing that God cares for you help you deal with worries?
- How can worrying about the future prevent you from living effectively today?

### Bible Discovery

Read the following Bible verses: Psalm 37:1-7; Matthew 6:25-34; Philippians 4:6-7; 1 Peter 5:7.

### Bible Point

Worrying about the future when coping with a disappointment or painful event only immobilizes a person and hampers his or her efforts for today. The Bible says to place our anxieties on God and trust in his provision for all our daily needs.

### Bottom Line

Instead of worrying, trust God and tackle one day at a time.

SKILLS FOR LIFE

# 15 How to Stay out of Trouble

## *Choose Right*

Brandy was sitting in the hall outside the assistant principal's office. The reason she was there had started at the beginning of the year. In English she sat beside a group of girls who liked to see how far they could push the rules. They worked really hard to get by with things they knew they shouldn't do. Brandy had tried a few of their stunts with them.

One day these girls decided to cut the whole last half of school. "Nobody will notice, and who would it hurt?" they said. Brandy was helping with some special testing, so she didn't go.

While the girls were out, a lot of money was discovered missing from the band room. Everyone wondered if they took it. Because Brandy was their friend, she was to be interviewed by the assistant principal.

While Brandy was waiting, another friend, Shawnda, sat down beside her. "Have they talked to you yet?" she asked.

Brandy shook her head.

"What are you going to tell them?" Shawnda demanded.

Brandy exploded. "What do you expect me to tell them? I don't know who stole the money. I don't know where Teri and the others were. I was here doing what I was supposed to be doing, or at least I was until I got jerked out of class."

"Whoa, girl!" said Shawnda. "I'm not accusing you of anything. In fact, I really want to help you, Brandy, before you get in real trouble."

Now Brandy was curious. "What do you mean?"

"I got mixed up with Teri last year. I had never been a trouble-maker, but somehow I got sucked in. Teri's a lot of fun, and I didn't want her to think I wasn't. Before I knew it, I had cut classes, lost my good reputation, and gotten distracted from schoolwork."

Brandy realized Shawnda really *did* know Teri. Shawnda's story was way too close to Brandy's own experience.

Shawnda spoke again. "Well, listen, hang in there, Brandy. And tell the truth no matter what."

Before Shawnda could walk away, Brandy asked, "When did you stop hanging around with Teri?"

"I cut the last half of school one day with Teri and some other friends. There was some stolen money, just like there is today. I got blamed for it, even though I didn't know anything about it. You were lucky, Brandy. You *couldn't* leave with them. Somebody was looking out for you."

Brandy felt sad after Shawnda left. She hadn't realized before that her own reputation at school was changing. She hadn't really thought about the real trouble she could have gotten into. Somebody *had* been looking out for her, and she knew it was God. As the assistant principal called her into the office, Brandy whispered a prayer of thanks. And she asked for God's help to do the right thing.

### Questions

- Why was Brandy sitting outside the assistant principal's office?
- Why did both Shawnda and Brandy do things they knew they shouldn't have?
- Do you know anybody like Teri at school?
- How can the wrong friends lead us into trouble?

### Bible Discovery

Read these verses: Proverbs 13:20; 24:1-2; 1 Corinthians 15:33; Romans 16:17; 2 Thessalonians 3:6.

### Bible Point

The Bible says a lot about people who cause trouble. According to these verses, if you don't want to be one of them, stay away from those people. Don't hang with them. Don't get near them. God very clearly says in his Word that if we stick around troublemakers long enough, eventually their trouble will become our own.

### Bottom Line

To stay out of trouble, stay away from people who get into it.

## *Warning Signs*

Allen was reading the comics while his dad watched the news on TV. The newscaster was telling about a horrible crime that had happened that week involving an adult and a little girl. The adult had abused the young girl cruelly.

Allen said, "Dad, it scares me that there are people who can do that kind of stuff. How does a person get to be that way? Doesn't it bother them that they hurt people? I feel guilty when I'm not truthful to Mom or you. I can't imagine how guilty I would feel if I hurt a little girl."

Just then the TV showed the man being taken away by the police. He didn't hide his face or anything. He looked like he just didn't care.

Allen's dad looked sad. "I'm not sure it's really possible to understand, Allen, so I don't know that I can really explain it to you. But I do know this. The first time you do something wrong it bothers you. The Holy Spirit convicts you, and your conscience makes you feel guilty. These are your warning signals. The next time it doesn't bother you quite as much. The third time it bothers you even less. Somehow your conscience just gets used to it and stops talking to you so loudly. The Bible says it's like deadening the nerves in your conscience with a hot iron."

Allen thought for a moment and then said, "It sure would take a lot of irons to deaden my conscience enough to do what that guy did."

"You're right," said his dad. "But the first step to never becoming like that guy is to listen to your conscience the first time it speaks to you about something. Don't ignore it even once."

"What if I don't recognize the voice of my conscience or of the Holy Spirit?" Allen asked.

"That's part of growing up," answered Dad. "You have to get to know your own instincts. If something feels wrong to you, either something you did or something someone else did, stop and think about it. Pray and ask God to direct your conscience and teach you to recognize his voice.

"Sometimes your conscience feels like guilt. Sometimes it is a quiet little nagging feeling, something bothering you, but you're not sure what."

"Do you still have to listen to your conscience, Dad?" Allen asked.

"Every day, but I also have to spend time in prayer and in God's Word to freshen up my conscience," Dad answered. "Our world doesn't try to stay away from sin like it should. So I try to read the Bible and remind myself that God wants me to be as concerned about sin as he is. That is what you need to do too."

"You mean I can train my conscience?" asked Allen.

"Exactly," answered Dad. "You can train your conscience to be sensitive to sin. But then it's up to you to listen to your conscience when it points sin out to you."

Questions

- Do you think the man on the news felt guilty?
- Why did God give you a conscience?
- Why is it important to listen to and obey one's conscience?
- When has your conscience "talked" to you?

Bible Discovery

Read these verses: Proverbs 16:17; 1 Thessalonians 5:22; 1 Timothy 1:5, 18-19; 1 Peter 3:15-16.

Bible Point

God built a conscience into each person. It's that voice that tells the person when something just doesn't feel right. It's the warning sign to help when a person gets close to sin. Listen to your conscience. Stay away from trouble. Keep your conscience sensitive to wrong.

Bottom Line

To stay out of trouble, listen to your conscience. If you have a gnawing feeling that you probably shouldn't do something, *don't!*

## *Negatory*

Jeremy and Joshua were best friends, but they were so different. Jeremy was tall for his age; Joshua was average size and thin. Jeremy was serious most of the time, and Joshua was funny most of the time. It was not surprising, then, that they handled trouble differently.

Trouble, around Jeremy and Joshua's school, meant Andy Johnson and his henchmen. Andy loved picking on anybody he could scare. He would wait right at the corner of the hall, so when the kids stepped around it, he would be right in their faces. "Where do you think *you're* going?" he'd ask in a sinister tone.

Jeremy and Joshua each had their own plan for handling Andy.

"I'd just stare him in the face until he looked away," said Jeremy.

"I'd just tell him a joke and get him laughing, and then I'd run for it," said Joshua.

They got a chance to test their ideas right before school ended. They rounded the corner from gym and *bam!* there was Andy's mug and his mean, little crooked smile.

"Where do you think *you're* going?" Andy asked.

Joshua and Jeremy didn't speak. They looked at Andy. They looked at each other. They looked at their shoes. Then before they realized it, they both ran as hard as they could the other way. Breathless and with hearts pounding, they finally stopped at the other end of the school building.

"Are we wimps!" said Jeremy between breaths.

"Where was the big stare?" said Josh with the beginnings of a smile.

Jeremy smiled back. "I guess it was out on the playground with your sad little jokes."

They started to laugh and laughed so hard they thought they might never stop. Old Stan, the school custodian, came sweeping down the hall and asked, "What is so funny?"

The guys told him about meeting Andy and how their brave ideas had fallen through. Old Stan just shook his head and replied, "I don't think running away from trouble is such a bad idea. It's a way to say 'No, I'm not getting involved.' Don't start a fight, but keep your wits about you. And go slow around the corners!"

Jeremy and Josh felt so much better after their good laugh that they didn't even expect Andy, but around the next corner *wham!* there he was.

"Where do you think—," he began.

"Hi, Andy. Do you guys want to play some ball?" interrupted Joshua.

Andy was completely surprised."Well . . . I . . . uh . . . ," he stuttered.

Jeremy stood by, calmly looking at Andy and his boys.

"Aw, come on," continued Josh, "it's a lot more fun than standing around here. Race you!"

Josh took off for the basketball courts, and all the other guys started following behind.

Old Stan watched them play for a while. He thought, *Sometimes saying no to trouble is more than saying no. Sometimes it's not saying anything, and sometimes it's just offering another suggestion. These are some smart boys.*

Questions

- Why was Andy a bully?
- What would you have done differently than Josh and Jeremy?
- Why was Stan's advice good advice?

Bible Discovery

Read these verses: Genesis 39:4-12; Psalm 26:5; Proverbs 6:35; 20:3; Daniel 1:3-16; Titus 2:11-12.

Bible Point

Daniel and Joseph said no in different ways just like Jeremy and Josh did. Joseph ran away from trouble. Daniel offered another suggestion. But all of them did what they had to so they could obey God, stay out of trouble, and keep away from troublesome people.

Bottom Line

To stay out of trouble, learn to say no. Leave the bad situation as soon as possible, even if it means running away.

## *Have Fun*

Vanessa and Constance had it all figured out. They would go to youth group tonight. Then the real fun would begin.

Vanessa had told her parents that she was going to Constance's house afterward. Constance had told her parents that she was going to Vanessa's house. What they were *really* going to do was go ice-skating at the mall. They knew their parents would never let them go by themselves. Somehow, it wasn't just shopping or skating that sounded fun. It was getting away with something sneaky.

After the opening announcements, John, the youth leader, began an activity. "Tonight we're going to talk about having fun," he said. "We're not going to talk about fun in general, however. We're going to talk about sneaky fun."

Constance and Vanessa looked at each other and smiled.

"Let's make a list on the board," John continued, "of all the sneaking-around activities that sound fun to you. It won't go past this room, so be honest."

The group started a list that grew and grew and grew. They could think of many ways to have fun by sneaking and doing something their parents wouldn't want them to do.

After they filled the board, John had them look up Scriptures. They spent a lot of time talking about a verse in Colossians that said, "Don't lie to each other." They talked about sneaking being a form of lying. They talked about remembering that God sees them always, sneaking or not. They talked about how God gives us guidelines to protect us, not to ruin our fun.

After all that discussion, the group went back to their list on the board and thought of nonsneaky substitutes that would be just as fun.

As the session wore on, Constance and Vanessa felt worse and worse. By the closing prayer they both knew they couldn't enjoy going to the mall without their parents' permission. Instead they went to Vanessa's house, and Constance spent the night.

The next morning as they were eating breakfast, Vanessa's mom said, "Oh, girls, some kids got hurt at the mall last night. They were there without their parents, and as they were walking through the parking lot, some guys from a gang started bothering them. Most of the kids got away, but one ended up in the hospital."

"Wow," said both Vanessa and Constance as they looked at each other through wide eyes.

"Vanessa's father and I wanted to remind you girls to always let us know where you are," she said. Then she added, "Constance, I see you brought your skates. Are you two going skating today?"

"Maybe later," Vanessa answered. Then to Constance she whispered, "First we've got to go up to my room and thank God that he kept us from sneaking around last night. I'd sure rather wake up in my own bed than in the hospital."

"Me too," whispered Constance. "That list we made last night just might come in handy."

### Questions

- What sneaky thing were Vanessa and Constance going to do?
- Why is it fun to sneak around?
- What is the danger in sneaking around?
- How does God feel about sneaking around?

### Bible Discovery

Read these verses: Proverbs 1:10-19; 15:21; Ecclesiastes 11:9; Colossians 3:9.

Bible Point

God wants his people to be happy. Part of being happy means having fun. But God doesn't tell us to have fun no matter how it affects anyone else. We have to find ways to have a good time without hurting someone, deceiving someone, making someone angry, or mistreating someone.

Bottom Line

To stay out of trouble, avoid sneaky fun.

### *Respect*

"She's just an old woman! Come on; it'll be fun," the guys called.

For some reason, it just didn't feel right to Tim. On their way home from school the guys would ride their bikes through old Mrs. Gillis's backyard and beat sticks on the metal fence. Most days she would run out on her back porch and yell at them to stop.

Tim told the guys, "Not today. I don't have time. You'll have to go on without me." He and Jerry both knew that the real reason was that Tim just didn't think it was right. What they couldn't figure out was why it bothered Tim so much when it didn't bother Jerry at all.

Later Tim walked down the street in front of Mrs. Gillis's house. She was talking loudly to her son in the yard.

"It's about respect! If I don't want them in my yard, they shouldn't be in my yard. What's the good of having your own house if little hoodlums don't respect you enough to keep away from it?"

As he walked on down the street, Tim thought about that word *respect.* Was respect why he didn't feel good about riding through an old lady's yard?

That night Tim told his mom about what the boys had been doing. He told her that they weren't damaging any of Mrs. Gillis's things, but he still felt badly about it. Then he told her about what he had overheard.

After he had finished, his mom said, "Tim, I don't know if I can tell you why you feel the way you do, but I can tell you this. I know Mrs. Gillis doesn't live right next door to us, but she is one of our neighbors. You might not remember, but before her husband died, he helped your dad several times when the car was broken down. When your sister was born, Mrs. Gillis and some other ladies brought food over for you and your dad. You were only four when Mrs. Gillis even called to ask what you liked so she would be sure to make something you'd eat.

"Mrs. Gillis has been a good neighbor to us. She has helped us, and she has respected us. It's our responsibility to be a good neighbor back to her. We should do it for her and for God because he commands us to love our neighbors."

Tim felt as though he had sinned, but he hadn't even ridden through her yard today. He told his mom that.

"There's a good chance that what you feel is conviction from God because you have failed to respect another person," said his mother. "But you don't have to mope about it. You can start being a better neighbor right now. I found an old tool in the garage today that your father borrowed from Mr. Gillis a few years ago. Why don't you return it to her?"

Tim did return the tool, and he chatted with Mrs. Gillis. After talking with her, Tim knew that he would never show her disrespect again. He even liked her. He knew for sure what he would say the next time Jerry came around. He'd ask him to come and meet Mrs. Gillis for himself.

### Questions

- How do you think Mrs. Gillis felt when the boys rode through her yard making all that noise?
- Why was that fun for the boys?
- Why do we get in trouble when we fail to respect other people?
- What other acts of disrespect lead to trouble?

### Bible Discovery

Read these verses: Deuteronomy 19:11-13; Proverbs 22:8; 3:29-30; 11:9; Romans 13:9-10.

### Bible Point

Both the Old and the New Testaments teach that God is very concerned about how we treat the people around us. Staying out of trouble means respecting people enough to be their neighbor. This makes our society healthier and happier and pleases God.

### Bottom Line

To stay out of trouble, respect other people.

# 16

# How to Make a Difference in the World

***The Neighborhood***

One night at the dinner table, Sharon's parents were talking about things that were happening in their neighborhood. They were discussing how they could do something to make a positive difference. The Millers lived in an older part of the city that was a mixture of individual houses and apartment buildings. Lots of kids lived in the neighborhood, and many of them were under ten. Mom was concerned that when summer vacation started, these children wouldn't know what to do all day.

"They will get bored, bored, bored just like me," predicted Kyle, Sharon's eight-year-old brother. "There's not much to do around here. Everything interesting and all the neat stores are on the other side of Lincoln Avenue. But we can't go there because there's too much traffic."

"Kyle's right," Sharon agreed. "There's really not much for the little kids to do. They can go to the park, but an older person probably has to go with them." Logan Park was a nice open space among the tall apartment buildings.

At the start of summer vacation, Sharon was reminded of the dinner-table discussion when she saw all the young kids. There seemed to be fifty right on her own block. She tried to remember what she liked to do in the summer when she was that age. A little flicker of an idea started to form. There just might be a way she could help some of these kids.

Sharon talked to her friend Dawn, who lived in one of the

apartment buildings. "I want to have a club for kids from five to seven years old. We would meet two mornings a week and do fun things like sing, play games, do crafts, and read stories. We could have snacks and maybe go to Logan Park sometimes. What do you think?"

"That's a really neat idea! I think it's so cool! We need to write down what we have to do. We can make a couple of lists. What should we do first?" Dawn was even more excited than Sharon was!

"Whoa! Wait a minute, slow down. I need to talk to Mom and Dad first. After all, we will be using our house and yard. I'll probably have to include Kyle too. He's the one who really started me thinking about this."

"OK, let me know when we can get started," Dawn said as the girls parted.

As Sharon walked home, she felt more and more excited by the possibilities of the idea. "I'll call it the Walnut Street Club or maybe the Creative Kids Club or . . . ," Sharon said to herself. She thought of several more possibilities but decided that whatever name she used, it had to sound like something fun and exciting.

Sharon hoped her family would be as enthusiastic about her idea as Dawn had been. She would need their help if she was really going to pull this off.

### Questions

- What was Mom's concern about the neighborhood where the family lived?
- How is your neighborhood similar to Sharon's?
- What are some concerns you have about your neighborhood?
- What one thing could you do in your neighborhood to make a positive difference?
- What do you think Sharon is planning?

### Bible Discovery

Read Luke 10:36-37 and Romans 13:9.

### Bible Point

No matter where you live, you are part of a neighborhood. If you live in the country, your neighborhood may cover several miles or be a town nearby. In a large city, one apartment building may be a neighborhood. You can make a difference in your own neighborhood by caring about the other people who live there. Just being friendly and helpful will help to improve any neighborhood.

Bottom Line

Making a difference in the world starts in your own neighborhood.

## About Time

Connor liked going to Sunday school because he had friends there. But the best part of Sunday school was the teacher, Mr. Schultz. He made learning fun and interesting. The students never knew exactly what to expect when they walked in the door on Sunday morning.

One Sunday the classroom was filled with clocks—big and small, ticking and quiet. There was also a big circle of cheese on the table. The kids tried to guess what cheese and clocks had in common. How could either one have anything to do with a Bible story?

After their curiosity was raised, Mr. Schultz settled the class. Then he asked, "How do you think these might go together?"

Connor blurted out, "All I can think of is the nursery rhyme, 'Hickory, Dickory, Dock, The mouse ran up the clock.'"

Kids giggled and snickered, but no one else ventured a guess.

"You're kind of right," said Mr. Schultz, "because we are going to talk about time today. That's why it looks and sounds like a clock factory in here. The cheese will stand for the amount of time we have in one week, which amounts to 168 hours. God gives everyone in the world the same amount of time each day, not one second less and not one second more. But we all use this time in different ways."

Mr. Schultz had the class tell how they spent their weekly hours, and he cut an appropriate size chunk from the cheese. The biggest chunk went to sleeping (56 hours). School time came next (30 hours). The cheese quickly disappeared as pieces representing hours spent eating, playing sports, personal time, leisure time, chores, and homework were chopped off. Finally, only one little chunk was left.

"This seems to be the time left for God and his work each week," said Mr. Schultz, pointing to the small remaining piece. "It's not very much, is it? Think of ways you can give more hours to God and how you can use them well. You really can make a difference in the world by giving of your time."

On the way home Connor told his family about Mr. Schultz's time lesson. "I want to make my 'God' chunk bigger and use it in a better way. Let's see . . . if I don't play soccer one afternoon, I will have two more hours. And, Mom, maybe I can go with you to the homeless shelter and help serve food on Thursdays."

Mom approved of Connor's idea, saying that it was a great way to give of his time to help others.

Questions

- What do people mean when they say that time raced by?
- Is that statement true? Why or why not?
- Besides sleeping, what do you spend the most time doing during your free time?
- Why is it important to give some of your time to God and his work?
- What are some ways you can give of your time to others?

Bible Discovery

Read Luke 2:36-38 and Acts 2:43-47.

Bible Point

Every person has the same amount of time each day, and it passes, minute by minute. Once time is gone, it is lost forever. It is important, therefore, to use our time wisely. We can give time to make a difference in the world by praying, volunteering to help someone in need, or joining a group that works to improve things or help others.

Bottom Line

Use your time to make a difference in the world.

## *Caring for Amee*

In a split second, Amee Wilson's life was changed forever. It happened as she was riding her bike home along a country road. A car came speeding around a curve, and the driver didn't see Amee until it was too late. The car hit the bike, sending Amee flying through the air and into a ditch. Her helmet saved her head, but she had several broken bones, deep cuts, and bruises. The doctors said it would take a long time and lots of work for Amee to get well.

Amee and her family were members of Oakwood Church. The people prayed for her, asking God to heal her. Their prayers were answered as Amee gradually started to show improvement.

When the people heard how expensive Amee's hospital stay and therapy would be, they wanted to help. After many ideas and much discussion about what to do, they decided to have an Amee Day. It would be a funfair with food, games, and crafts. Everyone in Oakwood Church was urged to help by contributing money, organizing games, or making something. All the profits would be given to Amee's family to help with the expenses.

Mr. Edwards told his Sunday school class about the event and asked the kids to think about what they could contribute. "Amee has to work hard to recover, and we need to help her in any way we can. We can show Amee that we really care about her. We can make a big difference when we give our money or use our abilities to help others," he said.

Cheryl said, "I do lots of baby-sitting. I can give a month's worth of baby-sitting money to help."

Susan and Carmen were excellent cookie bakers. They would bake one hundred cookies to sell. Ben would paint designs on faces and hands, Chris would run a free-throw-shooting contest, and Rex would make some birdhouses to sell.

Everyone except Ellie was excited and full of plans. She sat quietly at the table until Mr. Edwards asked, "Ellie, what would you like to do?"

"I don't know," she said. "I don't have any money, so I can't give that. And I'm not very good at anything like baking or making something."

Mr. Edwards said, "Oh, but you are very good at something, Ellie. You tell wonderful stories. Why don't you have a storytelling corner for people to visit?"

"I didn't think of storytelling as an ability," Ellie said. "That *would* be fun."

### Questions

- Why did Amee need help?
- How did the people of Oakwood Church respond when they heard of Amee's accident?
- How do you think Amee felt when she heard about what was being done?
- How can your family use money or abilities to make a difference in someone's life?
- Who would you choose to help?

### Bible Discovery

Read Luke 21:1-4 and Acts 9:30-41.

Bible Point

God wants his people to use their money and abilities to make a difference in the world. Some may have lots of money, and some may not have much. But God has given each person at least one ability. Maybe you can draw or play music. Perhaps you get along well with small children. Or maybe you are a good listener. Everything can be used to make a positive difference in the world.

Bottom Line

Use your money and abilities to make a difference in the world.

## *Adoption?*

"Hey, Mike! Guess what!" shouted Alysia as she burst into her big brother's room.

"Alysia, how many times have I told you not to just charge into my room? This is my private place. Knock before you come in," Mike said.

"OK, OK, next time I'll knock," Alysia promised. "But this won't be your own private room for very long. I know something you don't."

"Alysia, quit fooling around. What *are* you talking about?" Mike asked.

"Well," she said, "I heard Mom talking on the phone. She was talking about *adopting* someone. Mom said there were five in the family. Mike, maybe we're going to have five new brothers and sisters. What do you think?"

"I think you heard wrong," said Mike. "Where would we fit five more kids in this house? How could Mom and Dad buy food for seven kids?"

Alysia was a little upset. "I did not hear wrong," she insisted. "Let's go ask Mom."

When Mike and Alysia found Mom, she was reading a letter from church. Mike got right to the point. "Mom, are we going to have five new kids living with us?" he asked.

"What!" Mom exclaimed with a startled look on her face. "I sure hope not! What gave you that idea?"

Alysia spoke up. "I heard you tell Mrs. Bartlet that we were going to adopt someone, and there were five in the family."

Mom laughed and gave Alysia a hug. Then Mom showed the kids the letter she was holding. Across the top in bold letters it said "Make a difference in the world—adopt a missionary."

"You are half right," said Mom. "Our family is going to adopt a missionary family of five people. They are the Nichols family: the mother, the father, two sons, and a daughter. They are living and working in Africa."

Mike asked, "How can we adopt a family that lives in Africa?"

"Not everyone can be a foreign missionary," said Mom. "So we can do our part in bringing the Good News to people all over the world by helping the missionaries. Adopting a missionary family means remembering them and their work in our daily prayers. We will also send them cards on their birthdays or holidays. We will write them letters and encourage them as they spread God's Word. We will help them in any way we can."

Mom showed Mike and Alysia the picture of the Nichols family and the information about them. Alysia decided to write her own letters to the girl. Mike liked the idea of learning first-hand about mission work. He thought it was neat to adopt five people—and not have to share his room with two of them.

### Questions

- What were the kids concerned about when Alysia heard about the adoption?
- How would Mike's family help the Nichols family by adopting them?
- Why is adopting a missionary a good idea?
- How can adopting a missionary make a difference in the world?

### Bible Discovery

Read Acts 16:13-15 and Philippians 4:10-20.

### Bible Point

God wants all people to hear the good news of Jesus' death and resurrection. He wants them to know Jesus as their Savior. Not everyone can go to a faraway land, but we can help missionaries with our prayers, money, and encouragement.

### Bottom Line

Make a difference in the world by adopting a missionary.

### *The Best Life*

As Keith headed for his Sunday school class, he wondered what they would be talking about today. He was sure the teacher, Mr. Damion, would make the class really think about what was being taught.

Mr. Damion settled the class and began. "How many of you think you can make a difference in the world? Raise your hands." Not one hand went up.

"Why don't any of you think you can make a difference?" asked Mr. Damion. Everyone had an idea. Most of them thought they were too young and inexperienced. Some thought the world was in too much of a mess.

Mr. Damion said, "None of you are right. You *can* make a difference. You can influence another young person. You can get help to take care of one small problem in your neighborhood like cleaning up an empty lot. Don't think that you can't do anything. The very best way to make a difference in the world is to live in a Christlike way."

"How can I live like Christ?" asked Keith. "He is God, and he never sins. It's impossible for me to be like that."

Some of the other kids agreed.

Mr. Damion said, "You're absolutely right, Keith. We can't be exactly like Christ. But we can follow his example by doing what he did and behaving as he did. Let's do an acrostic to help us think of ways to live like Christ."

Mr. Damion wrote the letters *C-H-R-I-S-T* vertically on the board. Then the class thought of a Christlike quality they could copy in their own life for each of the letters. Here are their ideas:

Caring—We can show Christ in our lives by caring about others and how they feel. We can do this by being kind, helpful, and loving.

Happy—When we have a happy, optimistic attitude, other people notice. It cheers them up and helps them feel happy too.

Respectful—Jesus respected all different kinds of people. We can do the same thing, treating everyone in a fair way.

Involved—Jesus was involved with the people around him. We can become involved in the lives of our friends by being good listeners and encouragers.

Strong—With the Holy Spirit's help we can have a strong faith to fight against sin and temptations.

Trustworthy—We can always trust Jesus. When we keep our promises and do what we say we will do, people will trust us too.

"All right," said Keith. "I'm ready to make a difference in the world. Think I'll start by getting *involved* with old Mr. Peters next door."

### Questions

- Why did the kids think they couldn't make a difference?
- How do you feel about making a difference in the world?
- Which of the Christlike qualities above would be the easiest for you to do? Which one would be the most difficult?
- What other words can you fit into the acrostic?

### Bible Discovery

Read 2 Corinthians 3:18 and 1 John 2:3-6.

### Bible Point

Christians are to live like Christ. That means following his example and treating other people as he treated them. We can make a difference in the lives of others by being kind, loving, and trustworthy. This can also give us an opportunity to tell them the good news of salvation.

### Bottom Line

Make a difference in the world by living in a Christlike way.

# 17

# How to Spend Money

## *Wise Spending*

Deana Ruiz leaped toward the van. She took a series of leaps before settling into the front seat.

Mr. Ruiz shook his head. "Are you trying out for *Swan Lake?*" he asked with a smile.

Deana grinned. "Finally I'm getting my money out of the bank! I can spend, spend, spend!"

"Only *some* of your money," Mr. Ruiz said as he started up the van. "Your mother and I agreed to allow you to take $200 out to see how wisely you spend your money."

Her father had more to say, but Deana had tuned him out by that time. After six whole months of saving birthday money, Christmas money, money she had received from walking her neighbors' dogs, and some allowance money, she could shop till she dropped. First, she knew she had to give some of it in the church offering. After that, she had a whole list of things she wanted to get. At the top of her list were a new pair of Windspeed in-line skates—her dream skates—and a new CD-ROM game.

"We're here!" Her father's voice snapped her back to reality. She realized that they had arrived at the bank. "Are you coming in, or have you decided to stay in the van?"

Deana scrambled out of the van and raced her father to the door. Minutes later, she had the money in her hand—ten crisp twenty-dollar bills.

"Can we go to the mall now, Dad?" she asked. "I saw the skates I want at Ben's Better Sportstore."

"Were they on sale?" Dad asked.

Deana shrugged. "I don't know."

"Well, let's go home and check the sale flyers in today's paper," he said. "We might find them at a better price somewhere else."

Deana groaned. "Do we have to?"

"Deana, what did your mother and I tell you about being a good steward of your money?"

Deana wished she couldn't remember. But she did. *This is what I get for having a mother who is a financial planner and a father who is an accountant,* she thought. "God wants us to spend money wisely," she said dryly, repeating what her dad had once told her.

"And the way to do that is—?"

"Ask God for help in choosing what to buy," she finished.

"I know you're in a hurry to spend your money," said Dad. "But why pay full price for something if you can get it on sale? That way you get more for your money."

"But looking through sale papers takes forever!" Deana complained.

"Honey, I know you've waited a long time to spend this money," said Dad. "But once it's spent, it's gone. Your mother and I just want you to learn the value of a dollar. We don't want you to be foolish. That's why it's important to ask God to help you and to shop around for the best buy. Spending money wisely will help you avoid debt later on."

### Questions

- If you had Deana's money, what would you spend it on? Why?
- What are some ways you have used to save money while you spend it (for example, using coupons)?
- Why do you think God wants people to be wise about spending money?

### Bible Discovery

Check out Proverbs 1:7; 3:9, 13-16; 4:1-5; 17:16; 21:20.

### Bible Point

Solomon, the wisest man who ever lived, had a lot to say about wisdom. It comes from God and is necessary in all situations of life—especially money matters.

### Bottom Line

Ask for God's wisdom before spending money.

## *Reasons to Read*

When Deana and her father arrived home from the bank, Mrs. Ruiz met them at the door. She had a stack of magazines in her hand. "Deana, are you finished with these *Consumer Reports* magazines?" she asked. "I can take them back to the library today."

Deana didn't meet her mother's gaze. "Uh . . . yeah, you can take them back." She glanced at her mother and saw her mother exchange glances with her father.

"You didn't look at these magazines, did you?" Mrs. Ruiz asked.

"I looked at one of them," Deana said. She slid past her mother and went into the house. She busied herself with looking for Bólido (Spanish for "fireball"), her family's miniature schnauzer. She found him down the hall in the laundry room, curled up next to the dryer.

Mrs. Ruiz cornered her there. "Deana, I checked out these magazines for you so you could see if the skates you wanted were worth the price."

"But, Mom, everybody's got a pair of Windspeed skates!" Deana said. She picked up Bólido and rubbed his head.

Mrs. Ruiz sighed. "Come with me." She led the way to the kitchen. There she plopped the magazines on the table. "You see this microwave?" She pointed to it across the room. "Remember we wanted to get a MicroGlo 2000?"

"Yeah. We saw that on a commercial." Deana remembered the clever commercial with its catchy jingle.

"So your dad looked it up in *Consumer Reports.* Remember what he found out about it?" Mom asked.

Deana searched her memory. "Oh, that it was one of the most dangerous microwaves ever made."

"Yep. Uncle Luis had one, remember?" Mom asked. "It shorted out and caught on fire."

Deana shuddered as she recalled what had happened. She was glad they had managed to get the fire put out before the kitchen went up in flames.

"So, *mi hija,* what do you think you should do?" asked Mom.

Deana sighed and opened the first *Consumer Reports.* Soon she was involved in reading a report on popular kinds of in-line skates. To her dismay, the Windspeed skates were one of the lowest rated skates. "It says here that they're a big rip-off. Does this mean I shouldn't get them?" she asked.

"What do you think?" said Mom.

"But other kids have 'em," replied Deana.

"Honey, just because other kids have them, does that make them safe? Uncle Luis had the microwave we wanted and look what happened. We would have thrown our money away if we had bought the same microwave," she said.

Deana nodded and returned her attention to the magazine. "It says here that the Dynoblade 350 skates are better than the Windspeeds. And they cost $50 less!"

Mrs. Ruiz put her arm around Deana's shoulders. "Reading about a product helps you spend your money wisely. God leads us in different ways. The information you find could be his way of helping you avoid being cheated."

Questions

- Where can you find information on the things you want to buy?
- Why do people make mistakes and buy inferior products?
- Why is it important to find information on an item before you buy it?

Bible Discovery

Read Proverbs 4:6; 31:10, 16-18.

Bible Point

The woman of noble character described in Proverbs 31 provides a model of a careful spender. She inspected the field she wanted to purchase before giving up her money. God wants us to be careful about how we spend our money.

Bottom Line

The wise person seeks information to avoid being cheated.

## *Temptation*

Deana inspected her new skates, the Dynoblade 350s. They looked even better than they had in *Consumer Reports. And I still have $100 left to spend,* she thought. She was pleased with herself and even more pleased at the thought of going to the mall that afternoon. She looked at her list:

- skirt
- earrings
- CD-ROM game or music CD
- blue jeans

*I should have just enough to get everything on my list,* she thought.

Saturday afternoon Mr. Ruiz drove Deana and her best friend Giselle to the Clover City Mall. "I'll meet you by the food court in an hour and a half," he said.

"Let's synchronize our watches," Deana suggested.

They all checked their watches. "It's 1:30 now. Be back here by 3:00," Mr. Ruiz said.

The girls set off at a fast pace. "Let's stop at The Earring Place," Deana suggested, pointing to a small store. "I need a new pair of gold hoops."

"Ooh." Giselle paused by a knickknack store to gaze at the items in the window. "Look! They have those cute electronic pets," she said. "I want one of those."

"Ooh," Deana echoed. "They're only $15."

"Let's go look at them." Giselle led the way into the store. They quickly found the electronic-pet display. They each grabbed a demo to play with.

"It's sooo cute!" Deana said.

"They're pretty popular," a salesclerk said. "Better get one now before we sell out."

Deana was tempted. She noticed that there were only a few left on display. "Is this all you have?"

The woman nodded. "The next shipment won't be in until next week."

Deana took her list out of the pocket of her jeans. She hadn't gotten any of the things on her list. If she bought the electronic pet, she wouldn't have enough to buy everything else.

"A lot of kids have them," the salesclerk said.

"They sure are cool," Giselle said.

"I need a minute to think about it," Deana said. She put the demo down and walked around the store. *What should I do?* she thought.

She then remembered what her Sunday school teacher had said during class last Sunday. "Whenever you're tempted, pray. God can give you the strength to resist temptation," he had said.

*This is probably too minor to pray about,* Deana thought. But she kept thinking about her teacher's words and what her father had told her just days ago. "Ask God to help you," he had said.

*Lord, help me know what to do. I want to be wise in the way I spend money,* she prayed.

As she ended her prayer, Giselle tapped her on the shoulder.

"My cat's a lot more fun than that electronic pet," she said. "I don't think I'll spend my $15 on it."

Deana smiled. "Neither will I."

Questions

- Why was Deana tempted to buy the electronic pet?
- What are you usually tempted to spend your money on?
- How do you resist temptation?
- Why does God care how you spend your money?

Bible Discovery

Read Matthew 6:13; Luke 22:40; 1 Corinthians 10:13.

Bible Point

Temptation comes in many forms. Sometimes you can be tempted to spend your money in an unwise fashion. At other times, you can be tempted to impulsively buy something you hadn't planned to buy. When temptation comes, God can show you a way to resist and overcome it.

Bottom Line

When you are tempted to spend money unwisely, remember your values and pray.

## *The Value of a Dollar*

"What time is it?" Deana asked her friend Giselle.

Giselle looked at her watch. It was shaped like a fish and had fish fins for hands. "2:15."

"We have to meet my dad at 3:00," Deana reminded her. "And I've bought only one thing on my list." She had bought herself a pair of hoop earrings for $15.

Giselle had a few bags of her own. "I'm glad my grandma gave me money instead of pajamas for my birthday this year," she said. "Grandma finally realizes that I'm thirteen, not three."

Deana clapped a hand to her face. The word *birthday* had reminded her that her mother's birthday was coming up. "My mom's birthday is in three days! I haven't bought her anything!" she cried.

"What are you going to get?" Giselle asked.

Deana shrugged. "Well, I don't want to spend a whole lot on a gift." She wanted to buy everything on her list. After all, hadn't she waited six whole months to be able to spend money on herself?

By this time, they had wandered near a Christian bookstore.

"Let's go in here and see what I can get cheap," Deana said. "Mom usually likes books and stuff."

They searched the aisles.

"Hey, look at these," Giselle said, pointing to a display of ceramic angel figurines.

"My mom has one of these!" Deana said. "She loves this kind. I know she'd like one." She glanced at the price. "This is $30! I didn't want to spend that much."

"What about getting her a plaque?" Giselle suggested. She held up one that said "World's Greatest Mom."

Deana shrugged. "I gave Mom a plaque once. I'm not sure she really likes them."

"But it's only $12," said Giselle.

"Hmm. I like that price!" said Deana.

At that moment, a woman walked into the store with her daughter. The girl looked about Giselle's and Deana's age.

"Now don't buy anything stupid," the mother said loudly.

"But it's my money," said the girl.

"So? You don't have sense enough to know how to spend it," answered her mother.

"Did you hear the way she talked to her daughter?" Giselle whispered. "If that were me, I'd run away from home."

"My mom would never embarrass me like that," Deana said. She suddenly realized how much freedom her parents had given her to make her own choices about spending money. They just wanted her to be wise about spending it.

Deana looked at the plaque. "Come to think of it, my mom's worth a lot more than $12." She set the plaque down and headed back to the display of angels.

"What about the stuff on your list?" Giselle asked.

"Mom's worth more to me than having that stuff," answered Deana.

Questions

- What is the most expensive gift you have ever bought someone? Why did you choose that gift?
- Why was Deana's choice in the Christian bookstore a good one?
- What caused Deana to make the choice she made? Why was it a difficult choice?

### Bible Discovery

Read John 3:16; Romans 8:32; 2 Corinthians 9:7.

### Bible Point

How people spend their time and money shows what they value. God generously gave us everything, including his own Son. His gift of love can encourage us to be generous in our giving. Being generous does not always mean spending a lot of money. It can also mean being generous in love. God's "bank" of love is always full. Make a withdrawal today! "Spend" it wisely!

### Bottom Line

Because God gave generously, we can too.

## *A Collection of Value*

As Deana and Giselle walked through the mall, they heard their names being called. Soon Sean Crabtree, a friend of theirs from school, caught up with them.

"Where are you two headed?" he asked.

Deana looked at her watch. "We have to meet my dad in fifteen minutes. . . . Right now, I want to find someplace to sit down. My feet hurt."

"Where are you headed?" Giselle asked.

"To get some new CD-ROM games," Sean said. "Thought I'd check out Software Sal's."

"I wanted to get another CD-ROM game too, but I don't have enough money," Deana said sadly.

"Too bad. Say, you guys want to come with me?" asked Sean.

"Guess it couldn't hurt to look," Giselle said.

The three took an escalator down to the lower level. The software store was just to the left of the escalator.

"How many games do you have now, Sean?" Giselle asked.

He shrugged. "I don't know. Maybe fifty."

"Fifty?! Wow!" Deana exclaimed.

"I collect 'em. As soon as a new one gets popular, I bug my parents about it until they give in and give me the money." Sean looked proud of his strategy.

"What're you going to get?" Giselle asked.

"It's a toss-up between 'Serial Killer VI' and 'Blood and Mayhem II.'"

They worked their way through the crowd of shoppers until they found the new-games display. A still shot from the "Blood and Mayhem II" game had been enlarged to advertise the game. It showed a number of dead bodies and plenty of blood.

*Gross!* Deana thought when she saw the scene.

"Hey, cool," Sean said. "This looks much more real than 'Serial Killer VI.'"

"You're going to buy this?" Giselle asked. "It costs $79!"

Sean shrugged. "Everybody's playing this." He grabbed a box and headed to the cashier.

Deana and Giselle browsed while Sean made his purchase. "That game looks disgusting," Deana said. "I wouldn't spend my money on it." She picked up the game she had wanted to buy. It was a travel adventure that cost $39.99. "I can't even afford this," she said.

"Sean's got an expensive collection of games," Giselle said. "Everybody at school talks about his collection. Look at this." She pointed to a war game. "He told me two weeks ago that he got this for his birthday. It's almost $60!

"He told me about some of the games he has," said Deana. "I think I'd have nightmares just looking at that stuff. I hate looking at blood and guts! My parents would freak if they saw that 'Blood and Mayhem' game. I can hear my dad now: 'That just glorifies violence.'"

Giselle laughed. "You sound just like him."

"Well, I think he's right, though. Why should I spend my money on something disgusting? Sean's collection may be expensive, but to me, it's not worth a whole lot!"

### Questions

- How does what we buy reflect our values?
- Think about the last few items that you bought. How do they show what you value?

### Bible Discovery

Read about your "heavenly bank account" in Matthew 6:19-24.

### Bible Point

In the Sermon on the Mount, Jesus wanted people to think about something else of value—heavenly investments. Being obedient to God is a way to store up treasures in heaven. You can show you value what God values in the way you spend your money and your time.

### Bottom Line

Spend wisely and be sure to store up treasures in your heavenly bank account.

# 18 How to Manage Money

### *Resource-Full*

"Hey Dad, can you loan me $10?" Marty Kessler asked. "Me and Tony want to go to the movies. I'll pay you back, honest."

*"Tony and I,"* Mrs. Kessler corrected from her room upstairs.

"Marty, that's the second time this week you've asked me for money. You already owe me $15. What do you do with all your money?" Mr. Kessler asked.

Marty shrugged. "Can I borrow $10, Dad? Tony's older brother's coming any minute. He's driving us to the mall. Can we talk about this later, huh Dad? Please?"

Mr. Kessler sighed and took out his wallet. He quickly peeled off a ten. "We'll definitely talk about this later."

"Thanks, Dad. See you!" Marty hurried out.

Later that evening, Marty had just settled down to play a game on his Nintendo as Mr. Kessler entered the family room.

"OK, let's go to the computer. I just loaded a new finance program."

"Aw, Dad, I just got started! Can we do it in a minute?"

"Save it now or lose it. Your choice."

Marty saw that his dad meant business, so he saved the game, then flopped into a chair next to the one at the computer. Mr. Kessler clicked a few icons on the screen and launched the finance program. "Now," he said, "let's figure out where your money goes. OK, your mother and I give you how much for allowance?"

"You know," Marty said.

"Just play along," said Dad.

"Five dollars a week," answered Marty.

Mr. Kessler typed that information into the computer. "And you make how much from your paper route?"

"Practically nothing!" answered Marty, but after a look from his father, he added, "Thirty-five dollars a month."

Mr. Kessler added that information. "Tips?"

Marty shrugged. "Sometimes $12 a month. Sometimes $15. Sometimes $8. Depends on how cheap people are acting. One time Mr. Winchell—"

"Let's be on the safe side and put down $10." Mr. Kessler typed that. "So, let's say you get about $65 a month. Does that seem about right?"

Marty nodded.

"You look as if you're about to face a firing squad." Mr. Kessler suddenly smiled. "I guess I felt the same way when my dad first sat me down and asked me the same questions." He paused, then asked, "Why do you think I'm asking you about your spending?"

Marty shrugged. "To make sure I pay you back?"

"No," Dad responded, "to make sure you manage your money well. Managing your money can help keep you out of debt. One day you'll be on your own. You'll need to know how to budget, how to save, how to monitor your spending, how to—"

"I have to know all that?" asked Marty, rolling his eyes.

Mr. Kessler grinned. "We'll take them one at a time. First you should know that a wise person manages money with one thing in mind."

"Which is . . . ?" asked Marty.

Mr. Kessler answered, "How he or she can glorify God by being a good steward of God's resources. Money is a resource. It's how you use it that matters."

### Questions

- What do you do with your allowance?
- Why is it important to manage money well?
- What do you think God wants you to learn concerning the money you have?

### Bible Discovery

Check out Proverbs 1:7 and Luke 19:12-27.

### Bible Point

Jesus' parable shows the value of managing money wisely. God wants his children to be wise in all aspects of their lives.

That includes being wise money managers. The wisdom for that comes from God.

Bottom Line

Managing money takes wisdom, which comes from God.

### *Income and Expenses*

Marty Kessler watched his father typing away on the computer. Bored, he began to spin around on the chair. He accidentally swung his feet against a floor vase and sent it crashing to the floor.

"Whoops! Do you think it's broken?" Marty asked anxiously.

Mr. Kessler sighed as he held up a pottery shard. "Guess."

"I didn't mean it!" exclaimed Marty.

"Tell that to your mother," replied his father. "You should be glad it's not expensive . . . since you'll need to replace it."

"Replace it?! I've got to buy another one?" said Marty.

Mr. Kessler nodded. "You broke it, right? Good thing we're getting a budget planned for you, huh?"

Marty looked crestfallen. "B-but . . ."

"So, we'll work on getting the $40 to get another vase," Dad stated matter-of-factly.

"$40! But it was an accident!" exclaimed Marty. "I'll be broke till doomsday! And I wanted to buy another Nintendo game! It's not fair, Dad."

Mr. Kessler took off his glasses and swung them around by one of the temples. "OK. I'll make you a deal. I'll go halves with you. We'll both pay $20. How's that?"

Marty just sulked.

"Marty, I just want you to realize that money doesn't grow on trees. Your mom and I both work, but that doesn't mean we're rich. If something breaks, we can't always afford to pay to have it fixed. That's why we try to take care of what we have." Mr. Kessler looked hard at Marty. "That's why we gave you an allowance. That's why we wanted you to keep your paper route. Now—" Mr. Kessler pointed to the screen—"you get $65 a month, right?"

Marty nodded.

"When you make a budget, think of income and expenses," continued Marty's dad. "Any money you get regularly is income. Expenses are what you spend money on. A budget will help you avoid living beyond your means. Let's see . . . you owe me $25. And with the $20 you'll give me for the vase, you're in debt $45."

Marty groaned.

Dad continued. "So, let's see . . . instead of paying it all at once, we'll deduct it from your weekly allowance. How much should we deduct? How about $1.25?"

"That much?" Marty frowned.

"Keep talking and we'll make it $2," added his father.

"$1.25 sounds great, Dad!" said Marty.

"I thought so. In two months you will have paid off the $20 for the vase," explained Mr. Kessler. "Now, from your pay, we'll deduct $12.50. In the same two months you would also finish paying off the debt you owe me. So that's $17.50 a month altogether. OK?"

Marty nodded.

"So now you have $47.50 to work with for each of the next two months. Not bad, huh?" Dad asked.

"If you say so," answered Marty.

Dad continued. "Remember we talked about being a good steward with money? I want you to know how to manage your money wisely so you won't be stuck in serious debt someday."

"OK," said Marty.

Mrs. Kessler entered the family room. "Hey, who broke my vase? Whoever did better buy me a new one."

Mr. Kessler grinned. "Don't worry, dear. We've got that covered."

### Questions

- When you owed someone money that you couldn't pay back, what did you do?
- How do you feel when you're in debt?
- What are your "expenses"? What "income" do you have?
- Which is greater—your expenses or your income? Why?

### Bible Discovery

Read Romans 13:6-10.

### Bible Point

Getting into debt and staying there is not wise. God tells his people to pay what they owe.

### Bottom Line

Pay what you owe. Do what you can to stay out of debt.

### *First Things First*

"OK. Time to budget," Mr. Kessler said, rubbing his hands together.

Marty stood and stretched. "Can we take a break, Dad? I need a snack."

"Sure, go ahead," said Mr. Kessler.

Marty gratefully escaped upstairs to his room. Just as he crossed the threshold, he heard the phone ring. He grabbed the cordless phone in his parents' room. "Hello?"

"Hey, Mart. It's me, Ray."

Ray was one of Marty's friends. "Man, why do you always say, 'It's me, Ray'? I know it's you. I recognize your voice," Marty answered.

"It's a habit, man," answered Ray. "Listen, can I borrow $5?"

Marty sighed. "This is the third time this month! What do you do with your money?" He suddenly realized how much he sounded like his father.

"I can't help it," answered Ray. "My dad cut back on my allowance, man."

Marty shook his head. Ray's parents were wealthy, yet Ray always bummed money off his friends. "I don't know if I'll have enough to give you. I owe my dad money. He's deducting from my allowance for the next two months."

"Bummer. Well, maybe I'll try Sean. See you." Ray clicked off.

Marty returned downstairs, grabbed a Coke from the refrigerator, and returned to the family room.

"Who was that on the phone?" Mr. Kessler asked.

"Ray. He wanted to bum $5 off me. He still owes me $2 from a week ago." Marty shook his head. "His dad's loaded, too."

"Yes, but that doesn't mean they give him any of it, beyond what's needed," said Mr. Kessler. "Maybe they have him on a budget too."

"He never seems to have *any* money. He just bums off his friends," said Marty.

"Well, he must have generous friends," added Marty's dad. "It's great to help your friends, but be careful, OK? Now . . . you have $47.50 to work with. How much did your mother and I tell you to save each month?"

"Twenty percent of what I get," answered Marty.

"So that would come to about $9.50. Let's make it an even $10," said Mr. Kessler.

"Why not $20, Dad?" asked Marty, smiling.

"Sarcasm will cause me to deduct more from your allowance," said Mr. Kessler.

"OK, sorry," said Marty.

His dad continued. "So, we deduct $10 and come up with $37.50. Oh, I forgot about a tithe. We should have deducted that off the top."

"Do I have to give 10 percent?" asked Marty.

"It's not a question of *have to,*" answered his father. "The Lord loves a cheerful giver. He doesn't want any do-I-have-to money. Remember, God gives us everything we have. It's a privilege to give back to him. Anyway, your mother and I won't force you to give 10 percent, but we do want you to give something."

Marty thought a moment. "How about 5 percent for the two months until I pay my debt, then 10 percent afterward?"

"OK. So that would be $4.75. We'll make it $5." Mr. Kessler deducted the $5. "Now you have $32.50 to work with. Not a bad haul."

Marty smiled. "I guess not. Maybe I've been spending too much. Maybe I've been like Ray."

"Son, I think you've just seen the light," said Mr. Kessler with a smile.

### Questions

- How can you honor God with your money?
- Why do you think it's important to watch out for how much you spend?
- How much do you set aside for God each week?
- How can a budget help you manage your money?

### Bible Discovery

Read Proverbs 3:9, 13-16 and 2 Corinthians 9:7.

### Bible Point

Giving back to God is a way to say thanks to him for his provision. God never forces anyone to give to him. After all, he prefers cheerful givers.

### Bottom Line

Giving to God first and keeping a budget are steps that wise money managers take.

### *Money Matters*

"Thirty-two fifty." Marty thought over that amount. He had that much each month. Yet why was he always broke? He gingerly swiveled around in the chair, then realized that the vase he had broken had been moved. He gave a full swivel.

Mr. Kessler returned bearing a bowl of pretzels. "So, let's get to how much you're spending. What did you spend this month?" he asked.

Marty thought about that a minute and then said, "Well, I went to the movies four times. That was . . . uh-oh. That was $10 each time."

"So if you keep doing that, you'll be in debt before the month's out," said Mr. Kessler. "You're going to have to cut back on the movies. What else?"

"I went to the arcade a few times," answered Marty. "I don't know how much I spent there."

"You're going to have to keep track," said his dad. "That's your assignment for the next two weeks. Keep track of what you spend. Can you think of anything else?"

Marty thought for a few seconds and answered, "Well, I went bowling once. And I played golf with Uncle Frank. I bought some golf balls. Uncle Frank paid the green fees. There's no way I could afford that."

Dad agreed. "Definitely. Golf is out for you, my boy—unless my brother pays. It's too rich for your blood."

"Dinner!" Mrs. Kessler called. "Marty, you were supposed to set the table!"

"I thought it was Kassie's turn!" Marty yelled.

"Is not!" his younger sister called from somewhere else in the house.

During dinner, Mrs. Kessler said, "The front brakes on my car have been grinding again. I've got to get them replaced."

Mr. Kessler groaned. "Oh, great! We just replaced the windshield last month! Well, there goes $500."

"Whoa!" Marty said. "That would take me a zillion years to save up."

"Just wait till you start driving in two years," said his father. "We may get you in on car repairs."

"No thanks! About the car repairs I mean!" Marty replied.

"If we hadn't managed our money properly, we couldn't afford these emergencies," Mr. Kessler continued. "Speaking of emergencies, I'll need $250 tomorrow to pay the insurance deductible for Kassie's emergency-room bill from last month."

"You had to break your arm," Marty said.

"It wasn't my fault! Traci hit me with her bat during softball!" Kassie retorted.

"I'll write out a check tonight," Mr. Kessler said. "I'm glad the Lord provides for us."

A loud crash was suddenly heard from the direction of the family room.

"What on earth was that?" Mrs. Kessler asked.

"Another emergency?" Marty asked with a grin.

### Questions

- What emergencies have come up in your life where you needed money?
- Why is it important to prepare for things like emergencies?
- What can a person do to be prepared financially for emergencies?

### Bible Discovery

Read Proverbs 3:5-6; 4:1-6.

### Bible Point

God wants us to trust him. He also wants us to listen to and learn from wise advice from others.

### Bottom Line

To manage money, keep track of what you spend and plan ahead for emergencies.

## *Needs*

Marty gave a satisfied pull on his straw. "Nothing like a strawberry-banana Smoothie," he said.

"How come you didn't get the large size?" his friend Dean asked. "That's what you usually get."

"I'm on a budget now," Marty answered, reaching into his pocket and counting his remaining cash. "I've got $4 left to last the week."

"That's all?" Dean shook his head. "Your old man been cracking the whip?" He made a whip-cracking sound.

"Naw, man," Marty answered. "I've been trying to watch what I spend. I want to save up and get that 'Warriors of the Night' game."

"Oh, man, that's awesome, man!" exclaimed Dean. "My dad bought that for my birthday. It costs $89."

"Wow. Might take me awhile to save that," Marty said.

"Why don't you just ask your dad? Now that my parents are divorced, my dad gives me what I want." Dean reached into his pocket and pulled out a twenty-dollar bill. "Too bad, man. I was going to see if you wanted to play mini-golf this afternoon."

Marty shrugged. "Can't afford it." He felt a tug of envy. Dean always had money. *What good is being a Christian if you're always broke?* he wondered. *Dean's not even a Christian.*

Marty glanced at his watch. "I have to get home anyway. My mom's making me do extra chores around the house. She'll be at the front entrance waiting."

"Didn't you say they're deducting money out of your allowance?" Dean asked. "*And* they're making you do extra chores? What a gyp!"

"See you, Dean," Marty called as he left the ice-cream store.

Marty found Mrs. Kessler waiting at the mall's front entrance.

"Why the long face?" she asked when Marty climbed into the front seat.

Marty sighed. "Dean always has money, and I'm always broke. He's not even a Christian!"

"So you think being a Christian means you'll always have money?" Mrs. Kessler asked.

"Well, yeah. God's supposed to take care of us, right?" said Marty.

"Well, honey," answered his mom, "God never promised that everything would be easy when we follow him. He just wants us to be obedient." Mrs. Kessler glanced over at Marty. "Just think, you're almost out of debt. You'll have a little more pocket money next week."

"But next week's four days away," said Marty. "Can I have an advance on my allowance? Dean wants to go play mini-golf this afternoon."

Mrs. Kessler shook her head. "Nope. We discussed this before. No advances."

Marty sulked for a while. Why did his parents have to be so unfair? It was horrible that he had to stick to this stupid budget!

He thought about Dean's situation. His father practically threw money at him. Still, he had to admit that Dean hardly saw his father. His dad lived in another state. *I'd hate that,* he thought.

*At least my parents are together. I'm thankful for that. Maybe I have more to be thankful for than I thought.*

By the time they pulled up in front of their house, Marty felt a lot better.

"You're smiling now. Why?" asked Mom.

"I just realized that I have a lot to be thankful for, even if I have only $4," answered Marty.

### Questions

- Why was Marty feeling bad when he met his mother at the mall?
- What made him feel better?
- Which one does God promise to supply?
- How has God provided for your needs?

### Bible Discovery

Read Psalm 37:1-5; Philippians 4:11-13, 19.

### Bible Point

God promises to take care of our needs, but that doesn't guarantee that life will be smooth sailing. Even though others may have more than we do, we are still to trust God.

### Bottom Line

Trust God to supply your needs.

# 19

# How to Deal with Tough Questions

### *Is the Narrow Way the Right Way?*

"Hey, Adam, are you playing softball on Sunday?" Miguel Galanes asked. "My dad said he'd drive us."

Adam Bridgman shook his head. "No, I already told the coach I have church Sunday mornings. I don't like to miss it."

"Why do you always have to go to church?" asked Miguel.

Adam felt put on the spot. "Well, we're supposed to worship God," he answered.

"Let me ask you something. Why do Christians always say they know the only way to heaven?" asked Miguel. "My dad says you guys are just narrow-minded."

Adam didn't know how to respond to Miguel's question. Miguel didn't wait around for an answer either way.

Adam was troubled as he rode the bus home from school. His mother commented on his expression when she met him at the back door on her way from the garage.

"Did your team lose again?" she asked as she unlocked the door of the house.

"No, we won," Adam said with a brief smile.

Mrs. Bridgman's eyebrows rose. "You could've fooled me."

Adam headed to the refrigerator. "I was just thinking about something Miguel said. He said Christians are narrow-minded." Then Adam quickly related his conversation with Miguel.

Mrs. Bridgman shook her head. "Well, all you can do is point out that Jesus said he's the only way to God. That's John 14:6, I believe."

"But what about other religions like Hinduism and Buddhism?" Adam asked. "How do we know they're false? Are we being narrow-minded and judgmental?"

"Tell you what, Adam," Mom replied. "After dinner, let's go to the Christian bookstore. I believe it's open until nine tonight. We can look through some of the booklets they have on other religions and compare what they say to what the Bible says."

"But won't they just give the Christian view on those religions?" Adam asked. "Is that fair?"

Mrs. Bridgman shrugged. "If you like, we can stop by the library, too, to find some books on the subject. But the thing that I want you to understand, Adam, is that God expects us to have faith. Sometimes we won't find all the answers we're looking for. When that happens, we need to trust that God will help us be satisfied with what we know about him."

"But what will I tell Miguel?" asked Adam.

"The best thing to do is tell him about your relationship to Jesus," Mom answered. "Tell him what you know, not what you think he might want to hear."

#### Questions

- Why was Miguel's question tough for Adam to answer?
- Where do you go to find answers when you have hard questions?
- Why did Mrs. Bridgman suggest going to the Christian bookstore?

#### Bible Discovery

Read these verses: Proverbs 15:1; 2 Timothy 2:15; 1 Peter 3:15-16.

#### Bible Point

Study God's Word so you will be ready to answer those who ask you about your faith in Christ. Be sure to answer in a gentle and respectful way.

#### Bottom Line

When you are faced with tough questions, answer gently and with respect.

## *Study Time*

Allison was entertaining her four-year-old sister, Patti, while Mom was putting the finishing touches on a special meal. The Doyle family had been invited for dinner, and Mom did not need Patti asking her a million questions. So Patti asked Allison instead.

"Who's coming? Where do they live? Do they have kids?" Patti asked all in one breath.

Allison answered, "The Doyle family is from church. They live in a farmhouse outside of town. They have three boys."

Patti's lower lip stuck out. "Boys!" she said. "I want them to be girls. Boys don't like to play girl games." Patti put her hands on her hips and let out a dramatic sigh.

Allison tried not to laugh as she said, "Patti, you know Jimmy—he's in your Sunday school class. You can play ball or build blocks with him. You might have lots of fun."

Patti seemed to consider this. Then she said, "But will he know what to do? How will he know the right way to play ball or build? Guess I'll show him how. I'm going to look out the window till they come."

Now Allison let out a sigh of her own. Sometimes she wished she were four years old. It was easy to tell Patti what was right. But Allison found it very confusing to know what was right sometimes. Some of her friends had different ideas of right and wrong than she did. And then she might see or hear something entirely different on a TV show or read it in a book. It was hard to know what was *really* right. She wondered if anyone else faced these kinds of tough questions.

Dinner was very enjoyable. Mom's food was delicious, and the conversation was interesting. Mr. Doyle owned the hardware store in town, and he told some funny stories about things that had happened to him. Then he said, "Sometimes it's really hard to know what is right. Some people have one opinion and someone else thinks the opposite."

Allison gave her full attention to Mr. Doyle. Here was a grown-up who had the same problem she did. Mr. Doyle went on. "To really know what is right, I study the Bible. God tells us in the Ten Commandments and other places in his Word what is right and wrong. When I know what God says, it really doesn't matter what people say."

*Thank you, Mr. Doyle!* Allison said to herself. *I needed to hear that.* She decided that she didn't *really* want to be four again as she watched Jimmy and Patti giggling and poking each other.

Questions

- Why did Allison sometimes wish she could be four years old?
- What was bothering Allison?

- What tough questions do you wonder about sometimes?
- How can studying the Bible help you find answers to your questions?

Bible Discovery

Read Acts 17:11 and 2 Timothy 2:15.

Bible Point

The Bereans were believers who were taught by Paul, but they checked everything they heard against God's Word. When you need answers to hard questions, you can be a "Berean" by searching God's Word for answers.

Bottom Line

When you are faced with tough questions, look to God's Word for answers.

## *A World of Suffering*

Ginger Donatucci groaned as she shifted her sprained foot on the couch. "Stupid sprain!" she muttered. "Mom! Can you bring me some iced tea, please?"

Mrs. Donatucci carried a bottle of raspberry iced tea from the kitchen. "Ginger, I don't want you to lie around all day," she said. "That's why we got you the crutches."

"I know, but my foot hurts today. And I feel so weak," replied Ginger with a touch of a whine in her voice.

The phone suddenly rang, and Ginger almost dived off the couch to grab the cordless phone. Her friend Lynette was on the line.

"How are you feeling?" Lynette asked.

"OK," answered Ginger. "What's up at school?"

"Nothing much," replied Lynette. "There's a rumor going around that Sydney cheated on the algebra test."

"Ooh. Everybody knows he did," said Ginger.

"Stacey wasn't in school today, either," continued Lynette. "Our homeroom teacher said that her family's house burned down yesterday."

"Oh, that's terrible! Wasn't her mother just out of the hospital?" Ginger asked.

"Yeah. Bummer, huh?" said Lynette.

Ginger chatted with Lynette awhile longer and then hung up the phone with a sigh. She collected her crutches and went to find her mother in the kitchen.

"Well, I'm glad to see that you're finally up and about," Mrs. Donatucci said.

"Lynette told me about our friend Stacey's family," said Ginger and she quickly told her mother what happened. "Mom, why does God allow suffering in the world?" she asked.

"Hmm. That's a tough question," Mom replied. "I can't say I really know why. When sin came into the world, a lot of suffering came as a result. Some suffering we go through is the result of others sinning against us. Jesus said that we were to expect some suffering."

"But some things seem so unfair," said Ginger. "Like what's happening to Stacey's family. So many bad things have happened to them. Mrs. Mitchell's been in and out of the hospital. And last year Mr. Mitchell lost his job. Now their house burned down!" She glanced down at her sprained foot. "And I tripped over Robbie's stupid toy car and fell down the stairs."

"You think God has caused you to suffer?" asked Mrs. Donatucci.

"Well, he could have prevented it, like he could've prevented the Mitchells' house from burning down," answered Ginger.

"If you really want answers, you could read some of God's answers to Job in Job 38–41," said her mother. "Now there's a man who suffered. In the meantime, why don't we pray for the Mitchells? Let's also ask God to help us trust him with our lives, even in hard situations."

### Questions

- When you see someone suffer (especially if you're the one who is suffering), are you tempted to question God? Why or why not?
- Why doesn't God prevent suffering?
- What do you think God wants you to learn when you suffer?

### Bible Discovery

Read Isaiah 58:9; Job 40:1-8; John 16:33.

### Bible Point

God promises to answer if we call to him. During Job's suffering, he wanted answers. He questioned why God allowed such terrible suffering in his life. God's answer? "I'm God.

I don't need to justify myself to you." That may seem like a tough answer, but God wanted Job to look beyond his own need for answers and trust him instead. When we can't understand what God is doing or why, we still need to trust him.

Bottom Line

When you are faced with tough questions, trust God.

## *The Big One*

The Park Street youth group was in the middle of their evangelism weekend. The main activity for that Saturday involved going door to door in the neighborhood to distribute tracts.

Elliot Markham and his partner, Mitch Stevens, had started off the day with enthusiasm and a handful of tracts. But after a few encounters with some of the people in the neighborhood, they were discouraged. They returned to the church to look for Don, their youth pastor, who had to return early.

"You guys back so soon?" Don asked when the boys trooped into his office.

"You tell him," Mitch said to Elliot.

"Well, we sort of quit," Elliot said.

"Why?" asked Don.

"Well, after one guy yelled at us for ten minutes about why a loving God would send people to hell, we sort of got discouraged," answered Elliot.

"Oh. The big one," said Don.

"The big one?" Mitch echoed.

"Yes, that's the big question that a lot of people stumble over." Don waved his hand at a book-lined wall behind his desk. "See all those books? Many of them are commentaries. If you want to find the answer to that question, you're welcome to search through those books."

Elliot and Mitch looked at each other. Neither wanted to spend the time looking through all those books. "Isn't there a faster way to get the answer?" Mitch asked.

Elliot suddenly snapped his fingers. "The Internet! We could do a search on the Web browser and—"

Don laughed. "And where would you begin?"

That brought Elliot up short. "I don't know," he said.

"The Web can help you find answers if you need to know facts in encyclopedias. But you need a subject to begin the search."

Don paused, then said, "I know a faster way to answer your question."

Elliot looked disappointed. He had been itching to surf the Net.

"You sure know how to draw out the suspense," Mitch remarked.

"That's why I'm a youth pastor," said Don. "Anyway, I already know the answer to your question."

"And the answer is?" Mitch prompted, while Elliot mimicked a drum roll.

"The answer is . . . he doesn't," Don replied.

"Doesn't what?" Mitch asked, just as Elliot asked, "Who doesn't?"

"God doesn't send people to hell," answered Don. "They voluntarily go. It's our choice whether we accept Jesus or reject him forever. If it were up to God, we'd all be with him for eternity. But he gives us the choice. We can decide whether to trust Jesus and serve him or not."

"Why didn't you think of that?" Elliot asked Mitch.

"Me?" said Mitch. "You could've thought of that."

"No, I couldn't," answered Elliot. "It never would've crossed my mind!"

"Mine either," said Mitch.

The boys thanked Don, then headed out of his office.

"Going back out to pass out tracts?" Don asked.

"No," said Elliot. "We're going over to Mitch's house to see if his dad will let us use the Web browser."

"But I just told you the answer," said Don.

"Yeah, but suppose somebody asks us about free will?" said Mitch.

Don sighed. "Sit down, boys."

### Questions

- What is the most difficult question anyone has ever asked you?
- What do you do when someone asks you a question that you can't answer?
- Why is it helpful to talk to a knowledgeable person?
- To whom could you talk when you have tough questions?

### Bible Discovery

Read Luke 21:12-15 and James 1:3-4.

### Bible Point

We won't always have the right answers. But sometimes the hard questions help us judge and strengthen our own beliefs about God. That can help us persevere in seeking answers. We can ask other Christians, like parents or pastors, to help us find answers.

Bottom Line

When you are faced with tough questions, ask those who know the answers.

## *Lots of Questions*

"Type *S* for Subject," Colleen Phillips instructed.

Jennifer Edwards typed the letter. The computer screen went blank, then another screen popped up. "OK, what's our subject?"

"Average amount of rainfall in a Brazilian rain forest," Colleen answered.

"Is *Brazilian* spelled with one *L* or two?" Jennifer asked.

"Let's just ask the research librarian." Colleen pointed to a tall woman behind a nearby desk.

The girls trooped up to the desk. The librarian smiled at them. "May I help you?" she asked. Her voice had almost a musical tone.

"Yes. We need to find out how much rain falls in a Brazilian rain forest," asked Colleen politely.

"You'll need a book with statistical information," answered the librarian. "That's over in this section." She swept from behind the desk and led the way to one of the reference sections. Within minutes, the girls had the book they needed. They quickly returned to their table.

"Wow! This book has everything!" Jennifer whispered.

"Did you catch the librarian's accent?" Colleen asked. "Somebody told me she's from someplace called Belize."

"Where's that?" asked Jennifer.

Colleen shrugged. "I don't know. Let's ask her."

"I'd feel dumb asking her that," Jennifer replied. "Let's just find an atlas or something. I thought I saw one near the almanacs."

The girls soon found an atlas. "OK, how do you spell *Belize?*" Jennifer asked. "Is it *B-E* or *B-A?*"

"Maybe we should just stick to getting our report done," said Colleen.

The girls returned to their work. After a few minutes Jennifer looked up with a thoughtful expression on her face. "Do you suppose the library has the answer to every question we can think of?"

Colleen shrugged. "I don't know. Maybe."

"Let's think of a hard question and see if we can find the answer here," suggested Jennifer.

"Why?" asked Colleen.

"Well, if we really needed to find answers, we'd know where to look," answered Jennifer.

"OK. We can make a list." Colleen opened her notebook to a clean sheet and quickly wrote *Is there life on other planets?* Then she showed it to Jennifer.

"Good one," said Jennifer. "Let me think. . . . How about, Why is the sky blue?"

Colleen wrote that one down, followed by one she immediately thought of: *Why is the grass green?*

"That's not hard," said Jennifer. "We already know the answer to that—photosynthesis."

"I know that. I was just being goofy," Colleen replied.

"Let's think of a really hard one," said Jennifer.

The girls were silent for a few moments. Finally Jennifer took the paper and wrote *Why is there war and hunger in the world?*

Colleen wrote *Why do people stop loving each other?* She had been thinking about her parents' divorce two years ago.

Jennifer read what Colleen wrote. "Think we'll find the answers to these questions here?" she asked.

Colleen shrugged. "I doubt it. I think only God knows the answers to these."

### Questions

- What questions do you have that haven't been answered yet?
- What are some of the questions you know kids your age struggle with?
- Where do you think answers to those questions can be found?

### Bible Discovery

Read Job 11:7-8 and Ephesians 3:1-6.

### Bible Point

A research librarian and a computer search program can help you find answers to some tough questions, but others will remain a mystery. As Paul's and Job's friends explained, only God can reveal the answers to these "mysteries." Others he won't reveal in this life.

### Bottom Line

When you are faced with tough questions, remember that God holds the key that unlocks life's "mysteries." Some he'll reveal to us; some he won't.

# 20

# How to Be God's Friend

## *Getting to Know You*

"Stu, I need to use the phooooonnnnnne!" Joan Anthony complained to her brother.

"I can't hear!" Stuart yelled, his hand over the receiver.

"Why do you always have to talk to your girlfriend?" Joan sang the last word. "Nobody can get on the phone because of you. Always talking to Barbara. Babs, Babs." She made kissing noises. Stuart threw a plastic coaster at her.

"Joan, stop teasing your brother," Mrs. Anthony called from the family room.

"But I need to use the phone, Mom! I need to call Melinda and ask her something about our science homework."

"Come in here and keep me company while you wait."

Mrs. Anthony was in her favorite spot, the end of the love seat. Trigger, the family's Siamese cat, lay next to her with his head in Mom's lap. Joan flopped onto a nearby recliner.

"Mom, why is Stuart so goofy these days?" Joan asked. She twirled the newly clipped ends of her light brown hair. "I mean goofier than his normal goofiness."

"He's in love," Mrs. Anthony said dramatically.

Joan scrunched up her face. "Gross."

Mrs. Anthony laughed. "Honey, you're eleven years old. Some day it won't be gross to you. Trust me. Stuart's eighteen. This is his first serious girlfriend. He's just getting to know her."

"How long does it take to get to know somebody? He's been blabbing to her on the phone every night for two weeks!"

Mrs. Anthony laughed again. "Remember when you first met your best friend, Rosie? You wanted to go over to her house and play every day—except for the days when you weren't speaking to each other."

"That's different."

"Not really. In any good friendship you take time to get to know each other, especially when you're first getting acquainted. In fact, that's just what I'm doing." She held up the book she was reading.

Joan could see the name *One Year with Jesus* on the front cover. "What's that?"

"A book of readings from the Bible about the life of Christ. Your father gave it to me, and it's helping me get to know Jesus. It also encourages me to read the Bible." She sighed. "I'm sorry I let so much time pass before committing my life to him. Thanks to you and your father, I now know Jesus."

Joan looked doubtfully at the book. "The book looks boring."

"It's not. Nothing's boring when you love someone," answered Joan's mom. "This is my way of being God's friend. Just like you are."

Joan felt bad. She didn't read devotional books, and she barely read the Bible. Joan hardly thought about getting better acquainted with God. "I never thought too much about being God's friend," she admitted.

"Well, it's never too late to start, don't you think?" Mom said. Then she added, "Remember, good friends get to know each other better."

Stuart entered the family room. "I'm done with the phone."

"I don't need the phone now," Joan said with a grin. "Mom and I are talking about a friend of ours—God."

### Questions

- How does someone begin a friendship with God?
- How can reading the Bible improve a person's relationship with God?
- What are some of the ways you learned about God?
- What can you do to get to know God better?

### Bible Discovery

Read Exodus 33:11, 14-23 and James 2:23.

### Bible Point

Abraham was called "the friend of God." Moses was a man to whom God spoke "face to face, as a man speaks to his friend" (Exodus 33:11). There aren't many people in the Bible who were known as friends of God. Yet God wants to be known by his people, not only as God but as their friend.

Bottom Line

Being God's friend means working to get to know him.

## *In Touch*

Raymond Walters swiveled around on his stool, trying to avoid his mother's gaze. "Ray, why do I keep getting notes about your talking in class?" Mrs. Walters asked, after glancing once more at the note in her hand. "Why can't you and Dennis wait till after class to talk? . . . And what's this about your disrupting class by rolling an orange during a test?"

Raymond tried to look innocent, but the thought of that prank was too much for him. He couldn't help smiling.

"There's nothing funny about this, Raymond," Mrs. Walters said sternly.

"Mom, I wasn't going to do it, honest. Me and Dennis—"

"Dennis and I."

*"Dennis and I* were just joking around." Raymond smiled cheerfully, hoping his mother would smile too. Instead, her eyes narrowed.

"OK, spill it. Now."

Raymond sighed. "Dennis dared me to do it, but I wasn't going to. It just slipped out of my backpack. Honest, Mom."

"It just *slipped* out? Look at me, Raymond. It just *slipped* out?"

Raymond hung his head. "OK. I rolled it."

"I'm glad you're finally telling the truth," answered Mom. "No video games for two weeks—one week for getting in trouble and one week for lying to me."

Raymond groaned.

"I know that you and Dennis are best friends, but I don't think he's a good influence on you. Lately, he has been getting you into a lot of trouble."

"But, Mom!"

"But, Mom, nothing! Now I want you to think about this. Would a good friend encourage you to get into trouble?"

Raymond shrugged.

"Remember what you told me you talked about in Sunday school yesterday?" Mom asked.

Raymond wished he could have instant amnesia at that moment. "Being friends with Jesus," he muttered, barely above a whisper.

"Seems like you're more interested in being Dennis's friend than Jesus' friend. After all, you talk with Dennis a lot. And you always do what Dennis says." She raised his chin so he met her gaze. "Isn't that right?"

"I don't *always* do what Dennis says." Raymond didn't want to admit that his mother was right. Dennis *was* his best friend, had been since they were in third grade. He was the first friend he'd found after they moved to town.

Yet things had changed since then. For one thing, Raymond had become a Christian the previous year. He was supposed to be God's friend, too.

Raymond suddenly realized that his mother was still talking. "Good friends talk," Mrs. Walters was saying. "You talk with Dennis every day. Why not talk to God every day too?"

"You mean pray?" Raymond couldn't remember the last time he had prayed.

Mrs. Walters nodded. "In fact, why don't we do that now?" She leaned closer to him. "I'll let you in on a little secret. Talking to God regularly will make him more *real* to you."

"Really? Do you suppose he'd be willing to keep me out of trouble?" Raymond grinned.

"That's what friends are for," answered Mom.

### Questions

- Why do good friends stay in touch?
- What do you like to talk about with your good friends?
- What do you think would happen if you didn't talk to your friends?
- Why is talking to God important?

### Bible Discovery

Look up Matthew 6:9; John 17:6-10; 1 Thessalonians 5:17.

### Bible Point

Jesus always kept in contact with his Father, and he wants his followers to do the same. In order to be God'd friend and know what God wants, a person needs to stay in contact with him. That includes talking with God and asking him for guidance.

Bottom Line

Being God's friend means talking to him daily.

## *Standing Up for God*

*"¡Oye esé!"*

Eduardo Aguina reluctantly turned when he heard Hector's greeting from behind him. Hector stood on the corner with two of his friends.

*"¿Qué pasa, hombre?* Hector asked.

"Hey, Hector," Eduardo said, wishing he weren't carrying a Bible. He thrust it behind his back.

"What's that, *muchacho?*" Hector asked.

"Nothing," Eduardo mumbled.

"I think it's something." Hector waited for Eduardo to show what he was carrying. His eyes widened. "A Bible. Are you a Holy Roller or something now?" The two boys with Hector laughed.

Eduardo felt his skin grow warm. He hated being called that. Ever since he had become a Christian and started attending the Community Church, his friends had teased him. They always seemed to be around as he was leaving the youth Bible study. Why, oh why, did the youth pastor insist that everyone carry a Bible?

"Preach us a sermon, *predicador,*" Hector said.

"Ha, ha," Eduardo laughed as he began walking away.

"We're going over to Rhodes Street Park to hang out. Want to come?" Hector asked.

Rhodes Street was where they all used to hang out and get into trouble. Eduardo was tempted to go with them to prove that he was still cool. Each time in the past, he had given in and gone with them, even though he felt bad afterward. This time, however, he thought about what Guillermo, the youth pastor, had said earlier. "If you don't stand for God, you'll fall for anything. God expects his friends to be loyal to him. If you're not loyal to him, how can you expect him to be loyal to you?"

"Well . . ." Eduardo started back toward the boys, then paused. "No, man, I think I'll pass. I'll check with you all later." He turned and started to walk home.

"Maybe you're not cool anymore," Hector said.

"Maybe not. I just don't want to do anything that will hurt my relationship with God," Eduardo answered quietly.

As Eduardo walked away, he could hear the boys jeering and laughing. He kept on walking.

Later that evening, Eduardo joined his mother on the porch of their house. The refreshing cool breeze helped Eduardo put the afternoon run-in with Hector out of his mind. But the sudden sight of Hector coming down the street brought it all back.

"Here comes trouble," Eduardo heard his mother mutter under her breath.

As Hector approached the house, Eduardo could tell that he looked different somehow, less confident than before.

"*¿Hola, qué tal?*" he said.

"Hi, Hector," Mrs. Aguina said.

"Can I talk to you?" Hector asked Eduardo. "Hey, man, I see you're different, man. You don't hang with us anymore. You don't get into trouble either. I was wondering—" he shifted his feet uncomfortably—"if you would tell me about that church you go to."

Eduardo was surprised. "Sure, Hector. Let me tell you about a friend of mine first. His name's Jesus."

Questions

- Why is loyalty important in a friendship?
- When someone was loyal to you, how did you feel?
- How can you show loyalty to God?

Bible Discovery

Look up 1 Chronicles 29:18 and Matthew 7:21-23.

Bible Point

Loyalty is an important quality in a friend. God expects the same from his friends. This means standing up for him when talking to believers as well as unbelievers.

Bottom Line

Being God's friend means being loyal to him.

## *Keeping Close*

"Hey, Dad, did the mail just come?" Sydney asked excitedly. "Anything for me?"

"Well," Mr. Clarke said, a mischievous gleam in his eyes, "let me see." He thumbed through the envelopes in his hand. Sydney waited impatiently. Finally, with a laugh, Mr. Clarke produced a red envelope covered with stickers.

"I knew it would come today!" Sydney yelled. "Laura's letters always come on Fridays." She ran to her room and threw herself on the bed, almost landing on Beaver, the family's Angora cat. She felt the envelope. "This feels like a long letter, Beav." She carefully tore open the envelope and slipped out the seven pages of stationery. A few pictures slipped out too.

Soon Sydney was laughing at Laura's letter. Laura's letters always made her laugh despite how sad she felt knowing that her best friend lived over one thousand miles away. She went to the basement where her father was working in his photography studio. She found him staring at a photograph he had taken.

"Hey, Dad, look at these." She handed him the pictures. "Laura took pictures of her birthday party. She's wearing the sweater I gave her."

Mr. Clarke smiled as he looked at the photographs. "I'm glad you and Laura are still close friends. I know you worried about that when her family moved away."

"I'm just glad she likes to write letters as much as I do," Sydney responded. "Still . . . it's not the same as when she was here."

"I know, hon. At least you'll get to see her in a few weeks," answered Dad.

"I know. I can't wait." Sydney and her father were going to spend a few days visiting Laura's family. Sydney glanced at the photos once more. "At least I can see that she hasn't changed much in a year."

"She might've grown an inch or two," explained her father. "But try not to expect too much to remain exactly the same, Syd. The only person who never changes is Jesus."

"Yeah, but I can't *see* him like I can see Laura," answered Sydney.

"True, but you can look forward to seeing him one day like you look forward to seeing Laura," Dad explained. "In the meantime, all believers who want to be good friends with God will take his advice and remain close to him. A close friendship with God, just like with any person, doesn't happen overnight. You have to work at remaining close, just like you and Laura work at your friendship. What do you think would happen if you had decided that you didn't want to write to each other or talk on the phone?"

"We wouldn't be friends very long," answered Sydney.

"Well, that works the same way with your friendship with God," her father said. "True, he does most of the work in our relationship with him. But he does want us to make an effort too. Like praying to him and reading about him in the Bible."

"I hope Laura and I stay friends forever," said Sydney.

"What about you and Jesus?" asked Dad.

"I already know we'll be friends forever," answered Sydney. "But maybe I need to work on being a better friend to him."

Questions

- Why do good friends stay close? How do they stay close?
- Why is it important to stay close to God?
- How can you stay close to God?

Bible Discovery

Read John 15:1-8 and Hebrews 13:8.

Bible Point

God wants to be good friends with his people. We do that by remaining in him like a branch stays joined to a vine. A good friendship takes work. Staying close involves listening, talking, and obeying.

Bottom Line

Being God's friend means staying close to him.

## *The Choice*

"Can I talk to you a sec?" Mrs. Monroe asked.

"Sure, Mom." Dana made room for her mother on the couch and put down the book she was reading.

Mrs. Monroe touched Dana on the arm. "I saw you and your friends at the mall today."

"Why didn't you say something?" Dana asked.

"You know you don't like being seen with me or Dad when you're with a bunch of your friends," answered her mother.

"Mom, I've gotten over that," Dana said.

Mrs. Monroe did a dramatic double take. "You mean, it's OK again to acknowledge that I'm your mother when we're in public?"

Dana giggled. It seemed a hundred years ago, but she recalled being uncomfortable around her parents. Turning fourteen recently had changed everything. "What did you want to talk to me about, Mom?" she asked.

Mrs. Monroe looked a little embarrassed. "I couldn't help overhearing what you were saying. You were sitting at a table near mine in the food court. You couldn't see me because you were seated behind that pillar. Anyway, I heard you and your friends talking. Dana, do you realize how much they disrespect the Lord's name?"

Now Dana looked embarrassed. "I don't know what you mean, Mom."

"Well, that one girl, Tina, constantly used God's name with a curse word," her mother explained.

"Oh, Mom, that's just the way Tina talks sometimes," said Dana. "*I* don't talk that way."

"Have you ever said anything to her?" asked Mom.

Dana squirmed. "I . . . no. I just thought not joining in was enough."

"Remember how mad you got at your friend Becky because she criticized you during a softball game last week?" her mother asked.

"Yeah. But what has that—"

"Remember how hurt you felt?"

"Yeah, but—"

"Honey, that's how God feels when you don't speak well of him," Mom explained.

"But I didn't say anything bad about God."

"But you didn't say anything *good* either, when your friends said bad things about him," explained Mom. "Honey, if your friends don't know that you don't like something, they'll assume that you do."

Dana was silent for a few seconds. "I don't want to criticize my friends. They'll think I'm 'holier than thou' or something."

Mrs. Monroe put her hand on Dana's arm. "I'm not suggesting that you criticize them, Dana. Besides, if they're your friends, they'll know you're not trying to be that way." Mom stood. "Just think about it, OK? Would you rather be a good friend to them or a good friend to God?"

### Questions

- How did you feel when a friend said something nice about you?
- Why is it important for friends to stick up for each other?
- If a friend said something bad about God, how would you respond? Why?
- How do your actions show that you are friends with God?

### Bible Discovery

Read these verses: Exodus 20:7; 1 Kings 18:21; Psalm 148:12-13; Ephesians 5:19-20.

### Bible Point

Good friends compliment each other. *Praise* means saying nice things about God. God especially likes it when his friends praise him to others and acknowledge their relationship with him. This might mean risking embarrassment if your friends don't share your view of God. What choice will you make?

### Bottom Line

Being a friend of God means speaking well of him at all times.

SKILLS FOR LIFE

# 21 How to Feel Good about Yourself

## *God's View of You*

One morning as Katherine was getting ready for school, her college-age sister, Beth, stood at the door of her room observing Katherine.

"I hate you," said Katherine under her breath. "You can't do anything right. Nobody likes who you are and besides all that, you're hopeless." Katherine stared at herself in her mirror, convincing her reflection that she was absolutely no good. Her sister just leaned quietly against her door, unnoticed by Katherine.

It wasn't easy to be in junior high. That seemed to be when self-esteem was at its lowest. When Katherine looked in the mirror, all she saw was a gangly kid with zits.

Beth came into the room and sat down on the bed next to Katherine, who had plopped dejectedly onto her bed in tears. Beth said quietly, "Katherine, I know that when you look in the mirror, you see all your imperfections. And when you're in the middle of puberty, that can be a lot of imperfections! But what would happen if you realized God's view of the person you see in the mirror?"

Katherine shrugged her shoulders as if she had hardly heard the question.

Beth gently took the dusty Bible from Katherine's bedside table, opened it, and read aloud: "Thank you for making me so wonderfully complex! Your workmanship is marvelous—and how well I know it" (Psalm 139:14). She continued. "Katherine, God sees a wonderful creation when he looks at you. If you saw yourself through his eyes, you'd see the same thing. The bad news is, it's easy to forget how he sees us. Then we start to criticize and even hate ourselves. The good news is, puberty will pass. It did for me, and it will for you, too! Seeing ourselves as God sees us makes feeling good about ourselves so much easier."

Questions

- How did Katherine feel about herself when she looked in the mirror?
- What caused Katherine's low self-esteem?
- What do you think God sees when he looks at you?
- What should you do when you're feeling down on yourself like Katherine?

Bible Discovery

Read these Bible verses: Psalms 8:3-5; 139:13-16; John 3:16.

Bible Point

No matter how we feel about ourselves, God sees us as his wonderful and lovable creations.

Bottom Line

When you see yourself as God does, you see something wonderful.

## *I Think I Can*

"Are you listening to that thing again?" Tracy's mom asked as her daughter bopped through the kitchen, listening to her Walkman. It seemed as though Tracy was listening to music every time her mom turned around. "If you don't mind," her mother said as she gently lifted the headset off her daughter's head, "we'll put this away for now while we eat dinner!"

"Hey! Hey!" Tracy started to protest. Then she settled down at the table while her mom continued cooking.

"You look pretty today," Tracy's mom said as she stirred a pot of fresh vegetables.

"You're just saying that because you're my mom," Tracy responded. "I wish people at school felt that way about me." Tracy's mother gave her daughter a quick look, and Tracy continued. "Besides, I'm never going to look pretty to them since you won't even let me wear makeup yet."

"All right, that's enough," Mom said. "Tracy, do you realize that everything you say about yourself is negative lately? Every other word is somehow a put-down toward yourself."

Tracy's mother looked lovingly at her daughter as she spoke. Ever since Tracy had entered junior high, her struggle with self-esteem had grown greater. She picked up Tracy's headset and said, "If you keep thinking in a negative way, it's no wonder you have such a low opinion of yourself." She pointed to the headset and continued. "It's as if you're listening to a recorded message over and over again that says 'I'm no good. I'm no good.' It's time you started listening to a different message—positive thinking."

"What in the world does that mean?" Tracy asked.

"It simply means focusing on *good, positive* thoughts about yourself," answered her mom.

They talked through dinner that night about replacing her negative messages with positive ones. Afterward, they listed Tracy's good qualities—talents, abilities, personality characteristics—affirmed by family members and friends. Tracy and her mom focused on her positive qualities, not what she lacked. Tracy agreed to try telling herself things like "I can" whenever she felt like she couldn't. Instead of telling herself "You're stupid," she would start focusing on what she did right.

An hour later, after praying with her mom, Tracy said, "Thanks, Mom. I sure feel better right now. Please help me to remember the *good* stuff and to say 'I can!'"

### Questions

- What was wrong with the way Tracy thought about herself?
- What example did Tracy's mom use to illustrate Tracy's constant negative thinking?
- How can positive thinking help people feel good about themselves?
- How did Tracy plan to begin practicing positive thinking?
- What are some positive messages you can start "listening to" about yourself?

### Bible Discovery

Read these Bible verses: Philippians 3:12; 4:13; Ephesians 2:10.

### Bible Point

The Bible is the ultimate book on positive thinking. It teaches us we are extremely valuable because of Christ's love for us.

Bottom Line

We can think positively about ourselves because God created us, and we are valuable to him.

## *Refocused*

It seemed like Amy was always helping someone else. If she wasn't listening to a friend's sob story for the fifth time, she was encouraging someone else who was having a bad day. She was kind and considerate, and always seemed to make time for others. Everyone knew that Amy was a Christian—her actions made that very clear. But she didn't come across like a religious freak or anything. She seemed real.

Walking home from school on Friday, Tiffany came right to the point. "I feel so depressed, Amy. Nothing in my life is going right. Every time I turn around, something else has gone wrong."

Amy asked a few questions and listened carefully as Tiffany poured out her feelings. At one point, Amy nodded as though she understood and said, "I know what you mean."

Tiffany gave Amy a surprised look and exclaimed, "How could you possibly know what it's like? Your life seems so perfect. It's because you have God in your life and all that stuff, right?"

A bit startled by Tiffany's reaction, Amy stopped walking. Then she answered quietly, "Yes, it's true that God makes a difference in my life. But that doesn't mean I don't go through hard times. I get to feeling down on myself, too, sometimes."

Amy and Tiffany talked about how it's easy to get depressed if you're not careful. Then Amy said, "Once when I was really discouraged, my pastor gave me some good advice that I've tried to remember. He said that whenever I get depressed or down, I should try to do things for other people, like listen to their problems or do something nice for them. He said that focusing on the needs of others will take my mind off myself. I tried it, and it's true. When I help others, I don't feel so down anymore."

Tiffany smiled. "Hey, that's what you just did today, isn't it?"

"Yeah, I guess so," answered Amy.

Tiffany was glad to have a friend like Amy.

Questions

- What was Amy's reputation among her friends?
- Why was Tiffany surprised to learn that Amy had her own problems?

- What was Amy's advice to Tiffany whenever she felt down?
- Why will helping others help people feel better about themselves?

Bible Discovery

Read these Bible verses: Matthew 19:19; Acts 9:36; Romans 12:10.

Bible Point

Jesus focused on the needs of others. God wants us to do likewise—focus on others' needs, not just our own.

Bottom Line

Focusing on and serving others will help you feel good about yourself.

## *Respect Yourself*

Ron had stayed up late again, so it was no wonder he overslept again. As he sleepily squinted at his alarm clock, he figured he had exactly seven minutes to get ready for school and make it to the bus stop. No problem—he had a routine. He jumped out of bed and picked up the first thing he saw out of the crumpled heap of dirty clothes in the corner. Ron managed to get one half of his shirt tucked in with one hand, while he combed through his hair once or twice with his other hand. With sheet marks still pressed on the side of his cheek, he bounded down the stairs two at a time and breezed through the kitchen, grabbing a chocolate bar out of the pantry for breakfast. There wasn't time to brush his teeth, so a handful of mints would have to do.

At school Ron sat in the back of the class as usual. He didn't want anyone drawing attention to him. He stayed to himself at lunch, too, but he felt eyes staring at him as he tried to smooth the embarrassing wrinkles in his soiled shirt. After lunch he felt strangely sick to his stomach. He supposed that the chocolate bar hadn't settled well. Unfortunately, the coach wanted the students to run today in PE. As Ron tried to make it around the track, he discovered that he just didn't have the energy. He felt like a wimp, sitting on the sidelines while the others ran.

After PE class, his coach pulled him aside. Ron loved Coach Johnson because he really seemed to enjoy his job and the kids. "What's going on with you?" Coach asked. "You've barely got enough energy to walk a mile, much less run. Your eyes have got dark circles, and you look like you dressed in the dark. No wonder you don't have any confidence. If you took better care of yourself, you'd gain some self-respect."

"I guess you're right, Coach," Ron replied.

"You bet I'm right, Son," Coach continued. "God gave us bodies, and he wants us to take care of them head to toe. Eating healthy and getting plenty of rest is only the beginning. Self-respect also means that you want to look your best whenever you can. Try taking better care of yourself and your appearance for one week and tell me if you don't feel like a better person."

"I'll try it," Ron replied. He was already looking forward to the new Ron.

Questions

- What clues showed that Ron did not care about himself?
- Why does a person's outward appearance affect how that person feels about himself or herself?
- How can you take better care of your body?
- What is self-respect?

Bible Discovery

Read these Bible verses: Luke 12:22-24; Romans 12:1; 1 Corinthians 6:19-20.

Bible Point

Taking good care of ourselves pleases God and shows we respect the body God gave us.

Bottom Line

To feel good about yourself, eat well and get enough sleep—respect yourself.

### *Turning a Loser into a Winner*

Rhonda did not feel like going to Sunday school. She sulked in her room until the last possible minute before her family left for church. Her dad had to honk the horn a couple of times before she finally slinked out the door and slid into the seat next to her brother. All the way to church, Rhonda rehearsed in her mind all the things that were crummy in her life—bad grades, no friends, little money. Rhonda basically felt like a loser.

As she climbed the stairs to go to her Bible study room, she seriously considered skipping out. *Knowing my luck, this would be the day they decide to have refreshments, and I'd miss them,* she thought. *Besides, Mom and Dad would find out, and I'd be grounded for sure!*

In that frame of mind, Rhonda entered the room. She sat down at her table as Miss Brown began to teach. Her opening statement caught Rhonda's attention: "Today we're going to talk about how to CYB—Count Your Blessings. Whenever it seems like nothing's going right and you feel like a loser, God can help us feel better by helping us see all the things we do have going right."

*Oh great!* Rhonda thought to herself. *I don't have any blessings to count.* So she didn't say much when her small group began making a list. Others named simple things that they were grateful for: "Good health." "My family!" "A free country." "Great friends." "My dog." "God's love!"

As the list grew, Rhonda thought, *Maybe I* do *have some blessings after all.* She remembered her favorite teacher who seemed to like her. Rhonda was healthy and strong. Rhonda remembered that she had won an award at school a few weeks ago for an art project. She found herself suggesting blessings out loud to add to the list. As she added blessings, she felt better and better about herself.

*Hmmmm! This really works,* she thought. *I still have problems, but I feel better thinking of all the good things I have. I'm glad I learned to CYB."*

### Questions

- Why did Rhonda feel like a loser?
- What does it mean to CYB?
- How can counting blessings make a person feel good about himself or herself?

### Bible Discovery

Read these Bible verses: Matthew 5:3; Romans 10:12; 1 Thessalonians 5:18.

### Bible Point

Even when times are tough, we can always praise God for the blessings in our life.

### Bottom Line

Counting your blessings can help you feel good about yourself.

# 22

# How to Get Organized

### *Where Is It?*

Scott was trying to get ready for school. First he couldn't find a pair of matching socks. Then he found his favorite blue shirt in a wrinkled heap on his chair. "Can't wear that," he muttered as he grabbed something else. Now where was that permission slip Mom needed to sign? It had to be here somewhere. After rummaging through a small mountain of papers, Scott finally found it.

"Mom, the school is sponsoring a run for charity," Scott said. "Please sign this so I can get sponsors and run in it. I was supposed to bring it in yesterday, but I couldn't find it. The teacher said I definitely had to have it today or forget it." Scott tried to smooth out the rumpled paper.

Mom let out a big sigh. "Scott, you absolutely need to take better care of your things. Your room, your desk, and your backpack all look like they're the depositing place for every paper you've ever had your entire life. How about your desk and locker at school?" she asked.

"The desk sort of looks like it's growing paper hair. And it can be dangerous to open my locker. I may get buried in the avalanche," Scott admitted. "Sometimes I can't find an assignment, and then I have to redo it. Once I even got a lower grade because it was late. That's not too smart, I guess," Scott mumbled.

"No, Scott, that's not smart at all," Mom agreed. "It's a big waste of time and energy to do things over. You really need to get organized at home and at school. One of the first steps in getting organized is to *clean out the clutter.*"

"I don't know where to start," complained Scott. "Maybe I should just suck everything up with the vacuum. That would get rid of the clutter in a hurry."

"That might not be a bad idea," Mom said. "But there are some things that you really do need. So I'm afraid you'll have to pick through all your stuff, but *please* keep only what is current and important."

"Well, there goes my collection of doodle art and last year's football plans," said Scott. "They're all going to bite the dust. Maybe I'll find a treasure hidden in the debris, like lost lunch money."

Scott took the signed permission slip and his lunch and stuffed them into his overloaded backpack. When he saw Mom roll her eyes, he said, "This backpack will be cleaned and put in order by the time I get home from school today. Not only will it look better, but it won't weigh as much."

On the way to school Scott made plans for Operation Unclutter! He decided to tackle his desk first and then the locker. *I hope the teacher doesn't faint when I ask permission to do the cleaning,* he thought.

### Questions

- What was causing a problem for Scott?
- What was Mom's suggestion for being more organized?
- What clutter do you need to clear out?
- How will you tackle your clutter problem?

### Bible Discovery

Read Genesis 1–2 and 1 Corinthians 14:40.

### Bible Point

God is very organized. You can see that when you read the story of Creation or think about nature. Having a lot of "stuff" cluttering up our lives makes us unorganized because we waste time and energy looking for things. We may also need to do things over, and that's a real waste. Clearing out the clutter is a wise move.

### Bottom Line

Get organized by cleaning out the clutter.

## *Work Zone*

Scott's teacher almost went into shock when Scott asked permission to clean out his desk and locker. But she quickly recovered and said that he could do it after school, while she attended to things in the classroom.

*This is just like an archaeological dig,* thought Scott as he pulled stuff out of his desk. *The nearer I get to the bottom, the older the papers are.* Scott found notes, assignment sheets, two quarters, and some hard green things that may have been food at one time. The locker cleanup was the same. Scott's backpack also underwent major clutter removal. After forty-five minutes everything was neat and orderly, and a large garbage bag was overflowing.

At home when Scott dropped his backpack on the kitchen floor, it didn't make its usual *thud.* Mom commented, "It looks as though your backpack went on a strict diet. It's not nearly as fat anymore."

"Think I'll start my homework before dinner," said Scott. "Let's see, where should I work? I could move the dishes aside and work here on the kitchen table. Or I could lie on the family-room floor and study while I watch TV, or—"

"Scott, stop right there," said Mom. "Every day you sort of drift from one place to another doing homework. Your papers get scattered all over the house, leaving a homework trail. To get organized you need to set aside a special place to do your work. Then you'll know where to look for papers and homework assignments. Where do you want your special place to be?"

"I think I have a desk under the mountain of stuff in my room," replied Scott.

"Good thinking," said Mom. "It's quiet there and away from distractions. That will be much better than the table, floor, or couch for doing homework."

Scott took his homework and a garbage bag to his room. "Operation Unclutter goes to work on the desk of Scott Patterson," he said aloud.

Once again, Scott started at the top and worked his way down, sorting as he went. After a while the desk was bare, but now the floor was a somewhat organized mess—a pile of clothes, a bag of garbage, a pile of CDs and tapes, and a miscellaneous pile.

Scott was about to climb over and around the piles to reach his desk and begin his homework when he remembered what Mom had said: *Set aside a special place.* The desk didn't seem very special with all the stuff around it. So Scott disposed of the piles to the laundry, garbage can, shelves, and drawers.

*This is more like it,* thought Scott as he spread out his homework on the desk. *I'm on my way to being a truly organized person.*

Questions

- How do you think Scott felt as he cleaned out his locker, desk, and backpack?
- How does having a special workplace help you to be organized?
- Where is your special workplace?
- Is Scott completely organized now? (We'll find out tomorrow.)

Bible Discovery

Read Matthew 14:22-23 and Mark 1:35.

Bible Point

Jesus needed to be away from the distractions of the world to rest and be with his Father, so he often went away to a quiet place to think and pray. To be better organized, you need a special spot to do homework—someplace quiet and away from the distractions—to do your best work. Then you need to get into the habit of *always* doing your work at that special place.

Bottom Line

Get organized by setting aside a special place to work.

## *The Right Tools*

Scott was a talented artist. He liked working with all kinds of materials—watercolors, chalk, crayons, or markers. He also liked making collages and paper sculptures. Ms. Hanson, the art teacher at Scott's school, encouraged him to keep trying new things and to enter art contests.

During art class Ms. Hanson told Scott that she had a project for him. "The Charity Run is in three weeks," she said. "We want everyone in town to know about it so we can get lots of sponsors. The more sponsors we have the more money we can raise.I want you to make twelve colorful posters advertising the event. We'll put them in the store windows downtown. You can use school art supplies. You probably will want other people to help you. What do you think of the idea?"

"Wow!" exclaimed Scott. "That would be great. I'll make each poster different. I'll start tonight, and in no time, the downtown will be covered with posters. Thanks, Ms. Hanson."

Scott listened carefully as Ms. Hanson gave him all the information for the posters. Before he went home, Scott picked up some poster boards and other materials he thought he would need.

After dinner Scott sat at his desk, ready to start the first poster. But he couldn't find a drawing pencil. After ten minutes of pawing through drawers, he finally found one. He also needed colored paper, markers, and glue. Scott had remembered to bring home colored paper but not glue or markers. "Rats!" he said. "I'm sure there are glue and markers around here somewhere."

Scott ran downstairs to look for the supplies. Dad watched as Scott opened every cabinet drawer and rooted through it. "What are you doing?" he asked.

"I need to make these posters for school, and I can't find the glue or big markers. I'm sure there are some here, but I don't know where," said Scott, banging doors and drawers.

Mr. Patterson, who was a carpenter, said to Scott, "Part of being organized is to equip yourself with the things you need. Think of the problems I would have if I couldn't find my hammer, screwdrivers, or other tools. I'd never finish a job on time. Keep the things you need for art projects in one place, ready to use. You're wasting a lot of time playing hide-and-seek."

Just then Scott found the elusive markers and glue. "You're right, Dad," he said. "These are going up by my desk and staying there, even if I have to chain them."

Scott finally settled down to make poster number one. "Twelve posters is an awful lot," he mumbled as he carefully measured for the letters.

### Questions

- How do you think Scott felt when Ms. Hanson gave him the poster project?
- How would you react if you were given a big job to do?
- Why did it take Scott so long to get started on the first poster?
- How can having the right equipment help you be organized?

### Bible Discovery

Read Exodus 35:10-19 and Ephesians 6:10-16.

### Bible Point

In order to build the Tabernacle, Moses and the people had to have the proper equipment. Anyone who has a job to do can't do it without the right equipment; carpenters can't build without tools, and cooks can't cook without pots and pans. Collect the right equipment before you start a job, and keep it in a special place so you can find it easily.

Bottom Line

Get organized by equipping yourself with what you need to do the job.

### *What Did She Say?*

After working an hour, Scott had finished the heading. He had cut three-inch letters from brightly colored paper and glued them to the poster board. Then he had outlined the letters with a black marker. Scott propped the poster against the wall and stood back to admire it. He was quite pleased with the results. Just then his younger sister, Jenny, walked by. "Cool poster, Scott," she said. "Charity Run—nobody can miss seeing those words. What else goes on it?"

"I need to put on all the information like the time, place, and how to sponsor someone," Scott answered. "Think I'll use bright-colored markers for that. Do you *really* like it, Jen?"

"It sure would make me stop and read it," answered his sister. Scott felt pleased with this first poster, and he was happy that Jenny liked it. She didn't usually pay much attention to what he did, so it must be good. Scott started to whistle as he planned how to put the rest of the information on the bottom. Maybe if he hurried he could finish two posters tonight.

Carefully Scott started to pencil in the information. Place: Jefferson School Track. Date: Oh no! Scott's whistle faded. He couldn't remember what Ms. Hanson had said. Was it on the tenth at nine o'clock or the ninth at ten o'clock? No matter how hard he thought, Scott could not remember what was right. With a big sigh he flopped across his bed. "Rats and double rats!" he yelled.

Mom stuck her head in the door. "What on earth is wrong with you?" she asked.

Scott was embarrassed and mumbled, "I can't remember the information Ms. Hanson gave me for the posters, so I can't do any more tonight. And I need to have all of them done by next week."

Mom wanted to know if Scott had written down the information. Scott looked down at the floor and shook his head. "You have been trying to be more organized," Mom said. "An important step to being organized is to write down important facts. That way you don't have to remember everything."

"I will see Ms. Hanson before school. I'll be sure to have my notebook and pencil ready to write down every bit of information," Scott declared. "Now maybe I can do the heading on one or two more posters before lights-out.One of these days I'll get my act together, Mom. Just wait and see!"

Mom rolled her eyes and shrugged her shoulders, but there was a smile on her face. "Keep trying, Scott," she encouraged, "you're getting there."

Questions

- How did Scott feel about Jenny's comments?
- How do you know Scott was pleased with what he had done?
- What was Scott's problem?
- When you forgot important information, what did you do?

Bible Discovery

Read Luke 1:1-4 and 1 Timothy 1:1-2.

Bible Point

God gave writers like Luke and Paul the words to write down because the words were important. God gave you a good mind and a good memory. But sometimes your brain gets overloaded with too many things. Writing down important information will help you be more organized because you will have all the facts in front of you. Then you can do the task without wasting time.

Bottom Line

Get organized by writing down important notes and dates.

## *Panic Time!*

Before school the next morning, Scott was standing outside the art room door. He made sure he had a pencil and paper. Ms. Hanson looked surprised to see Scott waiting for her. "You're sure here bright and early, Scott," she said. "How are the posters coming along?"

"That's why I'm here," Scott answered. "I need to make sure of the day and time before I do any more. Could you please tell me again?"

Ms. Hanson gave him the information, and Scott very carefully wrote it down. "And remember, they all need to be done by Friday morning," she said. "That way we can get them in the store windows over the weekend. Can you have them finished?"

Friday! That gave him only three nights to finish twelve posters. Scott thought he had until next week to finish. Then Scott remembered that Grandma was coming to dinner on Thursday. He began to panic; his stomach felt like someone had tied a knot in it.

"I'll try, but there are so many posters, and I have some other things I have to do too," Scott said. How would he ever finish in time?

Ms. Hanson noticed the panicky look on Scott's face. She was a little disappointed by his response. "Scott, they *must* be done by Friday morning," she repeated. "Don't panic. Just get yourself organized and plan ahead. Think of how many you can do each day. Get other kids to help you. Do whatever it takes, but we're really counting on these posters to advertise the run."

Scott thanked Ms. Hanson and slowly slouched down the hall toward his first class. All morning Scott felt as though he were being attacked by bad thoughts. It almost became a song in his brain: "Twelve posters in three days. You can't do it."

"I *can* do it," Scott muttered at the lunch table.

"Do what?" asked Mac.

"I was thinking out loud," Scott said as his face turned red. "I need to make twelve posters to advertise the Charity Run by Friday morning. I just need to figure out *how* I'm going to do it!"

"Wow, man! That's a lot of work," said Mac. "You need to do four posters a night. Maybe you need help. I'm not an artist like you, but I can glue, and my printing is readable. Want me to come over?"

"Thanks, Mac. That would be great! In fact, that may be the answer: I'll make some plans for getting a bunch of people together to finish them up."

After dinner that night the "poster assembly line" got in full gear. Scott's friends Tom and Mac came over, Mom and Jenny helped, and even Dad got in on the action. Scott showed his helpers the plans for the posters. Then everyone got busy cutting, gluing, drawing, and lettering. Seven posters were finished by the end of the evening, and the other five only needed the information printed on them.

"Thanks a lot for your help. I couldn't have done it alone. Hmm. Maybe we should go into the poster-making business," Scott said as they were cleaning up. This brought groans and "No, thanks!" from the others.

Scott continued. "These posters look great. I can finish the others by Friday morning—no sweat. I'll even have time to visit with Grandma."

Saturday afternoon, Scott and Mac rode their bikes downtown to the hobby shop. "Well, look at that," said Mac. "That poster says there's going to be a Charity Run in two weeks."

Scott tried to keep a straight face as he said, "Such a great-looking poster! I'll bet it was done in a poster-making factory."

### Questions

- Why was Scott panicking?
- When you were in a situation similar to Scott's, how did you handle it?
- How did Scott solve the poster problem?
- How do you think Scott felt as his friends and family helped?

### Bible Discovery

Read Isaiah 14:24-27 and Romans 15:24.

### Bible Point

God plans ahead. This can be seen in the story of Creation and in God's plan for salvation. If you want to be truly organized, you need to plan ahead. Not planning ahead is foolish because it causes panic and frustration. Then you try to do too much in a very short time.

### Bottom Line

Get organized by planning ahead.

# 23

# How to Handle Arguments

### *Choose Your Battles*

Vince could hardly eat dinner, he was so upset. He went right to his room afterward. His parents tried to get him to talk about what was bothering him, but he wouldn't talk. Later, when his dad went up to check on him, Vince was talking into the mirror.

"And another thing . . . ," he said, full of anger.

"Vince, what are you doing?" his dad asked.

Vince was caught off guard. He just looked at his dad. Finally he answered, "I'm practicing."

"What in the world are you practicing?" his dad inquired.

"I'm practicing what I'm going to say tomorrow when I see Jeff." With that, Vince sat down on the edge of the bed and looked miserable.

"Vince, please tell me what has made you so unhappy," Dad pleaded.

"Jeff made me look like a fool, that's all," Vince answered. Then he explained that yesterday in school he was kidding around with some guys out on the grass. Tonya, a girl Vince really liked, was sitting on the steps with her friends, watching. Suddenly Jeff and four other guys from the baseball team ran out onto the grass and threw Vince on the ground. They didn't hurt him, but they humiliated him in front of Tonya. Vince was so angry that he hadn't even been able to talk to Jeff afterward.

Vince's dad remembered when he was Vince's age and the times he had been embarrassed. He remembered feeling that a friend had betrayed him. He also remembered that after a while it didn't seem like a big deal anymore. He wanted to help his son feel better. "Vince, would you like advice, or would you rather I just listen to you?" he asked.

"Well, if it's good advice, that would probably be OK," answered Vince.

Vince's dad continued, "I know you will find a way to talk to Jeff, but choose your battles wisely."

"What does that mean, Dad?" Vince said quickly.

"It means that you don't have to take part in every argument that comes along—," Dad began to answer.

Vince interrupted. "But he was wrong, Dad! He *knew* how that would make me feel—"

"I'm not disagreeing with you, Vince," replied Dad. "I'm just saying that you and Jeff have been friends for a long time, and before it's over, I'm sure you'll both let each other down a few more times. Sometimes you will need to fight it through to the end. But not *every* argument is like that. Sometimes you just let it slide."

"Is that what you would do in this situation?" asked Vince.

"I don't know," answered Dad. "But I don't think this will be as big a deal next week as it feels right now. So I'd hate for you to lose your friendship with Jeff over something that won't matter next week."

The next morning Vince left for school determined to figure out if he should confront Jeff or not.

### Questions

- Why was Vince angry?
- Why did it matter that Tonya was there?
- Why is it important to choose our battles wisely?
- What kinds of things are worth fighting for?

### Bible Discovery

Read these verses: Genesis 13:7-9; 26:20-22; Job 6:25; Proverbs 17:14; 26:17; Philippians 2:14-15; 2 Timothy 2:23-25; Titus 3:9-10.

### Bible Point

The Bible has much to say about taking a stand when you need to and about being smart enough to back down when it isn't worth it. Abraham backed down to keep peace in his family. Isaac backed down to find a peaceful new home. Having friends, getting along, and being happy are sometimes more important than proving you're right or getting your own way.

Bottom Line

Know what you are trying to win in an argument and decide if it is worth arguing about before you argue.

## *State Your Case*

When Vince got to school, he looked everywhere for Jeff. Today Vince was going to decide whether or not he would argue with him. Jeff had embarrassed Vince in front of Tonya, a girl Vince really liked. Was it worth arguing over?

Vince had just about decided that it wasn't that important, when he saw Jeff down the hall. He was laughing with those same three guys from the day before. Suddenly Vince was filled with anger. He wanted to march right down the hall and punch Jeff in the face. Actually, he did start walking toward Jeff. As he got near him, Vince just walked on by without saying a word to anyone.

"Hey! Come back here!" Jeff called out.

Vince didn't answer. He just kept walking. He avoided Jeff for the rest of the day. He did mention what a jerk Jeff was to several people, including Tonya. That night Vince didn't return Jeff's calls.

Just before Vince went to bed, his dad came into his room. He said, "Vince, I just took a call from Jeff, and he said he'd been calling all night and wondered where you were. What's going on?"

"I didn't feel like talking to him," Vince answered.

"I'm not going to make you talk to him," said Dad. "This is your friendship, not mine. I do want to remind you, however, that you and Jeff have been friends for quite a while. I think he deserves better than this."

"But, Dad, you know what he did," said Vince.

"I know that he embarrassed you in front of a girl," replied Dad. "I understand that you are too angry to let it slide. But you need to talk with Jeff and resolve it, instead of clamming up or talking to other people about him. It's only fair to the other person to let him know what he did wrong and why you're upset."

The next day, Vince was surprised to receive a note from the school counselor, asking him to be at his office at three. Vince was shocked to find Jeff waiting to see Mr. Leland, too. Apparently he had asked both boys to come to his office.

Mr. Leland began, "Look, guys, I've known you for a couple of years now, and I've always been impressed with your friendship. Because of that, I was concerned yesterday when I heard you, Vince, putting Jeff down to other people. Then this morning I heard you, Jeff, doing the same thing to Vince. I would like to do my part to help you guys work through this problem so you don't lose your friendship."

Mr. Leland asked questions to find out how it had all started. Finally, he got Vince to tell about his embarrassment two afternoons before when Jeff and some guys tackled him and teased him in front of Tonya. As Vince told the story, he got a little worked up. He thought Jeff would make fun of him, but Jeff was listening.

When Vince finished, Jeff asked, "Why did that make you mad? We always mess around like that."

"Not in front of Tonya," answered Vince. "You made me look like a fool, and you didn't even care."

"Tonya?" said Jeff. "I didn't realize she was standing there. I'm really sorry. But why wouldn't you talk to me about it?"

Vince didn't really have an answer for that. He wasn't sure why. Mr. Leland had some ideas. "Emotion and pride make it hard for people to resolve conflicts," he said. "We get so emotional that instead of stating our case and resolving the conflict, we run our mouth off to other people. Then we have to prove that we are right, that we are the injured party. Vince, you just stated your case. You described what made you upset and how you reacted to it emotionally. That gives Jeff an opportunity to talk with you about it and apologize if necessary." After looking at his watch, he continued. "It's getting late and we all need to get going, so let's meet a half hour before school starts tomorrow and finish this. Would that be all right?"

Both Vince and Jeff nodded. Then Mr. Leland concluded, "Thanks for stating your case, Vince. Thanks for giving your response, Jeff. See you guys tomorrow."

### Questions

- How did Vince's actions make Jeff feel?
- What did Mr. Leland hope to accomplish by bringing the boys together and talking with them?
- How did Jeff respond to the reasons for Vince's anger?
- How do emotion and pride make it difficult for people to resolve conflicts?

### Bible Discovery

Read these verses: Leviticus 19:16-18; Proverbs 10:18; 15:18; Colossians 3:8.

Bible Point

God gives specific guidelines for how people should treat their neighbors (this includes friends). He says to be kind and not to gossip. Those who have a disagreement or conflict should talk to each other, not to everyone else. Believers should be committed to obeying God and honoring their friendships, even when they are angry about something.

Bottom Line

To resolve an argument, talk to the person with whom you're arguing, not to everyone else.

## *Hold On to What You've Got*

When Vince and Jeff left Mr. Leland's office, they still felt a little funny about their relationship. This was their first big fight, and it didn't feel like things were right yet. They didn't talk that night on the phone, but both of them hoped things would get back to normal soon. They were both glad that Mr. Leland had made them talk about what was wrong.

The next morning while they waited for Mr. Leland, they talked a little about a test coming up in algebra. As soon as they got into Mr. Leland's office, however, they forgot about the test.

"What we have here, guys, is a conflict," began Mr. Leland. "In any conflict, we have a decision to make—whether to make it worse, leave it alone, or resolve it. The best way to end an argument is to resolve it. We started resolving it yesterday. Vince stated his case in the conflict. He was embarrassed in front of a girl, and he felt angry about it. Jeff seemed surprised and sorry about embarrassing Vince. That is an important step in resolving a conflict."

Mr. Leland paused for a second to let his words sink in. Then he continued, "The last step is to renew the friendship. It's one thing to say we're sorry and go on with our lives. It's another thing to trust the person again. Can Vince trust Jeff not to embarrass him again? Can Jeff trust Vince to come to *him* if Vince gets upset instead of clamming up and talking to everyone else?"

The boys knew that Mr. Leland didn't really expect an answer to those questions. But then he looked straight at them, and they knew he wanted a response when he asked, "Do you two want to go back to being good friends, or has this conflict ended that?"

Vince and Jeff didn't wait for each other to answer. Immediately they both replied, "Yes, we are still good friends!"

"Great!" said Mr. Leland. "Now Jeff, what will you do to make sure that this won't happen again?"

"Well," he answered, "before I clobber Vince the next time, I'll make sure there is no girl standing around that he likes." Jeff and Vince both smiled at this.

Then Mr. Leland turned to Vince. "What about you?"

Vince looked down at the floor, a little self-conscious, and said, "Jeff didn't really mean to embarrass me. He just made a mistake. But when I talked to other people about him, I *meant* to, and I made things worse. So I was more in the wrong, and I'm sorry. If Jeff ever makes me angry or embarrassed again, I need to go right to him so we can settle it between us."

"You guys are exactly right!" exclaimed Mr. Leland. "Do you think you can trust each other to do those things?"

Both guys nodded yes.

Mr. Leland ended the meeting but invited them to come back if they ever needed help again. They still had time to study a few minutes before class, so Vince and Jeff went down to their room to study together.

### Questions

- How did Mr. Leland help?
- Why was Vince's reaction to being embarrassed worse than Jeff's embarrassing him?
- What can good friends do to make sure that their conflicts get resolved and don't get worse?

### Bible Discovery

Read these verses: Proverbs 13:10; 17:19; 20:3; 25:24; Acts 15:36-41.

### Bible Point

Friends have conflicts. Paul and Barnabas were friends. They even took missionary trips together. But they argued. They even argued so badly once that they stopped working together for a while. But they didn't lose respect for each other, and they didn't lose their friendship. The Bible teaches that letting a quarrel or an argument ruin a friendship is wrong.

### Bottom Line

It's better to lose a little pride than to lose a friendship.

## *At Odds*

Several weeks after Vince and Jeff had resolved their conflict, Vince was thinking about talking to Mr. Leland again. Vince was having a conflict with someone he knew but didn't like—Marshal, a kid in his algebra class. Did the same rules apply?

Marshal was a bully. He acted nice in front of teachers, but when they turned their backs, he hit people, cheated on tests, copied homework, and was generally mean. Vince felt that Marshal deserved whatever bad stuff he got.

So it was easy for Vince to be really angry with Marshal. Marshal had knocked Vince's books out of his hands last week and had ruined a report that Vince had worked hard on. Since then, Vince had been looking for opportunities to get back at Marshal, whether it was through telling on him or being mean to him. Vince was even beginning to enjoy plotting his revenge.

Yesterday, however, Vince went to Sunday school, and the verse the teacher asked him to read: "You have heard that the law of Moses says, 'Love your neighbor and hate your enemy. But I say, love your enemies! Pray for those who persecute you!" These were Jesus' words. This had gotten Vince thinking about Mr. Leland: *What would Mr. Leland think about this verse? Would he expect me to state my case to Marshal the way he expected me to with my friend Jeff?*

After school Vince stopped by Mr. Leland's office to ask him about this. Vince explained the conflict with Marshal and then waited to see what Mr. Leland would say.

"First of all, Vince," Mr. Leland said, "I can understand why you aren't as motivated to resolve your conflict with Marshal as you were with Jeff. There is not a friendship at stake here. You probably don't even want to be friends with Marshal, do you?"

"I have no interest in having Marshal as a friend, Mr. Leland. I'm just being honest," said Vince.

"Then I guess the question in this situation is a different one," replied Mr. Leland. "The question here is what kind of person you want to be. I don't read the Bible as much as I should, but I am familiar with that Bible verse. It seems to me that Jesus isn't making a statement about your enemy as much as about you. He wants you to be a person who is honest, kind, and honorable. It sounds like he wants you to be that way all the time, no matter who you are dealing with—not just with friends. Does that sound right to you?"

"Yeah," said Vince. "But it's a lot harder with people you don't like."

"You're right," said Mr. Leland. "If you need any help from me, bring Marshal by. But it definitely sounds like you need to talk to him about the way he mistreats you instead of just mistreating him back."

### Questions

- Why did Vince feel that it was OK to get Marshal in trouble?
- Why did the Bible verse make Vince think about what he should do?
- How would Jesus relate to Marshal?
- How do you think Marshal will respond to Vince when they talk?

### Bible Discovery

Read these verses: Matthew 5:43-44; 2 Corinthians 12:20; 2 Timothy 2:14, 23-25; James 4:1-2.

### Bible Point

When God tells his people to love others and keep from quarreling, he includes enemies and those who are annoying. God wants believers to follow his principles with everyone.

### Bottom Line

It's up to you to be honorable in an argument, not because of who you are arguing with but because of who you are living for.

## *Challenge Authority?*

Jeff was not enjoying school this year. It wasn't just the conflict that he had had with Vince a few weeks ago—he just didn't like his teachers. *None* of them. He thought they were unfair, and he hated doing homework. The teacher he liked the least was Mrs. Hawkins.

Mrs. Hawkins was older, and she dressed like it. She expected the kids to stay completely quiet all the time, and she gave tough homework assignments. The worst part was that any time students tried to reason with her, she argued with them—especially with Jeff.

It seemed as though Jeff argued with Mrs. Hawkins every few days. He would stay after class and try and reason with her about an assignment or a deadline. He tried to explain to her how much time baseball practice took and how much time his other classes took. It would have been easier if she would just let him talk. It would have been better if she just hadn't said anything at all. But she argued. The more Jeff tried to explain, the more reasons she gave for things being the way they were.

One day Jeff decided to take up Mr. Leland on his offer to talk if he needed advice. Jeff stopped by the next day after school.

"Whew! That's a hard one!" was the first thing Mr. Leland said after Jeff told him the problem. He continued, "Disagreeing with someone in authority is a little different from disagreeing with your friends, Jeff. Friends meet on the same level. In other words, with a friend we expect to be heard, and we expect that our own opinion will have as much weight as the other person's. In a conflict with someone in authority, however, the authority is the one who makes the rules. That person also enforces the rules. It is our responsibility to obey the rules, even if we disagree with them."

"Well, I don't like that, and it's making me miserable," Jeff responded.

Jeff and Mr. Leland talked a little about why this was so difficult for Jeff. Part of it was that Jeff just needed to work harder, and he didn't want to. In other words, school used to be fun, and it wasn't fun anymore. And part of it was that Jeff kept feeling as though he needed to do something else to make the situation different.

Before Jeff left the office, Mr. Leland told him something important. "Jeff, it's OK to go to Mrs. Hawkins once if you want to talk to her about an unfair assignment. But after you have stated your case, it's over. You've done all you can. Sometimes ending an argument means accepting that you didn't get your way and making the best of it. That shows that you are treating the person in authority with respect. I've found that all people, even those in authority over us, respond better when they are treated with respect."

Questions

- Why was Jeff unhappy?
- What is an authority?
- Why do you think Mrs. Hawkins argued with Jeff when he disagreed with her?
- What can you do to treat a teacher with respect? How about a parent? a coach?
- How would Jesus relate to Mrs. Hawkins?

### Bible Discovery

Read these verses: Daniel 1:3-16; Romans 13:1-5; Titus 3:1-2; 1 Peter 2:13.

### Bible Point

Daniel disagreed with authorities and made some significant changes in his nation. He also got thrown into the lions' den. Disagreeing with someone in authority is tricky. Scripture teaches, however, that we are to honor the authorities over us because God has placed them there for our direction and protection. There may be a time, like there was for Daniel, to reason with, argue with, or even disobey authorities, but not until we have shown them respect and honor as God tells us to.

### Bottom Line

Respect those in authority over you.

# 24 How to Help Others

## *Help Needed*

*"Be a friend, be a friend, be a friend.*
*When somebody's sad, when somebody's glad,*
*Be a friend, be a friend, be a friend."*

Four-year-old Jimmy had just learned a new song, but he only remembered the chorus. He sang it over and over, louder and louder. After what seemed like a hundred choruses, Mom broke in and said, "Jimmy, that's a great song. But Aunt Liz and I want to talk, and we can't hear each other when you sing so loudly. Please play in the backyard for a while. You can sing really loud out there; the birds might sing with you."

Jimmy liked that idea and scooted out the door. "Here I come, birds," he shouted.

"Thank you, Mom!" said Angelica as she curled up on the sofa. She liked it when Aunt Liz came to visit. She was always interested in what Angelica was doing and had some really cool ideas about lots of things. She was also good at thinking of ways to solve problems.

"Hi, Angelica," said Aunt Liz. "What have you been up to lately? How's school going? What's new and interesting?"

Angelica laughed because the questions just tumbled out of Aunt Liz's mouth. You had to wait until she was done before you answered. "I'm playing soccer, and we won our first two games," said Angelica.

"Hooray!" cheered Aunt Liz.

"School's good," continued Angelica. "I like going to a bigger school this year and having a different teacher for each subject.

It makes it a lot more interesting. Most of the kids know each other, and that's good. But it's also kind of bad."

"Why?" asked Aunt Liz. "I'd think it would make school more fun."

"Oh, it's not bad for me," said Angelica. "But we have some new kids, and I don't think school's much fun for them. I especially noticed one girl, Yvonne, who's in three of my classes. Her family just moved here from Poland. She can speak English, but not very well, so she has to repeat a lot of words. Yvonne doesn't dress like the other kids, so some of them make fun of her. I'd like to help her, but I really don't know how to do it."

"Hmm," said Aunt Liz. "That is a sticky situation, but I think Jimmy has the solution."

"Jimmy!" exclaimed Angelica. "He's only four. What does he know?"

Aunt Liz chuckled at Angelica's surprise. "One of the best ways to help others is to be their friend," said Aunt Liz. "I'm sure Yvonne would love to have a friend—someone to help her understand all the new things she's being bombarded with. You can be that friend."

Just then Jimmy came charging in the back door, looking for a snack. His new song came bouncing in with him: "Be a friend, be a friend, be a friend."

Questions

- Why did Angelica like Aunt Liz?
- Why did Yvonne need help?
- Who in your classes needs help?
- How can you be a friend to that person?

Bible Discovery

Read 1 Samuel 18:1-4 and Proverbs 17:17.

Bible Point

Jonathan and David were best friends. Jesus helps us by being our friend. He wants us to follow his example by befriending those who need help.

Bottom Line

Help others by being a friend to them.

## *Powerful Help*

Mr. Sanders had asked his Sunday school students to bring the front section of a newspaper to class. As Elizabeth and Logan walked to the classroom, they speculated about why they needed the newspapers.

"Maybe we are going to make paper airplanes and have a flying contest," suggested Logan.

"No way," said Elizabeth, "not in Sunday school! Maybe we're going to see if we can find anything about churches or religion in the paper. But you know Mr. Sanders. Whatever it is, it will make us think."

After everyone had arrived, Mr. Sanders settled the class and began. "Today we are going to help others. I want each of you to name one person you know who needs help. You can't name yourself."

As the kids mentioned people, Mr. Sanders wrote their names on the chalkboard. Grandparents, aunts, parents, friends, and neighbors all were on the list. Some lived nearby, and some lived hundreds of miles away. Some were sick, some were unemployed, and some were lonely.

Then Mr. Sanders instructed the kids to quickly glance through their newspapers and read the headlines. "What would you say about most of these articles?" he asked.

Elizabeth answered, "Most of them are about bad stuff. I don't like to read them."

Mr. Sanders and the others agreed with Elizabeth. Mr. Sanders instructed, "Now I want you to choose one person from an article in the newspaper who needs help. Tell us his or her name and why he or she needs help."

Those names were also written on the chalkboard. Beside each name the class listed the reason the person needed help. "Whew! This is quite a list. So many people need so much help," observed Mr. Sanders. "OK. You can do it. I want you to help them right now."

Mr. Sanders got lots of puzzled looks, shaking heads, and raised eyebrows.

"I can't even help my own grandma. She lives in California, and she has cancer," said Logan.

"I can't help my uncle find a job, so how can I possibly help someone I never met and don't know at all?" asked Molly.

"But you *can* help," insisted Mr. Sanders. "A great way to help others is to pray for them. You can pray for the people you know, asking God to help them. And you can pray for the people you picked out of the newspaper. God knows everyone, and he hears our prayers."

Mr. Sanders continued, "We can't cure a grandma's cancer or find a job for an uncle. But we can always pray for them, and that's probably the biggest help they can have. Now let's all silently pray for the people we've listed on the board."

The room was very quiet as everyone was busy helping others by praying.

Questions

- Why did Logan and Molly feel that they couldn't help anyone?
- What was Mr. Sanders trying to teach his class?
- Who could you help by praying for him or her?
- How do you feel about praying for someone you don't know?

Bible Discovery

Read these Bible verses: Acts 12:5; Colossians 1:3-4; 3 John 1:2.

Bible Point

God wants his people to help others by praying for them. Often we can't do anything physically to help someone in need, but we can always pray and ask God to help others.

Bottom Line

Help others by praying for them.

## *Listening*

Jill had been Marianne's best friend since kindergarten. They lived on the same block, played on the same softball team, and went to the same school. Jill and Marianne agreed on many things, but they did argue at times. Then they became angry and didn't talk to each other. But their disagreements never lasted long, and in a day or two they were the best of friends again.

This time was different, however, and Marianne couldn't figure out what was wrong. Jill seemed to be avoiding her at school, and she hurried home by herself each day. Marianne was getting very upset.

"I give up!" Marianne said as she slammed the front door. She dropped her backpack on the floor and flopped on the couch. "I don't know what's wrong with her!"

Mom came into the room. "Marianne, what's the problem?" she asked. "You look like a thundercloud."

"Well, I feel like I'm going to shoot out lightning pretty soon," Marianne grumbled. "I just can't figure out what's wrong with Jill. She acts as if she doesn't even like me anymore. She's been this way for a week. I don't know anything I did to make her act this way."

Mom put her arm around Marianne. "Oh, honey, I don't think it's anything you did," she said. "It sounds like something is bothering Jill, and she doesn't know what to do. Maybe you can help her."

"How can I help when I don't know the problem?" asked Marianne.

Mom replied, "One way to help someone is to be a good listener. Being a good listener means to *really* listen and not offer advice or your own opinion. When someone has a problem, talking to a friend about it can be a big relief. Try to be a good listener for Jill."

Marianne left for school extra early the next morning so she could get to Jill's house before she left. When Jill came out, she looked worried and about to cry.

"Jill, what's the matter?" asked Marianne.

"Oh, Marianne, I'm so worried," said Jill.

Then Jill explained that her dad had lost his job a month ago. He had been looking and looking, but he didn't have a new job yet. The longer he was out of work, the angrier he became. Things were not very happy at Jill's house.

Jill talked all the way to school. Several times Marianne wanted to interrupt and say what she thought. But she remembered what Mom had said about being a good listener, so she kept her lip zipped.

"Thanks for listening, Marianne," Jill said as they walked up the school steps. "I feel lots better now. You're such a good friend."

Marianne felt lots better too, knowing she had helped Jill.

### Questions

- How was Marianne feeling about Jill? Why?
- Why do you think Jill was avoiding Marianne?
- What makes a good listener?
- How can you help someone by being a good listener?
- Why did Jill feel better after she talked to Marianne?

### Bible Discovery

Read Exodus 18:13-15, 24 and Luke 8:49-50.

### Bible Point

Jesus and Moses were good listeners; they listened to others' problems. Just plain listening can sometimes be difficult because we want to give advice or offer our opinions. But the best way to *really* listen is with our ears wide open and our mouths closed tightly.

Bottom Line

Help others by being a good listener.

## *You Can Do It!*

Peter was crazy about baseball. He watched every Major League Baseball game on TV. He read every article about baseball on the sports page of the newspaper. He could rattle off the batting averages, RBIs, home runs, and bases stolen for each of his favorite players. He collected and traded baseball cards. Peter knew everything about baseball except how to play it well.

Peter and his friends Andy and Henry had all signed up to play in the city baseball league. Andy and Henry had played in the league the last two seasons. Peter hadn't been able to play before this year, however, so the only experience he had was in neighborhood pickup games. Much to Peter's relief, all three were on the same team. Mr. Riley was their coach.

It didn't take long for everyone on the team to find out that Peter talked a great game of baseball, but he had a lot to learn about playing the game. The first practice was a disaster as far as Peter was concerned. He struck out three times, hit one little dribbler, and made two errors in the field.

After practice Peter said to Andy and Henry, "I think I'd better stick to watching baseball, reading about it, and learning statistics." He picked up his mitt and slowly started walking home.

"Hey, Peter, wait up," yelled Andy. "We'll walk with you." But Peter kept going.

"Let's talk to Coach Riley," said Henry to Andy.

They waited until all the boys had left and the coach was alone. "Coach Riley, Henry and I want to talk to you about Peter," Andy said. "He thinks he should quit because he can't play very well."

The coach answered, "Well, he does have a lot to learn, but I would hate to see him quit. You boys are his friends. Why don't you help him?"

"How can we help him?" asked Henry. "Should we practice hitting and catching with him?"

"That would be good," said Coach Riley. "But another way you can help is to encourage him. Keep telling him 'You can do it' when he becomes discouraged. Encouragement from you will make Peter try harder and keep practicing. Think you can do that?" Both boys nodded their heads.

"Thanks, Coach," they yelled as they headed home.

At the next practice Peter struck out twice. But then he hit a sharp single to center field.

"See, Peter? You can do it! Way to go, man!" Henry and Andy cheered from the bench. Peter grinned as he concentrated on his baserunning.

### Questions

- What could Peter do well? What couldn't he do very well?
- How do you think Peter felt during the first practice?
- How do you think the rest of the team felt about Peter's playing?
- How did Henry and Andy help Peter?
- In what ways does encouragement help a person?

### Bible Discovery

Read Acts 11:22-30 and 1 Thessalonians 5:9-11.

### Bible Point

Barnabas, an apostle in the early church, was called the Encourager because he was always encouraging other Christians. We can help others by encouraging them to keep on trying when they are discouraged about something. We can also be encouragers by praising and cheering others when they have done well or overcome some obstacle.

### Bottom Line

Help others by being an encourager.

## *The "You" Package*

Renae and her mom were enjoying an late-afternoon snack. They enjoyed spending this time together telling each other about their day. Mom was a social worker with the older people in town. She found transportation for them, helped them fill out complicated forms, told them about services for seniors, and did whatever was necessary.

"I had an appointment with Mrs. Carlson today," said Mom. Mrs. Carlson was their neighbor, a kind loving woman in her late 70s.

Mrs. Carlson had lived next door since Renae was three. Renae got a worried look on her face. "Oh, I hope Mrs. Carlson's not sick. She isn't sick is she?" she asked.

Mom answered, "She has her aches and pains, and her hearing isn't very good. But she's pretty healthy for someone her age."

"Then why did you have to see her? What *is* her problem?" Renae wanted to know.

Mom couldn't tell Renae a lot of details because what she and Mrs. Carlson talked about was confidential. But Mom mentioned that all of Mrs. Carlson's children lived out of state, so she got lonely. Also, she couldn't do all the work around her house anymore, like taking care of the lawn, washing windows, and other odd jobs.

Renae said, "I wish I could help. She's always been so nice to us kids. I'd like to give her something, but I don't know what."

"I know the perfect present," said Mom. "Give yourself to Mrs. Carlson."

"How do I do that?" asked Renae. "Wrap myself up in paper and put a bow on my head?"

Mom laughed. "Well, that's an interesting idea, but it's not quite what I had in mind. You can help others by giving of yourself. For example, you can spend time visiting with Mrs. Carlson, you can mow her lawn, or you can run errands for her. Mrs. Carlson does beautiful needlework; she would love to teach someone how to do it. How about you? You don't need the fancy paper and bow—just be yourself."

Renae started rummaging around in the cabinets, looking for the ingredients for chocolate chip cookies. She was also thinking about the wadded-up cross-stitch shoved into the back of her closet. Tomorrow afternoon Mrs. Carlson would have a surprise visitor.

"Maybe after Mrs. Carlson tastes my delicious cookies she won't mind helping me untangle that mess of thread and terrible stitches," said Renae. "Of course, it might take *lots* of visits to get that sewing to look like something."

### Questions

- How did Renae feel about Mrs. Carlson?
- Why was Renae concerned about her?
- How can giving of yourself help someone?
- How do you think Mrs. Carlson felt when Renae went to visit her?
- How can you give of yourself to someone? Who will it be?

### Bible Discovery

Read John 13:12-17 and Acts 16:14-15, 40.

### Bible Point

Jesus gave of himself when he served his disciples by washing their feet and when he died on the cross for us. God's people can give of themselves in many ways. This really means helping people because they need us and because we want to, not because we expect a reward or repayment of some kind. As Christians, we give of ourselves because Jesus gave of himself.

### Bottom Line

Help others by giving of yourself.

# 25

# How to Be Popular

## *Know What You Want*

Megan wanted to be popular. She studied the popular girls and tried to do what they did. She tried out for cheerleading even though she didn't enjoy it. (She didn't make it, either.) She joined a lot of clubs that she didn't like. She didn't do any of the activities that she truly enjoyed—playing basketball, making good grades, and being with her church youth group—because that wasn't what the "popular" kids did. Megan was very unhappy.

Aunt Grace could tell that Megan was unhappy. She knew that Megan was trying to be someone she wasn't. One Saturday, Aunt Grace decided to talk with Megan about it. She invited Megan to do all kinds of fun things and planned a special talk for after supper.

The day went great. They went swimming and horseback riding. They had Megan's favorite supper on the back patio with candles on the table. Afterwards they settled in on the big couch in the den. Aunt Grace had brought down all her high school yearbooks. She began, "I wanted to show you my life when I was your age."

A cloud seemed to settle over Megan. "Oh. I bet your life was a lot better than mine," she said.

"What makes your life so sad, Megan? What do you wish was different?" asked Aunt Grace.

Megan answered slowly. "I look at all those popular kids, the ones everybody knows and everybody likes, and I wish that I was like them. I wish I knew the right things to say all the time. I wish I had great clothes. I wish I enjoyed the things they do. Their lives seem like big-screen color TVs, and mine seems like Granny's little thirteen-inch black and white. How did your life feel, Aunt Grace?"

Grace swallowed her sadness and said, "I was *very* popular."

"Really?" Megan inquired. "Were you a cheerleader or a homecoming queen or a majorette?"

"Oh no, Meggie," Grace insisted, "I was none of those. I was a basketball player. Here I'll show you."

Megan and Grace began to look through the yearbooks. They found Grace's picture each year in the sports section. They found her in the honor society and in the Fellowship of Christian Athletes. But what amazed Megan the most was how many people had signed Grace's yearbooks. She must have known everybody at the school.

Grace was ready to tell Megan the most important thing. "Megan, you think being popular means acting and looking a certain way. But I'm living proof that being popular is doing what you are best at, being true to your beliefs, liking yourself, and helping other people enjoy life with you. And I know you can do that."

"Tell me more," said Megan. She knew that her unhappiness couldn't change with one conversation. But she also knew that she was about to learn something that would change the way she looked at her life.

### Questions

- Why was Megan unhappy?
- What does it mean to be popular?
- What made Grace popular in school?
- What are the popular people at your school like?

### Bible Discovery

Read these verses: Psalm 19:14; Proverbs 16:7; Romans 14:17-18; Galatians 1:10; 1 Thessalonians 2:4.

### Bible Point

There is nothing wrong with wanting to be liked. God created us to want approval. But our first priority should be to please God, not our classmates. If we understand that God approves of us, we will feel freer to be ourselves. If we feel free to be ourselves, other people will feel more at home around us and they will like us more. It all works together.

### Bottom Line

If you want to be popular, love and please God, learn to like yourself, and do what you do best. Let the rest take care of itself.

## *My Little Phony*

Al felt sorry for his cousin Candace. She had just come to live with them and was having a difficult time adjusting to school. He didn't understand it, but Candace seemed so uncomfortable being herself. Al liked Candace. She was funny and smart and seemed to be able to talk to anyone. But at school, Candace would get quiet and even snobbish.

Once Al sat behind her in the lunchroom; she had no idea he was there. She told more lies in that one lunch period than he could imagine. She lied about why she was there, making up some grand job that her parents had where they were living. *What is wrong with her?* Al wondered.

About four weeks after Candace had come, Al decided to say something to her, but he didn't want to hurt her feelings. One afternoon as they were working in the yard together, he said, "Candace, have you made a lot of friends at school yet?"

She didn't say anything, so he continued. "I bet you have because you are so easy to talk to and so much fun to be around. Anyone who gets to know you would like you a lot."

She still didn't say anything. Al began to think that maybe this wasn't the best time after all. So he waited a few minutes and then asked what time they were supposed to go inside.

After another minute or so, Candace stopped raking and admitted, "Al, I don't have any friends at all at school. In fact, I don't think anyone even knows who I am."

"Why, sure they do, Candace," Al said before thinking. "I hear them call you by name all the time."

"They know my name, but they don't know me because I've told hardly anybody about me, and the ones I've told I've lied to." As Candace finished her sentence, she started crying.

Al just sat her down right there in the grass and sat beside her. Even though she was still crying, he started talking."Candace, I know you've been lying. I heard you the other day in the cafeteria. What I can't figure out is why. Nobody at my school wants to be impressed. And what worries me is that nobody likes a phony. What's going to happen when they find out?"Al and Candace talked for quite a while about how she could get out of her mess.

The next day she went into school determined to be truthful. She went to the people she had lied to and set the story straight. It was not an easy thing to do, but Candace was glad that Al had talked honestly with her. She knew she would never be liked as a liar because no one likes a phony.

Questions

- Why did Candace lie to people?
- Why don't people like phonies?
- When have you ever lied so people would like you more?

Bible Discovery

Read these verses: Genesis 12:10-20; Leviticus 19:11; Psalm 51:6; Proverbs 12:22; 30:8; Ephesians 4:25.

Bible Point

God tells us to be truthful with our words and our lives. Believe it or not, this probably helps us be popular. People like those who are honest and whom they can trust. People like to know they don't have to pretend to be better than they are. The best way to be liked by people is to be who you are and to accept them for who *they* are.

Bottom Line

To be popular, don't lie about who you are—not with your words or your actions.

## *Making New Friends*

Mr. Baker was frustrated with his children, Mindy and Glen. They weren't even trying to fit into their new community. All they did was complain about how their new school was different from their old school. He was sick of it. So on Friday night he took them out for pizza and a good talk.

"Listen, kids," he said, "you aren't even trying to fit in."

"But the kids around here don't like any of the things we're used to," complained Mindy.

"And the things they like are just not cool, Dad," added Glen, continuing Mindy's thought.

"This may not seem fair to you, but you've got to remember that you are the new kids on the block," Dad replied. "You can't expect everyone to change their ways to suit you. An important part of fitting in and becoming well liked is learning the ways of a new culture."

"A new culture?" said Glen. "Dad, we didn't move across the ocean. We just moved across the state."

"I realize that, Son," said Dad, "but every group, organization, and place has its own culture, or subculture, if you want to call it that. Getting used to a new place means understanding that culture and then fitting into it where you can. What do these kids like to do anyway?"

In that town a popular game was Ping-Pong, which neither Mindy nor Glen knew how to play. And on weekends many of them went bowling, which neither Mindy nor Glen knew how to do.

"Hey! That's where I can help!" exclaimed their dad. After finishing their pizza, off they drove to the secondhand sports store. By Saturday evening Glen and Mindy had a Ping-Pong table in the garage and bowling balls and shoes in their closets. By the next weekend, Mindy could beat her dad and Glen at Ping-Pong, and Glen knew how to keep score at bowling (even though he hadn't made a strike yet).

By the next month, Mindy and Glen had been to several bowling nights and had even had friends over. They made so many friends that it was quite awhile before they ate out with just their dad again. When they did, however, things were going much better.

"Thanks, Dad, for helping us get to know these kids and this subculture." Glen was proud he could use one of his dad's words to thank him.

"You did the work, Son. I just gave you the tools," Dad replied. "I'm really proud of both of you. You were true to yourself, but you bent just enough to relate to the kids here. Good job."

### Questions

- What did Glen and Mindy *not* like about their new community?
- What is a subculture?
- Why do different subcultures have different interests and popular activities?
- What do the kids at your school like to do?

### Bible Discovery

Read these verses: Proverbs 19:20; 1 Corinthians 9:20-22; Romans 15:7.

### Bible Point

It takes work to get to know people. It takes a lot of work if you are new or different from them. Paul was a Jew, but he preached to Gentiles. He had to take on some of their customs to make them comfortable with him. That doesn't mean he gave up who he was; he showed them that who they were was important to him. That is important for us to do too. People need to see that we understand them and accept their ways. Then hopefully they will feel comfortable accepting us.

Bottom Line

To be popular, try new activities (within reason and righteousness).

## *Chitchat*

"The hardest part of going to a party is the chitchat," said Matt. "I think it is almost impossible to know what to say to people when you don't know them. I'm not going to be like my grandpa and talk about the weather that day."

"I agree," said Jessica. "I don't know what a guy I've never met is interested in. What kind of conversation should I have with him?"

This conversation occurred because Mrs. Baldwin had just come into Sunday school and invited all the upcoming seventh graders to the youth party next Saturday. This was supposed to be an opportunity for the seventh graders to be welcomed, but it was often such a stressful time for them that they left early or didn't come at all.

Mrs. Taylor, the group leader for Matt and Jessica's group, thought that maybe they should work on this chitchat thing. It certainly would affect how often these kids came to Sunday school once they moved into that age-group.

"Let's talk about some things you might say to open up a conversation," said Mrs. Taylor.

"How about," Mike said imitating an old man's voice, "nice weather we're having here, huh, sonny?"

They all laughed. "I'm serious," said Mrs. Taylor. "While you are growing up, part of going to church, as well as to a lot of other places, is being able to make conversation with people you don't know. How can you do that?"

Jessica spoke up. "My friend Val always starts a conversation with an introduction. She'll say, 'Hi. I'm Val.' Then she has at least started the ball rolling."

"That's good, Jessica," said Mrs. Taylor. "And that's a lot of what chitchat is. It's like tossing a ball back and forth. You don't have to play a whole ball game. You just have to be able to toss one ball at a time. An introduction is a good first toss. What would you toss back, Matt?"

"That one's easy. I'd say, 'Hi. I'm Matt.'"

"OK, Jessica, what would you say now?" interjected Mrs. Taylor.

"How about, 'Are you having a good time?'"

Matt answered, "It's OK. What is your favorite thing to do at parties?"

"Very good, Matt!" said Mrs. Taylor. "Now you are getting to know something about each other. You might also want to ask about the other person's favorite activities or classes in school. There's a lot to talk about. I think you'll do fine at the party. Just remember to always be gracious and interested. Stop thinking about yourself and show interest in the other person."

"And don't let the ball drop," added Matt.

### Questions

- What did Matt and Jessica dislike about parties?
- What makes chitchat difficult?
- What kinds of questions or statements can you start conversations with?

### Bible Discovery

Read these verses: Proverbs 12:25; 15:1, 23; 16:24; 25:11; Ecclesiastes 10:12-13.

### Bible Point

The Bible provides plenty of guidelines for using words. These guidelines help if we are learning how to get to know people. Getting to know people involves small talk, or chitchat. God tells us to be kind, pleasant, and gracious. These are good rules for any conversations you have with someone.

### Bottom Line

To be popular, be kind and gracious in your conversation and show interest in those you talk to.

## *Crash and Burn*

Rebecca had tried out for cheerleading for three seasons (a new squad was chosen for each season). When she finally got picked, she was overjoyed. She believed that now she would be popular. But that's not what happened. The other cheerleaders in the squad didn't like Rebecca. They excluded her from parties and conversations. They never saved her a seat on the bus.

After the last game of the season, Rebecca was glad that she would be rotating off the squad. The other cheerleaders had rejected her. They treated her as if she was unwanted and unworthy. Instead of feeling more popular, she felt less popular. That is how rejection works.

For several days after the last game, Rebecca hardly said a word. When she finally described the season to her mom, Rebecca's eyes filled with tears.

"Rebecca, honey, if only you had told me," said her mom, "I would have pulled you off the squad, and you wouldn't have had to go through all that."

"That's why I didn't tell you!" explained Rebecca. "I loved the cheering part, and I think I was really good. That's why I couldn't understand why they treated me that way."

"I can't answer that, Rebecca," said Mom. "Maybe because you were different. Maybe because they were a little intimidated. Maybe because the girls just aren't very nice. It might be that no matter who had been added to the squad, they would have treated her the same way. Usually, Rebecca, when someone rejects you, it is more about that person than about you."

"But it's me that it hurts, Mom," replied Rebecca.

"Rebecca, I'd like for you to pray about something," her mom continued. "If you truly love being a cheerleader, please pray about trying out again."

"What?" said Rebecca. "You just said you would have pulled me off the squad."

"Rebecca, I don't ever want you to be hurt," Mom said slowly. "At the same time, however, I don't want you to be robbed of something you enjoy. If you can be strong enough to cheer through their rejection, you might just be accepted by them the next go-around. Just think about it over the next few weeks.

"It's not that it is important to me that you are a cheerleader," Mom continued. "But it is important to me for you to learn that if God and your family are on your side, no person can tear you down. This might be a good way to learn it."

Rebecca did cheer again the next season. It was different, however, because she wasn't new anymore. The older girls accepted her, and she was able to help the new girl become accepted too. Because Rebecca didn't let rejection keep her from trying, she got to do something she loved and make friends while she did it. And she got her mom to come to every game.

### Questions

- What does it mean to reject someone?
- Why did the other cheerleaders reject Rebecca?
- What did Rebecca do to change the rejection pattern on the squad?
- When were you rejected?

### Bible Discovery

Read these verses: Deuteronomy 31:6-8; 1 Samuel 18:6-9; 1 Chronicles 28:2-7, 11-12; Psalm 69:18-20; Acts 7:35-39.

### Bible Point

Rejection is not pleasant. Saul was miserable when he realized that God wanted David to be king instead of him. It may have been difficult for David when he wanted to build a temple for God, but God said no, let your son build it. It certainly hurt when Moses' own brother and sister rejected him as ruler of the Hebrew people. We can learn from rejection, however, and move on. And we can be sure that God will never reject us, so there is always hope.

### Bottom Line

Rejection hurts, but God will heal you, and you can learn from it.

# 26

# How to Be a Better Family Member

### *The Golden Rule*

"I'm going to Konni's, Mom!" Janice Bergner yelled.

"Hey!" Blake, her younger brother, called from his room down the hall. "You said you were going to do the dishes for me tonight!"

Janice rolled her eyes. "Can't. I'm going to Konni's so we can work on our history project. Mom said I could go."

"But you said you'd wash the dishes for me! I washed *your* dishes last week!"

"Look, I'm busy right now. I'll make it up to you, honest." Janice quickly closed the front door, then strapped on her in-line skates.

Konni Andrews and her mother were cleaning the front windows when Janice arrived minutes later. They both called out enthusiastic greetings.

"What's going on?" Janice asked.

"Just a little late-summer cleaning," said Mrs. Andrews.

Janice was amazed that Konni didn't look upset about cleaning the windows. She would have hated that job. She remembered how her mother had wanted her to help, and she had found something else to do.

Janice played with Rollo, the Andrews' collie, while she waited for Konni. Finally, Konni was done. The girls went to Konni's room.

"How come your mom made you clean the windows?" Janice asked.

"She didn't. I volunteered."

"You volunteered? Ugh! Not me!"

"Well, I knew she needed help. Neither of my brothers is home—just me."

Janice shrugged. "I never volunteer to do chores. I got out of washing the dishes for my brother today."

"I would've waited for you if you had to do them."

Janice waved her hand. "It's his night anyway. He's just mad because he did them for me last week, and I said I'd do them this week. Nobody told him to volunteer."

Konni looked at Janice. "Do you think that's fair?"

"What?"

"You said you'd do the dishes for him and then you decide not to. What if he had done that to you when you needed help?"

"I've helped him lots—" Janice's voice cut off abruptly. She suddenly realized that she couldn't think of a time in recent months when she had helped Blake do anything.

There was a knock at the door. Konni called out, "Come in!"

Mrs. Andrews entered with two fresh pretzels. "Thanks for helping me with the windows, honey," she said, handing the girls the pretzels. "Here. I picked these up at the pretzel place for you."

"Mmmm! My favorite! Thanks, Mom."

"Wow, your mom's nice."

"Mom's in her 'do-unto-others' mode."

"What?"

"You know, the Golden Rule. 'Do to others what you would have them do to you.'"

"I've heard that before."

"If you want things to be fair, be fair yourself."

Janice looked thoughtful. She had been unfair to Blake. She stood up. "I'll come back later. Right now, I'd better get home and see if there are any dishes left to wash."

### Questions

- Why should Janice have washed the dishes?
- What happens when everyone at home doesn't do his or her share?
- How can following the Golden Rule make a family better?
- What can you do for others that you would want done for you?

### Bible Discovery

Read Matthew 22:39; Luke 6:31; 10:25-37.

Bible Point

We can learn from the Good Samaritan, who helped the wounded man by the road. If we want others to treat us well, we must first do our part and treat them well.

Bottom Line

Being a better family member starts by doing to others what you would want done for yourself.

## *Honoring Parents*

"Celina, I'm going to the arcade!" Sean Dunsmore yelled. He followed his friend Randy Beaman out the door.

Mrs. Dunsmore looked away from the television and frowned. "Honey, it's almost dinnertime. What time will you be back?" she asked.

"I don't know!" Sean slammed the door.

Neither Sean nor Randy spoke until they were on their bikes and headed toward the arcade.

"She gets on my nerves!" Sean said bitterly.

"You could've told your mom we'd be back in fifteen minutes," Randy said.

"She's not my mom! She's my *step*mom!"

"Whatever." Randy shook his head. He and Sean had discussed this before. Sean still was angry that his father had remarried after his mother's death.

Just as they were nearing the arcade, a car pulled up alongside them. Randy's mother poked her head out of the driver's side. After greeting Sean, she said, "Randy, I thought I told you to clean your room before you left."

"Can I do it when I get home?"

"I want you to do it now, Randy."

Randy sighed and nodded.

Mrs. Beaman smiled. "I'll be back in an hour." She waved as she drove off.

"Good," Sean said. He looked satisfied. "We'll be back before she gets back. C'mon. I want you to see this new game."

"What're you talking about? I've got to go home."

"But your mom won't be back for an hour!"

"You heard what she said. I have to go."

"I would've told my stepmother that I'll clean my room when *I* get ready." Sean looked defiant.

"My mom would never let me get away with that. I'd be grounded for a month!" said Randy.

"My dad grounded me once. I sneaked out of the house. Celina doesn't try that," said Sean.

"Well, sometimes I don't *want* to do what my parents tell me," commented Randy, "but I do it 'cause they expect me to respect them."

"Why?"

Randy stared at him. "Uh, I don't know. It's one of the Ten Commandments."

Sean rolled his eyes. "Whatever."

During dinner that evening, Randy suddenly asked, "Why should I respect you guys?"

His parents looked surprised. "What do you mean?" Mr. Beaman asked.

Randy told them about his conversation with Sean. "I couldn't think of anything else to say. Sean looked at me like I was crazy when I told him about the Ten Commandments."

"Well, honoring parents *is* one of the commandments," said Mrs. Beaman. "God put parents in authority over their children. It's a way to keep the peace in a household."

Randy shrugged. "I told him that you wouldn't let me get away with saying the stuff he says. Sean thought I was crazy because I came back here instead of going with him to the arcade. Do you think I should have said something else to him?"

Mrs. Beaman smiled. "No, honey. I think your actions said it all."

### Questions

- What kind of relationship do you think Sean had with his father and stepmother?
- Why is it important to honor your parents?
- How can honoring parents improve family life?
- In what ways do you show that you honor your parents?

### Bible Discovery

Read Exodus 20:12 and Ephesians 6:1-3.

### Bible Point

God commands us to honor and obey our parents, so it is important that we do so. Honoring parents is a way to honor God.

Bottom Line

Being a better family member starts with honoring your parents.

## *Pass On the Put-Downs*

Rochelle Watkins grumbled all the way home that Wednesday as she thought about the poem she had to write for school.

"Write a poem on a subject that is important to you," her teacher had said.

What a joke! Writing a poem was on Rochelle's list of top ten things *not* to do that year, along with things like growing a third arm and dyeing her hair green.

Rochelle's older brother, Bernard, was in the kitchen fixing himself a snack when she stalked in. "What's with you?" he asked, as Rochelle slammed her books on the counter.

"I have to write a stupid poem for stupid Language Arts!"

Bernard tossed a cheese puff into his mouth. "Hey, how 'bout this—Rochelle's no poet, and don't I know it."

"Shut up, Bernard."

"Rochelle's no poet, and *everybody* knows it!"

"You make me sick, you stupid slug!" yelled Rochelle.

"Girl, I'm just playing with you! Can't you take a joke?" Bernard laughed.

Their uncle soon entered the kitchen, sighing as he did. "I could hear the two of you all the way from the garage."

"He started it, Uncle Walt!" Rochelle yelled.

"Didn't we agree to cool it with the name-calling?" Mr. Watkins leveled his gaze at Rochelle.

"But he . . ."

Mr. Watkins stared at Bernard. "Bernard, you know better. A joke isn't a joke if it's at somebody else's expense."

Bernard threw up his hands. "OK, OK. I can't help it if she's touchy today."

Rochelle grabbed a piece of fruit and retreated to her room. She flopped down at her mother's old sewing table that served as a desk.

*Ooh, that stupid Bernard!* she fumed. Why couldn't he talk to her like a normal person? She couldn't remember the last time he had said something nice to her like a normal person. Come to think of it, she couldn't remember the last time she hadn't called him "stupid" or some other name to get back at him.

Half an hour later, Rochelle heard a knock at her door. "Enter," she said.

Mr. Watkins slowly pushed open the door. "Just thought I'd check on you. Dinner's almost ready." He came in and perched on the end of her bed. "Bad day at school, huh?"

"I have to write a stupid poem," mumbled Rochelle.

"You've been throwing that word around a lot today, Chel," said Mr. Watkins.

Rochelle muttered, "Bernard bugs me sometimes."

"You know your brother likes to tease you. Mainly because he's afraid you'll find out how crazy he is about his little sister," said Mr. Watkins. "Anyway, I'll talk to him."

"Hmmph," Rochelle muttered again.

"Anyway, Chel, you know how we feel about putting people down in this house. If you can't say something nice—"

"—don't say anything," Rochelle finished in a singsong voice. "But Bernard—"

"I'll handle Bernard," said Mr. Watkins. "We're talking about you now. You're getting to be a young lady. That means that soon you will be too old for baby stuff like calling people names, right? You know that's not the way God wants you to handle your business, right?"

Rochelle nodded.

### Questions

- How do you feel when someone calls you a name or says something mean to you?
- Why is it important to watch what you say to others?
- How can avoiding put-downs improve family life?

### Bible Discovery

Read Ephesians 4:29-32.

### Bible Point

"Foul or abusive language" is anything that puts another person down. Instead of using put-downs, we should be encouraging and helpful to others.

### Bottom Line

Being a good family member means being helpful, not hurtful, in what you say.

### *Togetherness*

Kennedy Adams glowed with excitement when she arrived home from school. Jelisha Sanchez, the coolest girl in the sixth grade, had invited her to eat dinner at their house once again.

"Mom," she called as soon as she opened the back door. "Jelisha's mom said I can eat dinner over there, OK? Say yes."

"No, it's not OK," Mrs. Adams replied. "I want you to eat here tonight."

"But—"

"I said no, Kennedy."

Kennedy stomped to the family room to use the phone. Her older sister, Angelica, was already on it.

"I need to use the phone!" Kennedy demanded.

"I'll be off in a minute," replied Angelica, before returning to her conversation. As soon as she was done, Kennedy snatched the phone out of her hand.

"Excuse *you,*" Angelica said sarcastically.

Kennedy quickly dialed Jelisha's number. As soon as Jelisha came on the line, Kennedy blurted out, "I can't go! My mother's making me eat here!"

"Too bad!" Jelisha said. "We're ordering your favorite—pizza."

Kennedy sighed in annoyance. "We hardly ever order pizza around here!" She sniffed the air. "Mom's making meat loaf tonight," she said sourly.

"Meat loaf? I love meat loaf! Maybe I should come *there.*"

"You *like* meat loaf?"

"Yeah. At least I used to. My mom, like, never cooks nowadays. We're always eating takeout."

"Go ask your mom, then. Call me back." Kennedy hung up. "Mom, can Jelisha eat dinner with us?"

Mrs. Adams's eyebrows rose. "I thought you wanted to eat over there."

"Well, I told her we were having meat loaf, and she wants to eat here." Kennedy shook her head in disbelief.

"Well, if it's all right with her mom, she can eat here. I'm glad you're inviting your friends over finally. I was beginning to think we have a disease or something."

"Mom, could you please tell Dad not to tell any of his stale jokes during dinner? And tell Jason not to pick his nose. He does that when you're not looking. And make Amy—"

"I'm sure we'll all try our best not to embarrass you," Mrs. Adams said sarcastically.

Kennedy wasn't sure, but she thought her mom looked a little hurt.

Dinner seemed to go fine. After dinner Kennedy and Jelisha played Ping-Pong in the basement. "Man, your family is so cool," Jelisha said, during a break. "I mean your dad, like, talks to you. My father never says anything at the table, when he's home to eat with us. Lately, that's not very often. And your mom's a great cook. My mom never cooks anything anymore. That's why we eat takeout a lot. I wouldn't mind hanging over here."

"You *like* it here?" asked Kennedy.

"Don't you? Man, you are soooo lucky," answered Jelisha.

Kennedy was surprised. She had thought that Jelisha's family was cool! She told her mother what Jelisha said after Jelisha went home.

"You sound surprised," Mrs. Adams said. "You know, honey, there's nothing wrong with spending time with your family. Some people don't have families to spend time with."

"I guess." As Kennedy looked at her mother, she thought, *Jelisha's right. My family is cool.*

Questions

- What do you like about your family?
- What would you like to change about your family? Why?
- How much time do you spend with your family?
- How can spending time together as a family improve family life?

Bible Discovery

Read Romans 12:16.

Bible Point

A part of being content means accepting family members for who they are, warts and all. It means spending time with them.

Bottom Line

Being a better family member means spending time with your family.

## *A-Grumbling We Will Go?*

"Do I have to go?" Chris Leonard asked his mother as he followed her to the driveway.

Mrs. Leonard sighed. A ray of early morning sunshine highlighted her tired expression. "We are not getting into this now, Chris. You've already made us late as it is."

Chris folded his arms and sighed loudly, causing his straight blond bangs to flutter. "Why do I have to go? Danny Peterson's parents don't make him go to church!"

"Well, *you're* going and that's that!" Mrs. Leonard snapped.

Chris glared at the backs of his parents' heads all the way to church.

"Can I go to the park with Danny, Mom?" Chris asked, waving the cordless phone at his mother later that day.

Mrs. Leonard looked up from the magazine she was reading at the kitchen table. "Did you do your homework?"

Chris threw his mother a look. "Most of it. Can't I just go for a few minutes?"

"You can go after you do *all* your homework and *after* we eat lunch," answered Mom.

Chris clicked off the phone. "I never get to do anything around here!" he said as he stormed to his room.

As soon as Chris was gone, Mrs. Leonard complained to her husband, "Bill, I can't take any more of this! Ever since he turned twelve, he's been so moody!"

"I've got an idea," Mr. Leonard said. He began to whisper in her ear.

Chris burst into the house and enthusiastically waved his notebook. "Look at this!" he said, waving a paper in front of his mother. On it was a large A-.

"A-? Is that the best you could do?" Mrs. Leonard grumbled.

Chris looked hurt. "This is the best grade I've got! You know how hard algebra is for me."

"Why couldn't you have gotten an A+?" she asked.

"I think it's pretty good!" He looked around the kitchen. "What's for dinner?"

"I don't feel like cooking. I was hoping your father would be here to start dinner," Mrs. Leonard said.

Chris looked at her as if she'd suddenly sprouted a second head. "Are you OK, Mom?" he asked quietly.

Mrs. Leonard just stood there huffing, just as Mr. Leonard arrived home. "What? No dinner?" he grumbled as soon as he walked in the door.

"I'm tired of having to cook!" Mrs. Leonard said. "I work all day too, y'know."

"Look at this, Dad!" Chris cut in before his father could reply. He proudly waved the paper.

Mr. Leonard glanced at it. "A-? Couldn't you have gotten an A+?"

"What's wrong with the grade I got? I did the best I could!" said Chris.

Mr. Leonard suddenly smiled. "That's how we feel whenever you grumble."

"You've been doing that a lot lately," Mrs. Leonard added. They both looked at Chris and smiled.

"Oh, I get it. You were just pretending." Chris didn't know whether to scream at them or laugh.

Mr. Leonard put an arm around Chris's shoulders. "Grumbling makes things a drag for everybody, Chris. It never solves any problems. It only creates more. Instead of grumbling, let's talk about things, OK?"

### Questions

- When are you the most tempted to grumble?
- When someone grumbles a lot, how do you think that makes others feel?
- How can a positive attitude improve family life?
- What can you do instead of grumbling?

### Bible Discovery

Check out Exodus 16:1-9; Philippians 4:4; James 5:9.

### Bible Point

Grumbling is a sign that something needs to change—either in the person who grumbles or in the situation. Either way, grumbling never solves anything. Instead of grumbling, we can thank God for his love and for what he's done for us.

### Bottom Line

Being a better family member means having a positive attitude and giving up grumbling.

# 27

# How to Get Along with Your Parents

***Loud Actions***

Mr. Martin was putting away the science-lab books when Andrew walked in. "Hey, Andrew, how's it going?" Mr. Martin said, as he turned to clear off his desk.

"OK," Andrew said with a shrug. There was something, however, in Andrew's voice that suggested that things were not OK.

Mr. Martin put down the stack of papers he had just picked up. "Want to talk about it?"

Andrew slumped into a chair. "This is going to sound stupid, but it seems like my parents just don't care about me anymore. I mean, they're hardly around much, with my dad's job and my mom's volunteering all over town. When I want to sit and talk with them, they're always too busy. I feel like I'm the last item on their to-do list."

Mr. Martin answered slowly, "I don't think that's a stupid issue at all, Andrew. In fact, I think a lot of families are going through the same thing that your family is experiencing. We *all* are so busy, sometimes the very thing that families are supposed to be about gets lost in the shuffle. Have you tried talking to your parents about this?"

Andrew nodded. "But every time I try to talk with them about *my* feelings, we get into a shouting match. I can't seem to get through to them at all. I'm seriously thinking about e-mailing them so they'll know I'm still around."

Mr. Martin smiled. "I suppose that is an option, but I think there's a better way. Let me ask you this: What is absolutely necessary to start a car?"

Andrew gave Mr. Martin a look that said "give me a break," but he answered, "A key."

"Right," said Mr. Martin. "Well, the same is true for families. You've got to have the right keys for keeping the doors of communication open in your family. And I think I've got just the book to help you find those keys." Mr. Martin reached for a stack of books on his desk and pulled out his Bible. It was a familiar book to Andrew because Mr. Martin always carried it with him to the early morning Bible study at school. "There are four keys essential to keeping the communication flowing on the home front," he said. "Let's look at one of them, and then you can look up the others at home. Take a look at Galatians 5:14-15."

Andrew flipped through Mr. Martin's well-worn Bible. Finally he found the verses and read aloud: "'For the whole law can be summed up in this one command: 'Love your neighbor as yourself.' But if instead of showing love among yourselves you are always biting and devouring one another, watch out! Beware of destroying one another.'" When Andrew finished reading, he gave Mr. Martin a questioning look.

"You see, Andrew," said Mr. Martin, "sometimes we need to use our actions to speak for us. Think about how you treat your parents when they get home from a meeting or from a trip out of town. Are you expecting them to meet all your needs immediately, or do you take time to find out what their day was like? God teaches us to treat others like we want to be treated. Putting that into action is a good first step to opening up those communication lines."

Andrew closed the Bible. "I think I understand. Like maybe I could have the table set when my mom is running late or help my brother get his homework started," he said, thinking aloud.

Mr. Martin clapped him on the shoulder. "You've got the idea. Give it a try and let me know what happens."

### Questions

- In what ways can a person's actions at home shut down communication? How can they keep communication open?
- How would you describe the communication at your home?
- Look at the three other "keys" to open communication

and describe how each helps promote communication: Ecclesiastes 4:9-10; James 1:19-20; 1 John 1:8-9.

Bible Discovery

Review these key Bible passages: Ecclesiastes 4:9-10; Galatians 5:13-15; James 1:19-20; 1 John 1:8-9.

Bible Point

Helping others, treating others as you want to be treated, listening without anger, and confessing our sins are keys to keeping the door of communication open.

Bottom Line

Choosing actions that open the door to good communication will help you get along with your parents.

## *Lend a Hand*

"Mr. Martin, I think I'm going to scream!" Erica cried as she flung herself into the chair by Mr. Martin's desk.

Mr. Martin had to smile to himself. Erica was one of his more dramatic students. Each week it seemed as though she had some new crisis, and she usually let everyone know about it in her own unique style. "What seems to be the problem this week, Erica?" Mr. Martin asked.

Erica crossed her arms angrily and launched into her list of complaints. "I can't stand it at home anymore. My mother is completely out of control. As soon as she walks in the door, she starts ordering me around." Erica began mimicking her mother's voice. "Empty the dishwasher! Fold the laundry! Pick up your room! Put away your books! Set the table! Honestly, you'd think I was her personal slave or something."

"What usually happens after your mother starts ordering you around?" Mr. Martin asked.

Erica thought a moment. "Well, my brother and I usually ignore her until she really starts to scream. Then it starts getting real ugly. By that time, everyone is screaming and mad at each other. Can you see why I can't stand it anymore?"

Mr. Martin said, "Sounds like you've got a real problem. Your mom is asking you to do a bunch of frustrating, dirty work."

Erica grumbled, "You got that right."

"You know, Erica, there was this man in the Bible who felt pretty much the same as you did about work. Let me find it here." Mr. Martin flipped through his Bible to Ecclesiastes 2:17-23. "Listen to some of the gripe words he used in describing work: *hate, meaningless, chasing the wind, disgusted, hard, despair, foolish, unfair, pain and grief, no rest.* Do those sound familiar?"

Erica nodded. "Boy, he's got that right," she answered.

"But you know, Erica, this man, Solomon, didn't stop there. He came to the conclusion that the solution to dealing with so-called meaningless work is to find satisfaction in that work. Here, read verse 24 aloud."

Erica took the Bible from Mr. Martin and began reading: "'So I decided there is nothing better than to enjoy food and drink and to find satisfaction in work. Then I realized that this pleasure is from the hand of God.'"

When she finished, Mr. Martin asked her, "How do you think you can find satisfaction in the work your mom asks you to do?"

"That's a tough one," Erica answered. She paused, thinking a moment, and then continued. "Well, I suppose I can take satisfaction in knowing I helped her out. Or that the house is clean when she walks in the door. Or that my room doesn't look like a total pigsty."

"That's a good start," Mr. Martin said encouragingly. "Now, think how your mom might react when she walks in the door and you already have done some of the work you know she wants you to do. Wouldn't that create a different scene from the one you described to me earlier?"

Erica had to agree that it would.

"Our chores can become a way of honoring God. If we do them as a service to God, our service honors him and draws others to him," Mr. Martin said.

Erica got up from the chair. "I never really thought about it that way before. I guess it's worth a try. It might be fun thinking of ways to find satisfaction in dusting!"

### Questions

- What chores do you have to do around your house? How can you find satisfaction in those chores?
- What would happen if no one did those chores?
- What could happen if everyone in your household shared the number of chores equally?

Bible Discovery

Read these Bible passages: Genesis 31:38-42; Proverbs 12:14; Ecclesiastes 2:17-25; 1 Corinthians 15:58; Ephesians 6:5-8.

Bible Point

God tells us to work hard. We should take satisfaction in knowing that God is honored by our work and will reward us for it.

Bottom Line

Looking for ways to help around the house is a good way to get along with your parents.

## *Pray to Obey*

Tim and his buddy Casey were getting dressed after basketball practice. The boys had just completed a grueling two-hour practice, preparing for the final cut for the school team. Tim was looking particularly discouraged. "What's up, Tim?" said Casey. "You had a really great practice today. I'm sure you will make the team."

"It's not that, Casey," said Tim. "It's my parents. They're really putting the pressure on me. If I don't get my grades up in math and science, they won't let me play basketball—even if I do make the team. I don't know what I'm going to do about it. I just have to play basketball—it's what I really want to do."

Casey felt bad for his friend. He knew how much Tim enjoyed the game, and he was one of the best players in school. But he also knew how much Tim struggled in math and science. Tim was in a really tight spot. "Hey, I know," Casey said, brightening. "Let's go talk to Mr. Martin. He's always willing to listen. He might have an idea or two."

Since the boys had fifteen minutes to spare before their ride came, they walked into Mr. Martin's classroom. He was still there, preparing things for the next day's lab. "Hey, guys, how's basketball going?" he asked as Tim and Casey walked in. Mr. Martin knew Tim and Casey well. He had the two in his science class last year, and both boys also attended his early-morning Bible study. Now he listened sympathetically as Tim related his dilemma. After Tim finished, Mr. Martin asked, "What do you think is most important here?"

Immediately Tim responded, "Playing basketball."

Mr. Martin chuckled. "I thought you would say that. But what do you think God would say is most important? Do you think his answer would be 'playing basketball'?"

Tim shook his head. "Probably not. I guess the most important thing is obeying my parents, isn't it? But if I obey them, I might as well turn in my basketball shoes right now. There's no way I'm going to be able to play. It's just not fair."

Mr. Martin considered Tim's last statement. "It may not seem fair to you because you want to play basketball so badly, but think about *why* your parents want you to do well in math and science. Do you think it's because they want you off the basketball team? Or because they enjoy seeing you suffer? Or do you think it may be because they want the best for you both academically and in sports?"

Mr. Martin opened his Bible. "In Colossians 3:23-25 Paul instructs us to work hard at whatever we do, as if we're working for the Lord not other people. When we obey our parents for God's sake, it not only pleases our parents, but it pleases God, too. The main reason we obey our parents is to glorify God, because God uses our parents to show us how to live for him. Does that make any sense?"

Tim considered what Mr. Martin said and nodded his head. Mr. Martin continued. "Now, Tim, do you think that perhaps some before-school sessions could help you with your science classes—and in obeying your parents?"

Tim gave a broad grin. "You bet I do! Thanks, Mr. Martin. Maybe there *is* a way to obey my parents first—and play some b-ball!"

### Questions

- How can obeying parents be a way to help a young person make smart decisions?
- How does obeying for God's sake make it easier to obey parents?
- How can you work together with your parents to do what is right?
- How can you draw on God's power to help you obey your parents?

### Bible Discovery

Read the following Bible passages: 1 Samuel 17:17-22; Luke 2:40-52; Colossians 3:20-25; Ephesians 6:1-3.

Bible Point

God is honored and pleased when children obey their parents.

Bottom Line

Obeying your parents is a good way to get along with them.

### *Show a Little Respect*

Mr. Martin's early-morning Bible study was buzzing with excitement. As a year-end celebration, the group had decided to invite their parents and serve breakfast, devoting part of the time to sharing some personal stories about how the Bible study had changed them during the year. The group energetically planned the event. "I'll bring the OJ," said one student. "Let me bring some muffins," said another. "I'll pitch in with some strawberries," called out another.

With the menu planned, the group decided that each student would write a personal invitation to his or her parents. As they worked, the students talked among themselves about the event—what they would share, the type of music they would play, the funny stories that occurred during the year together. As Mr. Martin observed the group, he noticed one student hanging back. Gregg, a new boy to the group, wasn't contributing anything to the breakfast, nor, as far as Mr. Martin could tell, was he writing an invitation. Mr. Martin pulled up a chair alongside Gregg.

"Hey, you're awfully quiet this morning," Mr. Martin said. "Aren't you planning to invite your parents?"

Gregg shrugged his shoulders. "Nah," he said, trying to act unconcerned. "I don't think they would like it."

Mr. Martin gave Gregg a long look. "Are you sure it's your parents who wouldn't like to come, or is it that you wouldn't like your parents to come?"

Gregg looked away. "I guess I don't want them to come. We just don't get along very well. They don't like anything I do, and they're always hassling me about something—keeping my room clean, the kids I hang out with, or studying. I get good grades, but that doesn't stop them from getting on my case all the time. If they came, they'd probably start bugging me about this, too."

Mr. Martin was quiet for a minute. Then he said, "Have you thought about *why* your parents are on your case? Maybe they hassle you about your room because they want you to learn good habits. Or maybe they hassle you about studying because they want you to succeed. Sometimes when we attempt to appreciate the *reasons* for parents doing what they do, we begin to respect them."

"I don't get what you mean. What does respect have to do with my parents? How can I respect them if all they do is yell at me all the time?" Gregg asked.

"That is hard," Mr. Martin agreed. "No one likes to be yelled at. But what if you began by showing your parents respect with actions, such as talking to them in a courteous tone, doing something kind for your mother, telling your dad that you appreciate his concern for you? All these actions show your parents that you are considering their views and wishes. Once you bring love and respect into the family, you will find yourself growing closer to your parents."

Gregg thought about it for a minute. "I guess that makes sense. But how do I get started?"

Mr. Martin picked up the crumpled invitation lying at Gregg's feet. "Here. Why don't you start with this?"

Questions

- Check out 1 Corinthians 13—the love chapter. What actions show respect?
- Which of these ways do you find easiest to express toward your parents? the most difficult?
- Why do parents need respect? Why do *you* need respect?
- How will respecting your parents help them respect you?

Bible Discovery

Read the following Bible verses: 1 Corinthians 13:4-5; Philippians 2:3-4; Hebrews 10:24-25; 1 Peter 2:17.

Bible Point

The Bible tells us to love, respect, and encourage each other. Showing parents respect enables families to work together and appreciate one another.

Bottom Line

Respecting your parents is a good way to get along with them.

## *Keep the Doors Open*

Austin and his friends were totally absorbed in the play on the field. The school's football squad was closing in on an undefeated season, but it was down to the last seconds and the team was down by three points. The team needed a touchdown to win and maintain their perfect record.

Their star quarterback had just completed a pass to the two-yard line, and it was down to the final play of the game. As the play unfolded, the team's running back, who happened to be Austin's older brother, pushed across the goal line. The crowd erupted into cheers. Austin and his friends ran excitedly onto the field to congratulate the players. As Austin looked for his brother, he bumped into his father.

"Hey, Dad, when did you get back in town? I didn't expect to see you here. It was a great win, wasn't it?" Austin shouted.

Dad gave Austin a brief hello and continued to scan the field for Austin's brother. "Just got in. Oh, wait a minute. I want to talk to Sam," his dad said and hurried off toward the crowd of jubilant football players.

Dejected, Austin walked off the field. He was gathering his books when Mr. Martin came up. "Hey, Austin, your brother was great. What a nail-biter," he said excitedly.

"Yeah, sure, it was great," Austin replied without much enthusiasm.

Mr. Martin stopped and followed Austin's gaze to where Austin's dad was talking animatedly with Sam. "Want to talk about it?" he asked.

"Oh, you know. My dad played football in high school and college, so he thinks Sam is just great. I mean, Sam is good, don't get me wrong, but I just don't seem to have anything in common with my dad. I'm not really good at sports, and my dad doesn't seem interested in the things I like. We just don't connect," Austin said.

Austin was about to leave when Mr. Martin stopped him. "Communication in families can be tough. It takes a constant effort, using all the skills we know to keep those doors open. But sometimes obstacles, like the one between you and your father right now, come up. That's when we need to work harder," Mr. Martin said as they walked back to the school. "I think you've got a head start on this situation because you've identified the obstacle—you feel you don't have anything in common with your father. Now the challenge is to think of ways to remove that obstacle," Mr. Martin encouraged him.

"Yeah, well, the only way I'm going to connect with my dad is if I put on football pads and slam into someone," Austin replied.

"OK, you're not going to become a football player," Mr. Martin answered, "but can you think of other ways to connect? Is there a project you're working on in school that you might get your dad to help you with? Think of ways you can get to know your dad that are different from Sam's."

"Well, maybe, I don't know," Austin said. "I'm doing a math project on statistics. Maybe I could ask my dad to help me work it through using sports statistics. He's got a million books with that kind of stuff in them."

Mr. Martin smiled at Austin. "That's a start, a good start. Just remember, God can help you understand and solve your communication problems. He can give you the skills and help you improve them. But you have to keep working at it. It's never easy, but it's always worth it."

### Questions

- What are some typical communication obstacles between kids and parents?
- What did Mr. Martin mean by finding other ways to "connect"?
- When you feel a lack of communication between you and your parents, what can you do?
- How does knowing that God cares about communication in your family help you?
- What are some ways you and your parents can improve your communication skills?

### Bible Discovery

Read the following verses: Psalm 133; Galatians 6:9-10; 1 John 1:7.

### Bible Point

We are to live in harmony and do good to everyone. God is pleased when we share our thoughts and feelings with others, but we need to work constantly to keep communication flowing.

### Bottom Line

Keeping the doors open to good communication helps you get along with your parents.

# 28

# How to Get Along with Your Brothers and Sisters

### *Private Property*

This summer Ryan's older brother, Dan, got a job at the neighborhood swimming pool. It certainly wasn't glamorous—emptying the trash cans and cleaning the bathrooms and eating area. But it was the first step toward becoming a lifeguard—a *real* job that Dan had wanted for a long time. With their mother working, both Ryan and Dan relied on their bikes as the main source of transportation. The boys would ride over to the pool each morning—Dan for his job and Ryan for swim-team practice.

The boys had strict rules about reporting in to their mother during the day; this was the first summer that they didn't have a "baby-sitter." Ryan was enjoying this newfound freedom. Today he and his friends were goofing off at Ryan's house after an afternoon of swimming. The boys were talking about a friend's brand-new, twenty-five-speed bike. It was the envy of their entire group. Ryan had hoped to save up whatever money he earned this summer mowing lawns to buy one for himself. As the boys were talking about this cool bike, Ryan remembered that his brother had the older model. It had twenty-five speeds and a totally cool ride. Every once in a while, Dan would let Ryan take it for a spin.

Ryan bet that his friends would enjoy a quick spin on Dan's bike. It was Dan's day off, and his brother had walked over to a friend's house for the afternoon. Dan would never know about it. And what he didn't know, Ryan figured, wouldn't hurt him.

"Hey, guys," Ryan said, walking over to the garage. "Want to try out my brother's bike? It's almost exactly like Zach's." Eagerly,

Ryan's friends gathered around him. Ryan gave each one explicit instructions: Only once around the block—no jumping curbs or popping wheelies; take it easy on the gears. His first friend took off around the corner, returning with an exhilarated look about five minutes later. "Awesome," he said. "I can't wait to get one of these bikes."

The next friend took off. After ten minutes went by and his friend hadn't returned, Ryan knew he was in trouble. The boys split up in different directions to look for Ryan's friend. Around the corner and half way down the street, Ryan spied his friend. A sickening feeling started in his stomach. His friend was crying, both knees were bleeding, and the bike was a tangled mess."What happened, Chris?" the boys exclaimed when they saw the bike.

"I couldn't change the gear, and I lost control of the bike and crashed," he cried. Ryan felt bad for his friend, but he felt even worse about what his brother would say when he saw the bike.

After his friends left, Ryan stared dismally at the bike. Maybe if he placed it in the driveway just so, he could say the mailman rode over it. Or he could hope his brother wouldn't notice the damage. But that was a long shot. Finally, Ryan decided to put the bike back where it was and see what happened.

That evening Ryan couldn't stand it any longer. His brother had given no indication that he had seen the damaged bike, but Ryan knew he had to do something before morning, when his brother was certain to discover it. Ryan looked for his dad and poured out the horrible story.

Dad listened quietly and then said, "I'm disappointed that you used Dan's bike without his permission, but I am glad you came and told me. You know how important the bike is to him this summer—and how expensive it is. More important, you know how we are to respect one another's belongings. I think you need to tell Dan the truth right now and offer him your bike for the remainder of the summer or until you can pay for the repairs."

It was a steep punishment that would mean a lot of walking this summer. And it would mean the end of buying his own bike. But Ryan knew that Dad was right. Respect for each other's property was an understood rule at his home. You didn't take things without asking first. If you did borrow something, you returned it in the same condition. Ryan had broken the rules big time. Now he had to face Dan and tell him the bad news. He only hoped that Dan would be as forgiving as his father had been. Ryan knew that next time he would think twice about showing off to all his friends—especially with stuff that belonged to his brother.

Questions

- How do you feel when a brother or sister borrows something without asking?
- What happened when you borrowed something from them without asking?
- How do you want your brothers and sisters to treat your belongings?
- Why is it important to show your brothers and sisters the same consideration?
- What would you say to Ryan if you were Dan?

Bible Discovery

Read the following Bible verses: Matthew 5:25; Luke 6:37-38; 1 Corinthians 10:24; Philippians 2:4; 1 Timothy 5:1.

Bible Point

The Bible tells us to treat others with respect and consideration. This also applies to others' property. We show love to our brothers and sisters when we respect their belongings and privacy.

Bottom Line

To get along with your brothers and sisters, respect their belongings.

## *Stand Together*

It was Chelsea's first year at her new school. Slowly she was beginning to make new friends. Lately, Chelsea had been eating lunch with some of the most popular girls in the school. Several were on the junior cheerleading squad, and they had promised to help Chelsea train for the squad next fall if she was interested. Interested? She couldn't think of anything more exciting. You bet she was interested!

Chelsea did have some concerns about her new group of friends. They tended to be a bit snobbish toward the other kids at school. At lunch their favorite pastime seemed to be making fun of the other kids—what they were wearing, who they were with, and what they looked like. Chelsea didn't usually participate in these critique sessions, although she did have to admit that most of what they said was true. That boy did wear geeky glasses, and the girl over at the other table was wearing the worst-colored dress that she had ever seen. Secretly, however, Chelsea was glad to be sitting at their table and not an object of their stinging remarks. She enjoyed the attention that she received from the girls and decided to overlook this one little fault.

Today Chelsea's English class was putting on a small production they had worked on as part of their unit on drama. Chelsea was excited because her mother and younger brother were coming to see the afternoon production. Several of her new friends were in the class, and Chelsea was eager to have them meet her family. She was especially excited about her brother visiting the class. Chelsea loved her brother. He had a number of disabilities—both physical and mental—because he had Down's syndrome, but he was an affectionate and endearing little boy. She knew her friends would just love him.

Chelsea was busy preparing for her role in the drama when she overheard a twittering of giggles from two of her friends. "Hey, who brought the geek to school?" one girl said, while the other replied, "Hey, don't they know he should be down the road at the school for the rest of the retards?"

Chelsea looked up and saw to her horror that her friends were talking about her brother, who had just entered the classroom. Chelsea's face turned a bright red. What was she going to do now? She could pretend that she was too busy to notice her mom and brother and find a way to talk to them after the show when her friends weren't around. If her friends knew that he was *her* brother, they probably would drop her like a rock.

While all these thoughts were flying through her mind, Chelsea remembered her Sunday school lesson about David and Mephibosheth and David's kindness to Jonathan's crippled son. She thought about Jesus' example and his love for those who were shunned by the rest of society. She knew she couldn't just sit and not do anything. If it meant losing these girls as so-called friends, then it probably was for the best, Chelsea thought. Her brother was definitely more important to her than being popular or making the cheerleading squad.

Quietly, Chelsea left her friends and walked over to her brother. She gave him a big hug and told him, "Welcome to my classroom,

Nathaniel. I am so glad that you are here. Just wait until you see the show!"

Questions

- Why is it important to stick up for a brother or sister?
- When did you stick up for a younger brother or sister? How did you feel when others were picking on him or her?
- When has your brother or sister stuck up for you? How did you feel when he or she came to your defense?
- How do you think Chelsea felt toward those girls when they began making fun of her brother?
- How do you think Chelsea's friends felt when they discovered that the "retard" was Chelsea's brother?

Bible Discovery

Read the story of King David and Mephibosheth in 2 Samuel 9:1-13. Discuss David's kindness to the lame son of his best friend Jonathan. Also read: John 13:34-35; Colossians 3:14; 1 John 3:18-19.

Bible Point

Jesus commands us to love one another in the same way he loves us. The way we fulfill this commandment is through our actions—caring, encouraging, supporting, and standing up for each other. David showed his love for his best friend, Jonathan, by showing kindness to Jonathan's disabled son, Mephibosheth.

Bottom Line

To get along with your brothers and sisters, stand up for them, even when it's tough to do.

## *Stop the Teasing*

Mom sighed. Sometimes it felt just like a war zone around the house. Her sons, Kirk and Trevor, were constantly teasing each other. At times it got so bad that she would send them to their rooms to let them cool off a bit. Today was no exception. It had begun this morning. Kirk adored his older brother, Trevor, and tried to master the same activities at which Trevor excelled. But he was still too little to succeed at many of them.

This morning Kirk had gotten up early, gone outside, and was trying to master a trick turn on the skateboard that he had seen Trevor do the other day. Mom watched from the kitchen window as Kirk practiced tirelessly. It was obvious that he was trying to perfect the trick and surprise his brother. When Trevor finally had breakfast and came outside, Kirk immediately called, "Hey Trevor, watch this!"

Kirk lined up his skateboard, but he hit the turn too hard. He sprawled on the ground. Trevor cracked up laughing at his little brother. "Nice fall there, Squirt. I like your style. Maybe you should enter the skateboard-falling contest."

With that, Kirk had stalked into the house and up to his room, his feelings and his backside wounded.

Kirk found his revenge later that day. Trevor was outside talking to one of the girls from down the street. Kirk knew from eavesdropping that Trevor liked this girl. He called out, "Hey, Lover Boy, is that your girlfriend? Does she know you spend hours combing your hair just for her? Does she know you walk up and down the block about a million times waiting for her to come out and talk?"

Trevor was steaming when he finally came into the house. He headed straight for Kirk, and Kirk ran laughing all the way down the hall. That's when Mom stepped in, and, once again, the boys were in their rooms.

*I have got to do something, or none of us will make it through the summer,* Mom thought. Grabbing a white handkerchief, she knocked on the boys' doors. "Truce," she announced. "Come downstairs. I want to talk to you both."

When they were all seated around the kitchen table, Mom gave them each a piece of paper with the words *E-A-S-E UP* on it. "What's this, Mom?" Trevor asked, rolling his eyes. "Another one of your games?"

"Nope," Mom answered. "This is my plan to stop the teasing that goes on here constantly. This is a little gimmick to help you remember *how* we're going to accomplish this. *E* is for Eliminate harmful words from your conversations—like calling each other names such as Squirt or Lover Boy. The *A* is for Adopt an attitude of caring for one another. *S* is for Show—show that you care through your actions."

Mom continued. "We can show we care when we don't laugh at each other or by respecting each other's time with their friends. That brings us to *E*—Exalt each other—which means to find ways of praising one another or looking for the good in each other."

The boys looked at Mom and then at each other. They both began to laugh. "When you describe what we do and say, it does sound pretty ridiculous," Trevor had to admit. "OK, Mom, I'm willing to ease up. How about you, Kirk?" Kirk nodded in agreement. "Say, Mom, can we come out of our rooms now? I'd like to help Kirk with that turn of his," Trevor said. "You know," he said to Kirk, "you almost have it down. With a little more practice, you'll make it."

Questions

- Why do brothers and sisters tease each other?
- Why do we seem to always hurt those we love?
- Why is teasing so harmful to family relationships?
- How do you feel when you are at the receiving end of teasing?
- Why do you think Kirk wanted to get back at his brother?
- How can you "wave the white flag" at your house to stop the teasing?

Bible Discovery

Read these Bible verses: Proverbs 11:9, 27; 12:18; Colossians 4:6; 1 Thessalonians 5:11.

Bible Point

Words can be hurtful and damaging. God wants our conversations to be controlled and "gracious and effective." Instead of teasing, we should encourage and praise each other.

Bottom Line

To get along with your brothers and sisters, stop the teasing; instead, be loving and encouraging.

## *Celebrate Your Differences*

Stephanie is going into eighth grade this fall at the middle school—tops in the school. But she isn't looking forward to this school year at all. In fact, she dreads it already, and school hasn't even begun yet. The problem isn't eighth grade; it's her younger sister, Jackie. Jackie is entering sixth grade, and she is everything that Stephanie is not.

Jackie has an outgoing personality and lots of friends. Stephanie tends to be more reserved, a quiet and loyal friend. She has had the same best friend since third grade. Although Stephanie knows many of the kids at school, she doesn't have a large group of friends. Jackie is a natural athlete. Everything comes easy for her. Stephanie tries hard and enjoys playing the games at school, but she never will be a star, and no one will ever pick her first for the team.

*That isn't the worse of it,* Stephanie considers grimly. The worst will be orchestra. Both girls play string instruments: Stephanie, the cello; and Jackie, the violin. Stephanie has worked very hard over the past two years and has finally earned a chance to play first-chair cello. She is proud of her accomplishment but is afraid that no one will even notice her once Jackie arrives on the scene. Jackie is a gifted musician. She far surpassed the other students at her elementary school and is quickly reaching—and passing—Stephanie's level of playing. Now, once Jackie arrives, Stephanie might as well pack up her cello and take up archery.

Orchestra auditions are tomorrow, and all Stephanie can think about is how awed her orchestra leader will be when Jackie plays. There is only one thing to do—quit!

Stephanie looks for an opportunity to talk with her mom without Jackie listening. While they are doing the dishes, Stephanie abruptly states, "I want to quit cello."

Her mom nearly drops the dish she is holding. "Quit cello? But you've been working so hard. Mrs. Mills would be so disappointed. Why would you want to quit?" When Stephanie doesn't answer, her mom speaks up. "This doesn't have to do with Jackie coming up there, does it?"

Miserably Stephanie nods her head. "Oh, Mom, once Mrs. Mills hears Jackie play, she's going to expect me to do as well, and I can't. I'm just not as good as Jackie—and I'll never be. I might as well stop wasting my time now."

Putting her arm around her older daughter, Mom says, "Stephanie, before you make a final decision, I want you to think about a few things. First of all, I want you to realize that God has created each person as unique and special. We all have different gifts, different abilities, different qualities as people. Being able to play the violin better than the next person doesn't make someone more important or better. What counts is how we use the gifts we have been given and how we live our lives.

"Think about the special abilities that God has given you," Mom continues. "You have a real gift for working with younger students. I know Mrs. Mills is counting on you to help with the new students this year. Can you imagine Jackie doing that?" Stephanie laughs a bit at that. Jackie has a volatile personality, and patience with new learners is not her strength. "We each have something unique to bring to a group. And every contribution is important and needed."

"I guess I was feeling a little jealous," says Stephanie.

Mom smiles and answers, "I think we all do at one time or another when it comes to our brothers and sisters. Fortunately, there's a cure for that: Remember that God made you special and that he has a special plan just for you and no one else. Also remember that we need to celebrate the differences in each other and not wish to be like everyone else."

Putting away the last glass, Stephanie says, "I'll try and remember that the next time I'm feeling a bit green with envy. Now I think I'll see if Jackie wants to go over the audition music with me again. Maybe we *can* help each other after all."

### Questions

- What causes brothers and sisters to be jealous of each other?
- What makes it difficult to live in the shadow of a brother or sister?
- What are some of your strengths and abilities?
- What are some of your brother's or sister's strengths and abilities?
- How can you use your abilities to help your brother or sister? How can your brother or sister use his or her abilities to help you?
- Why can knowing that God created you to be unique make a difference when you see someone do something better than you?

### Bible Discovery

Read these Bible verses: Psalm 139:13-15; Luke 12:6-7; Romans 12:3-5; 1 Corinthians 12: 4-7.

### Bible Point

Each person is a unique and special creation of God, and he gave each of us different abilities. God cares and values each person, and he wants each one to use his or her gifts and abilities to help others.

### Bottom Line

To get along with your brothers and sisters, celebrate your individual strengths and the differences between you.

## *My Brother's Keeper*

"This is absolutely the last time," Nathan grumbled under his breath while he picked up the cluttered floor in the basement. Company was coming over tonight, and, once again, Nathan had been asked to clean up his brother's mess. He kicked one of Simon's toys across the room. It scudded underneath the sofa. *There,* he thought triumphantly. *See if you ever find that toy again!*

Simon was the baby of the family, and as far as Nathan was concerned, he got away with *everything.* Just look at this basement. Maybe Nathan and his friends had forgotten to pick up a few of their things, but the majority of junk on the floor definitely belonged to Simon. And where was the little boy? Simon had wheedled his way out of cleaning the basement because it was his turn to walk the dog. Nathan wondered how Simon always managed to come up with a halfway decent excuse for not doing any of the dirty work around the house. "I'd rather be walking the dog and goofing off outside than picking up your toys any day," grumbled Nathan, sending still another toy flying across the room.

Not only did Simon skip out on the hard work, but he also was careless. Nathan always found Simon's library books thoughtlessly strewn about the house. Simon never managed to make it through the winter with less than six pairs of mittens because he would either lose them or leave them at school. Nathan often wondered how Simon managed to get by in school. *He must drive the teachers crazy,* he thought. Simon's worst offense, however, was his bike. He was forever leaving it out on the driveway so Dad couldn't pull the car in. Or he would forget it at the park; then Nathan or one of his older brothers would have to walk over with Simon to get it. "Face it," Nathan grumbled again, "the kid is a total loser."

When Nathan finally finished cleaning up the basement, he took off for a pickup game of basketball with his friends. They played for several hours until it began to rain. "I'd better get going," Nathan called to his friends. He picked up his pace as the rain began to fall in big, heavy sploshes. This was going to be a real drencher. As Nathan ran past the park, he noticed a bike over by the jungle gym. He took a closer look. Sure enough, it was Simon's bike. Nathan slowed down. It would serve Simon right if he left the bike out in the rain. Not only would he get in trouble for leaving his bike again, but it would be ruined for sure. *That would serve him right,* Nathan thought again.

Nathan continued walking. He thought about his own bike and what he would do for an entire summer without one. He thought about how mad his dad would be about a ruined bike—Simon would be in enough trouble for leaving the bike at the park again. But if Nathan brought it home, at least it wouldn't be ruined. Then he thought about the time he left his new starter jacket at the gym, and one of his brothers saw it and brought it home for him. He thought about how his brother had helped him find his lost wallet one day at the pool. *I guess Simon isn't the only one who forgets stuff,* Nathan told himself. He turned around and went back. Picking up the bike, he got on it and quickly rode home.

As he pulled into the driveway, he was met by an anxious-looking Simon. Simon flew to meet him. "Thanks, Nathan. You saved me and my bike again. You're the best brother a guy could have," he said gratefully.

Nathan smiled. "I know that you'll do the same for me someday."

### Questions

- What would you do if you were Nathan?
- When were you helped out by a brother or sister?
- When did you help out a brother or sister when you didn't feel like it?
- How do you think Nathan felt at the end of the day? How would he have felt if he had left the bike out in the rain?
- Why is it important for family members to help each other out?

### Bible Discovery

Read these Bible verses: Romans 12:9-10; 2 Timothy 2:24; 1 Peter 4:8.

### Bible Point

God wants his people to show that they are his followers by loving one another—not just with words but with their actions. This means showing genuine affection and care for each other.

### Bottom Line

To get along with your brothers and sisters, care for one another.

# 29
# How to Know What Is Right

***God's Guidance***

Alex loved basketball. He went to all the local high school games, and he watched games on TV—both college teams and the pros. Alex studied the players and how they moved the ball. Then he tried to do the same thing in his driveway as he practiced countless layups and free throws.

Alex thoroughly enjoyed playing basketball, and he was very good. Because he was tall and a good ball handler, Alex was a starter on his junior high team, the Falcons.

The Falcons were competitive, and they had a winning record. Near the end of the season, they were tied for first place with the Jefferson Cougars. The Falcon players were excited and a little nervous about the upcoming game between the two teams.

In the locker room after practice the boys discussed ways to beat the Cougars. "We'll just have to play our best and concentrate," Alex said.

"Oh sure," replied Cliff, "but that might not be good enough. Those Cougars are tough. You know they beat us the first time."

"Only by four points," Alex reminded him.

"I have a few ideas of how to win," said Joe. "When the refs aren't looking, we do some elbowing and a little pushing."

Next Paul gave his opinion. "We can also say things to the players when we're guarding them or when they're shooting free throws. That will break their concentration. How about it, Alex?"

Alex had listened to his teammates but had kept quiet. "I don't know," he said. "I think we can win without that."

The boys just looked at him. Finally Joe replied, "Hey, the college players and the pros do it all the time. What's the big deal?"

That evening Alex kept thinking about the locker-room discussion. In some ways it made sense, but it still didn't seem right. Finally he told his father about the important game coming up and what his teammates had suggested they should do to win. "I just don't know if it's the right thing to do," said Alex.

Dad answered, "It's hard to know what's right or wrong sometimes. Some things sound OK and others are doing them, but that doesn't mean they are right. But one way to know what is right is to pray for God's guidance. He will help you know what's right and how to play that game."

Alex prayed for God's guidance every day until the big game. And he knew what he should do.

Alex felt great when the Falcons played the Cougars because he knew what was right. He concentrated and played his very best, but he didn't talk trash, and he didn't play dirty.

Questions

- Would you like to have Alex on your team? Why or why not?
- What was Alex's problem?
- When you have been in a situation similar to Alex's, what did you do?

Bible Discovery

Read these Bible verses: 2 Samuel 5:17-19; Philippians 4:6-7; 1 John 5:14-15.

Bible Point

Like David, we need to ask God for guidance when we need it. God promises to help and guide his people when they are confused about what is right. Sometimes it sounds very logical when your friends give reasons for doing something that doesn't seem right. "Everybody else does it," they might say. That's when you need to ask for God's guidance and then follow it.

Bottom Line

Know what is right by praying for guidance.

## *Friends*

Jasmine looked in the bathroom mirror and wrinkled her nose. She didn't like what she saw looking back at her. Jasmine thought her curly black hair looked like a frizzy mop. Her nose seemed too small and her mouth too big. Her eyes were all right, but nobody noticed them behind her glasses.

*What's the use?* she thought as she washed her face. *Let's face it, Jasmine, nothing helps.* Mom and Dad called her Princess and said she looked great. But, well, they were Mom and Dad.

As Jasmine trudged to school, she thought about her looks and how she got along in school. Jasmine's grades were pretty good, but she was quiet and shy. She felt uncomfortable when everyone was laughing and joking. She wished she had some friends in the popular crowd.

Along the way, Jasmine stopped at Linda's and Susie's houses. The three friends were a lot alike. They went to the same church and were in the same Sunday school class. They liked chatting as they walked to school together.

"Know what?" asked Jasmine. "I wish I had a magic pill that would change me so I wouldn't be so ordinary."

"What's wrong with ordinary?" asked Susie. "How would you change?"

"I'd have long straight hair, a better nose and mouth, and no glasses. And I would joke with others and never be embarrassed," Jasmine answered.

"Oh sure," said Linda, "dream on."

In history class, Jasmine sat next to Cindy. In Jasmine's opinion Cindy was everything Jasmine was not. Cindy looked good, had lots of friends, and was never shy. Cindy also totally ignored Jasmine. That's why Jasmine almost fell over when Cindy stopped her in the hall.

"Hi, Jasmine," she said. "I really need your help. And I know Mrs. Burton likes you."

Jasmine had no idea what Cindy was talking about. She asked, "What do you want me to do?"

Cindy gave her a dazzling smile. "Some of us are going to cut classes this afternoon and watch a video at Pat's house." Jasmine didn't like the way this conversation was going. This sure didn't seem right.

"So when Mrs. Burton asks if anyone knows where I am, just say I got sick at lunch. She'll believe you," Cindy went on. "Nobody really cares anyway. Please, you'll be my friend forever."

Wow! Be a friend of the most popular girl in school. Jasmine was almost ready to say OK. Then she remembered something she had heard in Sunday school. The teacher had said, "One way to know what's right is to associate with Christian friends. They won't ask you to do something wrong."

"Sorry, Cindy. That would be lying, and lying is not right," Jasmine said quietly.

Cindy turned and stomped off down the hall. Jasmine hurried to meet her "ordinary" Christian friends, Susie and Linda. She looked forward to having lunch with them.

Questions

- What bothered Jasmine?
- When have you felt like Jasmine?
- What do you think would have happened if Jasmine had done what Cindy asked her to do?
- How can having Christian friends be helpful?

Bible Discovery

Read these Bible verses: Proverbs 12:26; 17:17; 18:24; 1 Samuel 18:1-4; Ephesians 4:32.

Bible Point

The old saying "Birds of a feather flock together" implies that people can be influenced by those with whom they associate. A good friend is loyal and trustworthy and will not ask you to do anything wrong. Christian friends can help you know what is right. Having close friends who are not Christians could be asking for trouble.

Bottom Line

Christian friends can help you know what is right.

## *What's Up, Peanut?*

Each summer Brigette spent a week with Grandpa and Grandma Larson on their farm. Her grandparents lived only seven miles from her own home in town, but Brigette felt as though she entered a whole different world on the farm. At home she was the only girl in a family of five kids, but on the farm Brigette was the only kid, *period.*

Brigette loved Grandma and Grandpa, and they loved her. They were always interested in what she was doing and wanted to know all about her friends, school, and other activities.

"What's up, Peanut?" was Grandpa's favorite expression. Brigette would probably fight her brothers or anyone else who called her Peanut, but it was OK when Grandpa called her that.

Brigette even liked doing chores on the farm. She helped Grandma in the garden. They chatted about anything and everything while they pulled weeds and picked vegetables. But Brigette's favorite farm chore was helping feed the animals. She and Grandpa did this every morning and evening.

One night at dinner Grandpa asked, "How's your baseball team this year? I want to come and see some of your games." Brigette played on a Junior League team with both boys and girls. It was fun, but lately she hadn't enjoyed it so much.

When Brigette didn't answer, Grandpa cocked an eyebrow and said, "Hey, what's up, Peanut? Has your team lost every game?"

"No, we've won more than we've lost, but it's just not so much fun anymore," answered Brigette.

"And why is that?" Grandpa wanted to know.

"We have this one boy named Chuck Latimer on our team," Brigette explained, "and he's not very good. He can't run very well, misses balls in the outfield, and hardly ever hits the ball. Chuck sits on the bench a lot, and the other kids talk about him. They call him 'Weirdo' and 'Space Cadet,' and they laugh at how he runs. They think it's funny to do this, but I don't know if it's right."

Grandpa was quiet a minute, and then he said, "I'm glad you told me this, Peanut. It's good to talk to a grown-up when you don't know what's right. And it is *not* right for the kids to make fun of Chuck or anyone else.

"I know Chuck's father. Chuck has an illness that affects his coordination, so it's hard for him to control his movements," Grandpa explained. "You can do the right thing by trying to encourage him."

Brigette felt lots better. It was good to have such a wise grandpa to help her figure things out—even if he did call her Peanut!

### Questions

- Why did Brigette like visiting her grandparents?
- What special things do you do with your grandparents?
- What was bothering Brigette about her baseball team?
- What helped Brigette make the right decision?
- When you were in a similar situation, how did you handle it?

Bible Discovery

Read Luke 2:43-47 and 2 Timothy 1:1-5.

Bible Point

Even at twelve years old, Jesus could teach the religious leaders what he knew; Timothy learned from Paul. Knowing what is right can be very difficult, but certain people can help us. We have trustworthy adults such as parents, grandparents, teachers, and others, who have had many years of experience and can help us know what is right or wrong. Ask for their advice and then follow it.

Bottom Line

Know what is right by talking with trusted adults; ask and then follow their advice.

## *Danger Zone*

Dimitri lived in a large city apartment. His family had moved to the neighborhood several months ago, but Dimitri still felt like an outsider. Some of the boys went to Dimitri's school, and he saw them around, but he didn't really know them.

In the middle of the apartment complex was the Community Center. It had a swimming pool, baseball and soccer fields, and a gym; it offered all kinds of classes for the kids in the apartments.

Dimitri started spending time at the Community Center after school until Mom got home from work. He also went there Saturday mornings and sometimes on school holidays. In warm weather Dimitri went swimming or played baseball. He also participated in the basketball or volleyball games in the gym.

But Dimitri's favorite place at the Center was the arts-and-crafts area. One of the reasons he liked it so much was Ms. Gomez, the director of arts and crafts. Ms. Gomez was a professional artist who believed everyone had talent. Her enthusiasm was catching, and she brought out the best in the kids.

While she taught arts and crafts, Ms. Gomez talked to the kids about their lives and about living in the neighborhood. "You need to be careful of what you do—to know what's right," she said. "Some kids will try to get you to do wrong things. A good way to know what's right is to avoid actions and situations that seem wrong. If it doesn't feel right, don't do it."

Dimitri learned a lot from Ms. Gomez, both about art and life in general. Dimitri also found a friend. Greg lived in the same apartment building as Dimitri, and both of them liked painting. Soon they started doing other things together in the neighborhood.

One Saturday, Greg invited Dimitri to go with him and some other friends to the Main Street Music Store. They wanted to check out the latest CD of their favorite group. Dimitri told Mom where he was going, stuck his allowance money in his jeans, and joined the others.

The store was huge, with rows and rows of tapes and CDs. Dimitri looked through the CDs until he found one he wanted. He was walking up to the cashier, money in hand, when Greg grabbed his jacket. "Put your money away," he whispered. "Just stick the CD under your jacket and stroll out. Look at all these CDs. They'll never miss one or two. They cost too much anyway."

Dimitri just looked at Greg. He sounded so convincing, but what he was suggesting didn't seem right. Then Dimitri remembered what Ms. Gomez had said: "Avoid actions and situations that seem wrong."

Quietly Dimitri said, "No way!" He put the CD back, stuffed the money in his pocket, and walked out of the store. Greg scratched his head and stared after him.

### Questions

- How was Dimitri feeling in his new neighborhood?
- What was one good thing about the apartment complex?
- What helped Dimitri do what was right?
- When you were in a situation similar to Dimitri's, what did you do?

### Bible Discovery

Read these Bible verses: Genesis 39:6-12; Proverbs 1:10-15; Titus 2:11-12.

### Bible Point

Like Joseph did, it is best to avoid situations that make you feel uncomfortable and actions that seem wrong. Sometimes kids can get caught in sticky situations and be confused about the right thing to do. That's the time to get out of there as soon as possible.

### Bottom Line

Do what is right by avoiding actions and situations that seem wrong.

## *Listen Carefully*

"He's the crankiest person I ever knew!" fumed Rich.

"I think he eats pickles and lemons every day," chimed in Kirk. "That's why he's such a sourpuss."

"He probably never smiled in his life—he was born crabby," decided Al.

Then Derek reminded his friends, "No matter what we say, he probably won't change. And he still has the two of the baseballs we hit over his fence."

"Yeah," mumbled Rich. "Game called because of Mr. Grouch, the ball stealer."

As the boys gathered their bats and baseball mitts, they kept complaining about Mr. Kanza, an old man who lived in a big spooky-looking house at the end of the block. The yard was wild and overgrown, surrounded by a tall board fence.

Some people said that Mr. Kanza used to be friendly and visit with the neighbors, but after his wife died, he changed and shut himself up in his house. The neighborhood kids thought his house might be haunted, and they were kind of scared of him.

The large empty lot next to Mr. Kanza's house was the favorite place in the neighborhood for baseball games. But it seemed as though Mr. Kanza hated baseball, noise, and kids.

Sometimes Mr. Kanza would come to the fence and yell, "Go away. You're too noisy. Playing ball is a waste of time. Now get out of here!" Any ball that went over the fence was gone forever. *No one* was going over the fence after it.

Kirk, Al, Rich, and Derek were still steaming mad as they tromped home. They had lost four balls in the last month to the black hole of Mr. Kanza's weedy yard. They didn't have a lot of baseballs left, and it's hard to play baseball without a ball. "Maybe we should just ring Mr. Kanza's doorbell and ask him to give the balls back," Derek suggested.

"Are you crazy?" exclaimed Rich. "He'd never give them back. He would probably call the police and say we were trespassing."

"Hey! I have an idea," said Al excitedly. "Let's teach Mr. Kanza a lesson. We can get some spray paint. Then we can sneak over there when it's dark and spray words on his fence."

"All right!" agreed Kirk. "We can write all his names: Grouch, Crab, Cranky, Ball Stealer. Let's do it tonight."

Derek didn't like the way Mr. Kanza acted either, and maybe he needed to know how the kids felt. But this didn't seem right. Then Derek recalled a devotion he had just read. It had said that when you want to know what's right, listen to your conscience. Derek's conscience was saying loud and clear, *"This is not right!"*

"Sorry, guys," Derek said, "that's not the way to solve the problem."

### Questions

- Why did the neighborhood kids dislike Mr. Kanza?
- What was Al's solution to their problem?
- What is a conscience?
- How can your conscience help you know what is right?

### Bible Discovery

Read these Bible verses: Genesis 42:21; Acts 24:16; 1 Corinthians 4:4.

### Bible Point

The conscience is sometimes called an inner voice. It is given to us by God, and it helps us know when something is right or wrong. When we go against our conscience, we feel guilty. God wants us to listen to our conscience and follow it. It can guide us to do what is right and keep us from doing what is wrong.

### Bottom Line

Know what is right by listening to your conscience.

# 30 How to Do What Is Right

***Listen and Act***

April Rogers thumbed through the racks of CDs, keeping time with the store's background music. As she pulled out a CD, she said, "I'm glad Mama gave me money for my birthday, instead of those old tired sweaters she usually gives me."

"I'm saying!" her best friend, Shannielle Moore, agreed. "Your mama has no taste in clothes. . . . Sorry to say," she added.

April nodded in agreement. "Hey, I like this song. I should get this CD."

"You should. It's the latest from Rap Master DJ Tuff," said Shannielle.

Suddenly April could hear some of the lyrics. The rapper used a lot of bad language. She knew her mother wouldn't want her to buy that CD.

"Mama would have a fit if she heard the words to this song."

"She doesn't have to hear it," said Shannielle. "Didn't your pops give you a portable CD player last Christmas? It comes with headphones, right?"

April nodded.

"So get the CD, girl! Everybody's got it." Shannielle grabbed it herself.

*Hmm. Nobody would have to know,* thought April. So she purchased the CD, feeling slightly uneasy.

The next day was Sunday. April and Shannielle both attended the church in their neighborhood.

Normally April liked her Sunday school class and the teacher, Jade Reynolds. But that Sunday, April could barely concentrate on what was being said. She kept thinking about the CD. She hadn't had the nerve to take it out of the bag. Instead, she had stuffed it in the bottom drawer of her dresser.

"How do you do what's right?" Jade's voice suddenly snapped April to attention. "Is that what you're asking, Archie?"

A teen to the right of April nodded.

"Doing what's right is part of what you believe about God," Jade said. "God tells us in the Bible how to obey him. But knowing what to do and acting on it are two different things. James 1:22 says, 'It is a message to obey, not just to listen to.'

"Let's say a friend asks you to go to a movie that you know your parents wouldn't want you to see. But your friend tells you that everybody's going to this movie. And your parents aren't around at the time. What do you do?"

No one spoke until Archie raised his hand. "I know you're supposed to not go to the movie, but sometimes it's hard when you're with your friends and they want you to go. You don't want them to laugh at you."

"I know," said Jade. "That's when you have to decide what's more important—listening to your friends or to your parents. To whom do you think God wants you to listen?"

April suddenly knew what she needed to do. She slowly walked out of the room at the end of the class time.

Shannielle caught up with her in the hall. "What're you doing after church?" she asked.

"I'm going to ask Mama if I can go back to the mall." April took a deep breath. "I need to return that CD."

"Why?" asked Shannielle.

"Weren't you listening? I know I was," said April. "I think I know what's more important."

### Questions

- How can the Bible help you know what is right?
- What does it mean to be one who obeys the message?
- How do your actions show that you trust in God?

### Bible Discovery

Read Matthew 7:21; Romans 2:13; James 1:22.

### Bible Point

The teacher in the story quoted James 1:22. Listening to God's Word is important, but doing what God says is even more important. We must know God's law and obey it.

Bottom Line

To do what is right, don't just listen to God's Word—do it.

## *Just Ask*

"Ow! Stupid hammer!" Rick Sanders yelled as he dropped the hammer on the workbench.

Mr. Sanders looked over Rick's shoulder. "What happened?"

Rick just grunted in pain."I keep hitting my thumb with this stupid hammer!" Rick pushed the hammer.

"Here. Let me show you how to keep from doing that," Mr. Sanders said and then patiently showed Rick how to keep his hand out of the way when hammering. "Don't be afraid to ask me for help when you need it," he added afterward.

"But I wanted to do this myself," Rick said.

"There's nothing wrong with asking for help every now and then, especially when you don't know how to do something. It'll save you trouble in the long run."

Rick returned to his hammering. Soon he dropped the hammer in frustration again. "I can't do this!" he yelled.

"Slow down. There's no race to building this birdhouse," explained Mr. Sanders.

"I keep driving the nails in crooked," said Rick.

Mr. Sanders showed Rick what to do; then he watched Rick pound a few nails. "Good. You've got the hang of it now," he said.

"Thanks, Dad." Rick returned to the birdhouse instructions he was following. "Now I need to connect the back. Or should I do the front?"

"Troubles, son?" asked Mr. Sanders.

Rick looked embarrassed. "I'm having trouble reading these directions. This part doesn't make sense." He pointed to instruction number five on the sheet.

Mr. Sanders read over the directions. Within half an hour the birdhouse was completed. They both stepped back to admire their handiwork.

"That looks pretty good," said Mr. Sanders.

"Thanks for your help, Dad," Rick said, but he looked a little disappointed.

"Are you sorry you asked for help?" Mr. Sanders asked.

Rick shrugged. "I just wish I knew what to do without having to keep asking you. I mean, I'm not a little kid anymore."

"You think only little kids ask their parents for help?" asked Mr. Sanders.

Rick shrugged again.

"I still ask my father for his advice every now and then," Mr. Sanders said. "But mainly, when I don't know what to do about a problem, I ask God for help. Your grandpa does too. Sometimes when a problem is too hard for us to solve on our own, we need to ask for help. That's the best way to start when we're not sure what to do." Mr. Sanders grinned at Rick. "Like you say you sometimes feel about algebra."

"I know! I know! I failed the quiz last Thursday! I've been trying to study. I just don't understand it," said Rick.

Mr. Sanders continued. "Rick, we want you to make good grades, so if you're having trouble, ask for help. Sometimes asking for help is the right thing to do."

### Questions

- In what situations do you often find it difficult to know what is right?
- To whom can you turn for help?
- When do you find it hard to ask for help? Why?
- How can talking with God help you know what to do?

### Bible Discovery

Read Proverbs 1:7 and James 1:5.

### Bible Point

Solomon, the wisest man who ever lived, and James, the brother of Jesus, both knew the value of wisdom. And both knew the source—God. Wisdom helps you do what is right. It also helps you know when you need to ask for help.

### Bottom Line

To do what is right, ask God for wisdom.

## *Follow the Leader*

Trish Baxter stumbled along the forest trail after her friend Sabrina Matthews. "Why did she pick Sue to be a hike leader?" Sabrina complained. "She's just fifteen. That's only a year older than we are. We went on this nature hike last year and know the trail better than Sue does! *Shhh!* Here she comes now."

"But you were the one who was talk—"

Sue strolled to the back of the line of hikers. "You guys OK?" she asked.

Sabrina and Trish nodded.

"All right, let's go!" Sue called. "Keep behind me and stay together." Sue gradually made her way back to the front of the group, and the hikers followed her.

Sabrina and Trish remained in the back. "You guys OK?" Sabrina mimicked.

Trish giggled. Sabrina was pretty good at imitating Sue's voice.

When the group reached a fork in the trail, Sue headed off toward the left fork. "Isn't that the wrong way?" Sabrina called. "The right fork takes us back to the picnic area."

"We're going this way," Sue replied.

Sabrina nudged Trish to the right, while the rest of the group went left. "Let's go this way," she said.

"But Sue's going left!" Trish said.

"But this is the shortcut. We'll reach the picnic area way before they do. Come on." Sabrina led the way onto the dark forest path. Trish shrugged, then followed Sabrina.

Sabrina paused by an oak tree. "See? This is the way we came last year." She pointed to a mark. "I carved my initials in this tree."

Fifteen minutes later, the girls were back at the picnic area. They were stunned to find their youth leaders scrambling around with balloons in their hands. The tables were half decorated with streamers.

"What are you girls doing back so soon?" Mrs. Winters asked.

"What's going on?" Sabrina asked.

"If you must know, we were planning a little surprise party for you all. That's why we had Sue take you around the long way." Mrs. Winters's eyes narrowed. "Why didn't you girls follow Sue?"

Trish looked at Sabrina and then lowered her eyes.

"I'm sorry, Mrs. Winters," Sabrina spoke up. "My leg was bothering me, so Trish helped me back here."

"Well, maybe you can help blow up some balloons." Mrs. Winters handed the bag of balloons to them.

Soon the rest of the group returned, and the party was in full swing. But Trish was bothered the rest of the afternoon. She hadn't liked lying to Mrs. Winters. Finally she couldn't stand it anymore. "Can I talk to you, Mrs. Winters?" she asked, pulling the youth leader aside.

"Sure, Trish," said Mrs. Winters.

Trish couldn't look her in the eyes. "We, uh, got back early because we didn't want to follow Sue."

"The leader you pick to follow will either lead you in the right way or get you lost," said Mrs. Winters. "I'm glad you told me the truth, Trish. Next time, follow a better leader than Sabrina."

Questions

- Who are possible leaders to follow in this world?
- How do you know which leaders to follow?
- Why is it important to follow the right leader?

Bible Discovery

Read 1 Samuel 8:4-9, 14-21 and 1 Corinthians 11:1.

Bible Point

God knew the people of Israel were making a big mistake when they insisted that Samuel find them a king. The Israelites wanted a king to lead them rather than God. Jesus is the only leader who will always lead us in the right direction.

Bottom Line

Follow the leader who will help you do what is right—Jesus.

## *An Act of Love*

Raymond Evans raced toward the basket and launched himself for the slam dunk . . . and missed. He could hear the laughter of his friend Dorian. "Michael Jordan you ain't," Dorian said, slapping him on the back.

"Ha, ha," Raymond replied.

The boys returned the equipment to the church office and went out to enjoy the cool breeze, a welcome relief from the usual August heat.

"Let's get some juice at the grocery store," Dorian suggested.

The boys hurried into the air-conditioned store and scanned the refrigerated case for their favorite juices. Just as Dorian made his choice and turned away, he froze. "Uh-oh. Here comes trouble."

Raymond looked away from the case and saw Clarence Franklin walking toward them. He wore the uniform of one of the store's baggers.

Clarence nodded in their direction. After a pause, Raymond said, "Hey, Clarence."

Once Clarence had gone on his way, Dorian blurted out, "Boy, I'd like to punch his face sometimes!"

"I used to feel like that, but not now. Besides, he doesn't run with that gang anymore," said Raymond.

"But he stole your bike! You saved all year for that. And your dad's lawn mower two years ago. He's probably stealing from this store," exclaimed Dorian.

"The police never proved that Clarence stole those things," answered Raymond. "Besides, he stopped hanging with that gang."

"Maybe we can get him fired," said Dorian.

"No." Raymond's voice was firm. "I don't want to get him in trouble."

"Don't you want revenge?" asked Dorian.

Raymond shook his head. "For what? It won't bring my bike back. Anyway, it's wrong."

As the boys left the store, Dorian asked, "How can you defend him? Nobody in the neighborhood likes him."

Raymond shrugged. "I don't like him, either, but that doesn't mean I have to treat him badly. God would want me to treat him nicely." He grinned. "At least that's what my dad's been telling me. And that's what I want to do. Dad said, 'When you're thinking about somebody you don't like, think about how much you love God.' When you love God, you want to do what's right—even to people who don't deserve it."

"Wow! Turning fourteen really changed you." Dorian suddenly grinned. "Hey, my birthday's next month. Maybe I'll change too."

"It's not turning fourteen that changed me," answered Raymond. "It's believing in Jesus that did it."

### Questions

- How do people's actions show what they believe about God?
- What does it mean to "love your enemies"?
- Would others say that you loved God by looking at your actions? Why or why not?

### Bible Discovery

Read 2 Corinthians 5:17; 1 John 2:29; 4:11, 19-21.

### Bible Point

Certainly actions speak louder than words. Those who truly love God show love to others, even to their enemies. We can't mistreat others and love God at the same time. Jesus helps us have the desire to treat others in the right way.

Bottom Line

Loving God helps you do what is right.

## *Helpful Advice*

"So, did you get invited to Countessa's party on Saturday?" Phyllis Weston asked. She was on the phone with her friend Helen.

"Yeah. I'm surprised her parents are letting her have one," answered Helen.

"Well, it's her birthday. Mom's letting me go. Are you going?" asked Phyllis.

"Let me check my horoscope. I don't make any decisions until I read the horoscope," answered Helen.

Phyllis soon heard the crinkle of newspaper pages being turned. She suddenly remembered how she used to look up her horoscope each day. But that was before she became a Christian.

The conversation ended soon after that. When Phyllis hung up, she went looking for her mother. She found Mrs. Weston in her baby sister's room. Mrs. Weston sat in a rocking chair with the usually wiggly baby quiet in her arms.

"Mom, can I ask you something?" asked Phyllis.

Mrs. Weston nodded. "Sure," she said, barely above a whisper.

Phyllis lowered her voice. "I was talking to Helen just now. She's still reading horoscopes and stuff. Do you think I should've said something to her about God?"

Mrs. Weston placed the now sleeping baby in her crib. She beckoned to Phyllis to follow her out in the hall. "Honey, I think you should just pray for her. You remember when you believed that reading horoscopes was all right?"

Phyllis nodded. "It seems silly now."

"Well, Helen doesn't think so," said Phyllis's mom. "A lot of people don't know where to go for help when they don't know what to do. They read horoscopes or write to advice columnists. They don't realize they can get better advice from the Bible. Sometimes they do know about the Bible but don't want to be led by God."

"But what should I tell Helen?" asked Phyllis.

Mrs. Weston answered, "Just be her friend. Pray for her. Ask God to help you do the right thing and be a good example. But don't forget."

"Don't forget what?" said Phyllis.

"You were once where she is," her mom answered. "Don't tell her what she *should* do. Tell her what she *can* do. She can turn to the Lord for help."

### Questions

- To whom or what do you turn when you need advice?
- What advice have you heard this week? How helpful was it?
- How do we get God's advice?

### Bible Discovery

Read these verses: Psalms 25:5-6; 37:5; Proverbs 21:3; Jeremiah 29:13.

### Bible Point

Many people turn to whomever they think will give them an easy answer. But God wants us to look to him for answers. Sometimes God's answers aren't easy or comfortable. But they are always right.

### Bottom Line

Turning to God for answers helps you do what is right.

# 31

# How to Handle Your Emotions

### *Get a Clue!*

When Audrey woke up late Friday morning, she could already tell that it was going to be a bad day. She had stayed up late the night before, frantically trying to complete a homework assignment that was already overdue. She had been so tired last night she could hardly stay awake as she had stared at her assignment. So it wasn't a real surprise when she slept through her alarm.

As Audrey rushed around the house trying to pull herself together, she encountered a number of setbacks. First of all, she could not get her hair to look right. Ponytail. Barrettes. Hair gel. Mousse. More gel. Nothing seemed to help. She forgot about her toast, which soon burned to a crisp in the toaster. To top it all off, her dad got on her case about her grades just as she was trying to walk out the door.

When Audrey got to school, her friend Susan ran up to her all excited about something great that had happened to her. Audrey just mumbled sarcastically, "Terrific. Wow" and walked away. A few minutes later, another friend greeted her with a smile, but Audrey dismissed her with a grunt and a wave. That's the way the whole morning went until she saw Susan again at lunch.

"Boy, you're in a bad mood," Susan exclaimed as they both opened their lunch bags. "What's wrong?"

"Nothing," mumbled Audrey as she sipped her milk.

"Well, you sure weren't nice to me this morning," replied Susan, obviously annoyed. "I just wanted to tell you about the party . . . get a clue!"

Susan had barely gotten that phrase out of her mouth when Audrey remembered what her Sunday school teacher had said last Sunday. Her teacher, Debbie, had been talking about how being tired and stressed out can cause emotions to change, sometimes putting a person in a very bad mood. Debbie had encouraged the class to pay attention to their emotions and think about how they feel in certain situations. "Get a clue!" she had said. "If you catch yourself snapping at everyone, put a name on what you're feeling—in that case, anger. Practice asking yourself, 'What are my emotions right now?'"

Audrey put down her sandwich and looked up at Susan. "You're right," she said. "I'm sorry I talked that way to you. I guess I'm really tired, and I'm frustrated about our English paper. And I'm having a bad hair day." She pointed to her hair and pulled a few of the loose strands as both girls laughed. "So I guess I've been snapping at everyone this morning."

Although she was still tired and frustrated, Audrey was glad that she had apologized to Susan and was learning to think through her emotions.

#### Questions

- What emotions do you think Audrey was feeling that morning?
- How can lack of sleep affect a person's emotions?
- Why did it help Audrey to think about how she was feeling?
- How do you usually feel when you are in a bad mood?

#### Bible Discovery

Read these Bible verses: Psalms 31:7-10; 55:2; 139:13-14, 23.

#### Bible Point

God knows our every thought and emotion because he created us and loves us. Many factors affect the way we feel: sleep, weather, circumstances, etc. The first step toward handling your emotions is to be aware of them and of their possible causes.

#### Bottom Line

To handle your emotions, start by naming them—be aware of what you are feeling.

## *Cause and Effect*

Look out! Jeremy was in one of those moods again. Everything seemed to be going wrong. Nothing seemed right. He moped around the house and sighed loudly enough to let everyone in his family know that he was depressed.

Finally, his father had had enough. After sitting Jeremy down, Dad said, "Look, Jeremy, everyone knows by now that you're in a bad mood for whatever reason. But I'm not going to let you ruin our weekend. We have chores to do and some fun activities planned. I expect you to participate with a positive attitude." Then Dad paused, took a breath, and in a softer tone continued. "Now, what's going on? What's bothering you?"

"I don't know what's wrong," was Jeremy's first response. "I just feel down, like I'm depressed or something."

Dad asked him to think about recent events—maybe something had happened to make him angry, upset, or worried.

When his father said "worried," Jeremy remembered that in a couple of days he had tryouts for Chamber Singers, a special choir at school. He really wanted to make it this year. Last week in chorus, Mr. Wilson, the choir director, had announced that auditions were coming up this week. Everyone would have to stand and sing a solo in front of the rest of the class. Jeremy hated to sing by himself—he was afraid his voice would crack—but he really wanted to be in Chamber Singers.

Jeremy explained what he was feeling, especially his fears about the solo tryouts. "I guess it bothered me more than I realized, Dad," he admitted. "I was feeling depressed just thinking about it. I'm sorry I took it out on everyone at home."

"Look, Son," Dad began, "it's all right to be nervous and even to be afraid at times. I certainly can understand your feelings about the audition. Let's pray about it, and later I'll work with you on your voice." Jeremy's face brightened a bit. Dad continued, "One of the most important steps in handling emotions is to find the underlying causes. In this case, you identified your fear and anxiety. I'm proud of you for figuring out what was causing you to feel so down. It's important to know how you feel, Son. It's even better to realize what caused that feeling in the first place. That will help you work your way out of it."

Questions

- What caused Jeremy to be in a bad mood?
- What emotions was Jeremy experiencing?
- What things typically cause you to be in a bad mood?
- How can discovering the cause of a bad mood help a person get out of it?

### Bible Discovery

Read these Bible verses: Psalm 42:11; Proverbs 3:13; 4:5.

### Bible Point

The Bible tells us to put our hope and trust in God when we are sad or discouraged. But it's not enough to know what we feel. We need to discover *why* we feel strong emotions so we can deal with them.

### Bottom Line

An important step toward handling your emotions is to identify the underlying causes.

## *A Careful Choice*

Karin could not believe her eyes! Sitting right in front of the TV was her brother, eating the sandwich that she had made for herself and drinking her juice. "What are you doing?" she screeched as she flew into the room. "I leave for one second to get something else out of the kitchen and you steal my sandwich! You're unbelievable!"

Her brother lazily took another bite of her sandwich, completely unmoved by her temper tantrum. "Get over it, Sis," he mumbled and turned back to the TV.

Thad was three years older than Karin and twice her size. Her hopes for wrestling the food away from him were pretty slim, and he knew it. Angry and frustrated, Karin threw the closest pillow at Thad (who just ignored her) and stormed out of the room. She slammed the door to her room and began to wail.

A few minutes later, their mother arrived home from work. As she walked into the house, she heard Karin and quickly walked to her room. Mom sat on the edge of Karin's bed and asked, "What in the world is wrong, honey?" She smoothed Karin's tearstained face.

"He makes me so mad, Mom!" Karin said through gritted teeth as she explained the story.

"I'll talk with your brother," Mom promised, "but I want you to know that no one can *make* you mad. You *choose* to be angry. It's a fact of life that we can't control what others do to us. We can, however, control how we react. It certainly is not wrong to be angry with Thad—what he did was not right. But you are allowing his actions to get you all upset and ruin your day. Actually, if you think about it, Thad is now controlling you!"

Karin dried her tears and looked up at her mom. Then she said,

"I see what you mean. But he makes me . . . I mean . . . I get so mad at him. What should I do?"

"Well," Mom answered, "it won't be easy because your natural reaction would be to yell and scream. But the best way to handle your emotions in a situation like that is to calmly and firmly explain to your brother what you are feeling. You could say, 'Thad, I am really upset with you. Eating my sandwich and drinking my juice was a very selfish act.' He might not change or apologize, but at least he would know how you felt, and his actions and attitude wouldn't ruin your day because you would be in control of your emotions."

Karin understood and determined to work on being more in charge of her reactions so her brother couldn't get to her so easily.

Questions

- Why was Karin so upset?
- How did her angry reaction hurt the situation?
- How would you have responded in a similar situation?
- How might you respond to demonstrate you were in charge of your reactions?

Bible Discovery

Read these Bible verses: Proverbs 25:28; 2 Timothy 1:7; 2 Peter 1:6.

Bible Point

Uncontrolled emotions can hurt us and others. God's Word instructs us to be self-controlled. Self-discipline is an important aspect of handling our emotions in a positive, constructive manner.

Bottom Line

To handle your emotions, remember that you can't help the way you feel—but you *can* help the way you react to your feelings.

## *Rocky Road*

Sarah had been looking forward to today's health class. Her Christian middle school was having a "Health Awareness" fair this week with a special emphasis on human emotions and how to learn to control them. Today's topic was one of the most emotional in a teenager's life—relationships with others. As Sarah sat in class, she listened to Mr. Meyer tell a story about two girls as an example.

"Kathy had a feeling from the beginning that something wasn't right with her new friend Amy. She felt uneasy when Amy talked about her wild past—parties, stealing, lying. Some of Amy's stories were so wild that Kathy wondered if she hadn't made them up. But Kathy desperately wanted to have friends, and Amy always included her in conversation. Soon Amy also began to invite Kathy to go to parties and other places Kathy was not allowed to go. Kathy would have to make an important decision.

"When Kathy's parents asked about her new friend, she was reluctant to tell them the whole truth. 'Who's this Amy you mentioned from school?' her mom asked one day. Frightened by the thought that her mom would be upset, Kathy nervously said something about Amy sitting next to her in one of her classes and quickly changed the subject. Later that night Kathy's stomach was in knots with worry, and she was unusually quiet at dinner. She soon mumbled something about wanting to go to bed early and went to her room before it was even dark."

At this point in the story, Mr. Meyer paused and asked, "What do you think Kathy should do?"

Students made a few suggestions, but most felt that Kathy should talk with someone about her feelings, probably her parents.

"That's good thinking," said Mr. Meyer. "Sometimes we keep our feelings bottled up inside. Instead, we should look for someone with whom we can talk them out. The best person would be someone who can listen and offer help. That's exactly what Kathy did. When she honestly shared her feelings with her parents, her mom and dad helped her realize what she should do about her relationship with Amy. They also explained that Kathy felt uneasy about becoming close to Amy for a reason. Her emotions were sending her a good message. Kathy could see that her friendship with Amy meant too much to her and could lead her into trouble.

"To handle your emotions, share your feelings with a trusted friend or parent who will listen and can help," concluded Mr. Meyer.

### Questions

- What were some of Kathy's feelings concerning Amy?
- How would you have responded to such emotions?
- Why do we experience strong emotions in our relationships with others?

- Why is it helpful to talk with others about our strong emotions?
- How can others help us handle our emotions?

Bible Discovery

Read these Bible verses: Psalms 25:5; 34:1-6; 64:1-2

Bible Point

David shared many of his deepest emotions with God through the psalms that he wrote. Relationships can produce a wide variety of emotions. We shouldn't keep our feelings bottled up inside us. Instead, we should find a positive way to express our emotions. The best way is to share our feelings with people who love us, will listen to us, and can help us.

Bottom Line

To handle your emotions, tell someone you trust what you are feeling.

## *Failure Isn't Final*

At the end of the week, Sarah's health class had learned a lot about emotions. The final lesson in the series focused on failure. Sarah was all too familiar with failure. Over the past few years, she had been cut from a variety of athletic teams at school. And she had just learned that her ensemble had *not* been chosen for the variety show.

After class, Sarah approached Mr. Meyer to ask him some questions. "You said this morning that failure isn't final," she began. "But it sure does feel like it sometimes."

Mr. Meyer smiled knowingly and replied, "You're right, Sarah. Failure can cause us to feel terrible about ourselves and our abilities. That's why we have to be in charge of our emotions and not let them be in charge of us."

Sarah explained to her teacher about her recent failures. She concluded, "Honestly, I really feel like a failure!"

"I think I understand what you are feeling," said Mr. Meyer gently. "I never did make the basketball team, although I tried out every year in junior *and* senior high school. Believe me, I really felt like a failure at times, especially in sports. Emotions run strong, but we should build our lives on the facts—the truth—and not emotions. So here's a truth that I want you to hold on to—someone shared it with me many years ago, and I've always remembered it, especially when I've been let down or rejected: *No matter how much you fail, you are not a failure.* You see, God created us, he loves us, and he has great things planned for us. Our failures hurt, but instead of focusing on them and feeling sorry for ourselves, we should learn from them and look forward to the opportunities that God is going to give us to excel." He paused and looked Sarah right in the eye and continued. "Sarah, you are a very sensitive, kind, and bright young woman. You are *not* a failure. God has a terrific future for you. Trust in him. Whenever you feel like a failure, turn to God—he really loves you." Then Mr. Meyer prayed for Sarah.

Sarah left class that day feeling better than she had in a long time and determined not to let her emotions get the best of her.

### Questions

- Why did Sarah feel as though she had failed?
- Why did Sarah feel like a failure?
- Why do emotions seem to get the best of us?
- What happens when we are controlled by emotions?
- When does failure sometimes feel like it's final?
- What advice would you give to someone who feels like a failure?

### Bible Discovery

Read these Bible verses: Psalm 34:18; 2 Corinthians 4:8-9.

### Bible Point

Feelings can betray us, and emotions can control us. We should build our life on the truths of God's Word, remembering that God created us, loves us, and has a great plan for our life. He is with us through every failure and can help us learn from them. Because of God's love, failure is never final, no matter how we feel at the time.

### Bottom Line

To handle your emotions, build your life on facts, not on feelings.

# 32

# How to Get the Most Out of Church

## *Get Ready, Get Set, Go!*

"Is everybody ready for church?" Nancy's father yelled up the staircase. With four girls in the house, it was quite a feat to get everyone up and going early Sunday mornings. There were curling irons and hairbrushes everywhere as the family rushed around, attempting to leave on time.

Nancy checked how she looked one more time. The dress she bought last week looked even cuter than it did in the store dressing room. She hoped to get lots of compliments on it. Her younger sisters, Tracie and Katie, came rushing through the bathroom one last time. Katie could find only one shoe at the moment, and Tracie was doing her best to find it in all the junk piled in a corner of the closet.

Meanwhile, Mom and Dad had their own concerns as they rushed around the house doing last-minute preparations before walking out the door. "Let's go!" yelled Dad one more time up the staircase. *Boom. Boom. Boom. Boom.* Four girls came bounding down the stairs, each fully dressed and with both shoes, too. The family quickly piled into the car and pulled out of the driveway only minutes behind schedule.

"Is everybody ready for church?" their mother asked.

"Well, it's too late now if we're not!" Nancy chuckled.

"Actually, I think we did forget something, and it's not too late," her mother suggested. "We need to ask God to make us ready to worship him today. We rushed around getting ourselves ready for church this morning. But now we need to ask God to get our hearts and minds ready to worship. That's one way we'll get the most out of church today."

"I agree," said Dad, "but I'm getting tired of all this last-minute rushing around. So I'm calling a family meeting for this afternoon after dinner."

After everyone had eaten and the food and plates had been cleared away, everyone settled in the family room.

"OK," Dad began, "we have a problem. This morning was pretty typical of our Sundays, and, as Mom implied in the car, that's not the way to get ready for church. What can we do to better prepare ourselves to meet the Lord in worship?"

At first, suggestions came slowly because no one really wanted to get up earlier. Eventually, everyone agreed that they needed to set aside enough time in the morning to get ready so they could prayerfully prepare and not feel hassled and rushed.

"I think our preparation really begins on Saturday night," said Mom. "We need to go to bed earlier if we want to wake up earlier . . . and in a good mood. To do this, we'll all have to sacrifice a bit. It means no Saturday-night sleepovers or late baby-sitting jobs for you girls—"

"And no late-night TV or sporting events, Dad," interjected Nancy.

"You're right," Dad replied. "All of us will have to work at making Sunday special."

### Questions

- Why was Nancy's family unprepared for church?
- How does being relaxed and rested help a person get more out of worship?
- Why does preparation for Sunday morning really begin on Saturday night?

### Bible Discovery

Read these Bible verses: 1 Chronicles 16:25; Psalms 29:1-4; 66:4.

### Bible Point

Worship is when believers meet God. They should come to this very special meeting prepared. This means being rested, relaxed, and prayerful, not hurried, hassled, and worried about appearances and schedule.

Bottom Line

To get the most out of church, begin your preparation on Saturday night.

## *The Offering*

The topic for the junior high Sunday school class focused on church, especially the worship service. "I don't get it," Tommy said in an exasperated voice. "Why does the pastor have us pass around the offering plates each Sunday? Does God need money that much?"

Everyone else in the class agreed that Tommy was making a good point.

Mr. Edwards held back a grin and replied, "No, it doesn't work like that. God doesn't need our money. He is *God.* He owns everything in this world and beyond."

"So why does it matter if I bring my money or not?" Tommy asked.

"To answer that question, let's look at a familiar Bible story," said Mr. Edwards. "Turn to John 6:1-15."

After reading the story, Mr. Edwards asked, "Could Jesus have fed the crowd all by himself, without anyone's help?"

"Sure," answered Melinda. "He's God. Look how he multiplied the few loaves and fish."

"Good answer," said Mr. Edwards. "But why, then, do you think he had the disciples check the crowd to see what food they had? And why did he take the young boy's five barley loaves and two fish?"

After a few answers, Mr. Edwards explained, "What happened on that hillside is similar to what happens in church when we give our tithes and offerings. Although God doesn't *need* the money, he has chosen to work through his people and their gifts to further his work in the world. Just think of how that young boy must have felt when he saw Jesus multiply his small gift to feed those thousands of people. What a blessing! Well, that's what God does with what we give in the offering plate. He takes our small gifts and multiplies them to further his work around the world. Where do you think that money goes?"

"I know," answered Erik. "The deacons take it to a back room and count it. Then they put it in a safe. I saw them one Sunday."

"That's right," said Mr. Edwards. "But eventually the money goes to help pay the pastors' salaries and other church expenses. Some money goes to missionaries. Some goes to ministries that help feed hungry people, counsel expectant mothers, and so forth. So you can see, God uses our offerings. Through them he uses us to reach people for Christ, here and around the world."

"Even in Africa?" Tommy asked. "I've seen those commercials on TV about helping the children and all."

"Yes," Mr. Edwards responded. "God is working in Africa, too."

Tommy thought for a minute and said, "I get it now. It really does matter if I bring my money or not—even if it isn't much. When I give an offering to God, he uses it."

#### Questions

- What is an offering?
- Why does God want us to give a portion of our money to our church?
- How can we participate in God's work around the world?

#### Bible Discovery

Read these Bible verses: Psalm 96:8-9; Mark 12:41-44; 2 Corinthians 8:3-4, 7-8.

#### Bible Point

We give tithes and offerings, not because God needs it but because we need to. Giving an offering to God through the church is a great privilege and a great way to participate in God's work. It is an act of love to God.

#### Bottom Line

To get the most out of church, give an offering to God.

### *The Experiment*

"Score! Score! Score!" Coach Lee yelled at Kevin, his best player, as Kevin raced down the soccer field toward the goal. The stands were filled with parents who roared with delight as they watched Kevin single-handedly slam the ball into the opponent's goal with a swift kick. Everyone could see that Kevin was putting his whole heart into the game.

Kevin didn't let up the entire time. He raced to defend his goal when the other team got dangerously close. He dove wholeheartedly into the pack when control of the ball was up for grabs. He was the first one to huddle with the coach at a time-out and the first one back out onto the field and in position. Every move he made during the game, he made with gusto.

After the victory, as Kevin was walking off the field, he heard someone call his name. "Kevin! Hey, wait up!" It was his youth director, Randy. He and Randy had a great relationship and spoke openly with one another about most subjects: girls, God, grades. Kevin respected Randy and tried to listen to what he said. Kevin could always count on Randy to watch him play in at least a couple of his games during soccer season.

"Hey, man! That was a great game!" Randy said. "Too bad you weren't really into it, though!" he joked.

Kevin grinned and said, "Those guys were tough competition! I was determined we were not going to lose if I could help it!" Randy and Kevin continued walking, dramatically recalling aloud some of Kevin's best plays of the game.

When they got to Randy's car, Kevin stopped and said thoughtfully, "You know that verse in Colossians you told us about at youth group last week? Something about working at whatever you do with your whole heart?"

Randy responded, "Sure. Colossians 3:23. I like that one a lot."

Kevin continued, "Well, I kept thinking about that verse when I was playing today. It really made a difference when I put my whole heart into it. That's why I played so well."

"That's great!" Randy said. "God wants us to be fully devoted to whatever we're doing. It brings glory to him when we do our best in all our activities. Just think what a difference that kind of attitude could make in other areas of your life—school, church."

"Yeah, church," Kevin said, shaking his head. "I can see getting better grades at school and all. But how would church be any different? It's just the same old thing every Sunday: Sit. Stand. Pray. Sing. Sit. Listen. Go home. No offense, but I just don't see how things could change for me there."

"Are you up for an experiment?" Randy asked with a twinkle in his eye.

Kevin wasn't sure how to answer. "What do you mean, an 'experiment'? Is this some kind of trick question or something?" Kevin asked.

"Oh, come on! Trust me!" Randy said. "What if you picked one thing in the service this Sunday that you're really going to throw your heart into like you did today's game? Like the singing, for example."

"You mean like look up the songs in the hymnal? And sing them out loud?" Kevin asked hesitantly. Kevin had a decent voice, but he was no choir member!

"That's a good place to start. God doesn't care how you sound. It's your heart he's interested in hearing. You can pick any part of the service you want to really focus on and then do what the verse says. Do it with your whole heart!" Randy challenged.

"It's worth a shot," Kevin said confidently. "Look out, Sunday! Here I come!"

Questions

- What did Kevin say helped him do his best in the soccer game?
- What does it mean to work at something with your whole heart?
- How can you participate more in your own church's service?
- Why do you think active participation makes a difference in a person's church experience?

Bible Discovery

Read these Bible verses: Psalms 81:1-2; 111:1; Colossians 3:23.

Bible Point

Participating in church means paying attention. When we focus on what we're doing in the service and actively participate with enthusiasm, we can give God the attention and praise he deserves.

Bottom Line

To get the most out of church, participate with your whole heart.

## *The Sermon That Made a Difference*

*Ho-hum,* Susan thought to herself as she sat down on the hard, uncomfortable pew. *Another hour in church to do absolutely nothing.* Each Sunday it was the same routine. Her family filed into the pew, third row from the front. They stood up when it was time to stand. They sat down when it was time to sit. And when it was time for the sermon, the youngest child lay down comfortably in Mom's lap while the middle child colored on the church bulletin.

As she sat, Susan ran down a mental list of things she could do to entertain herself this week: *Count the number of people in the congregation with glasses. See who's the first choir member to fall asleep. Circle all the vowels printed in the church bulletin.* This list got her through most of the singing and prayer. But the sermon was yet to come. Typically, the start of the sermon was Susan's cue to stare at the pastor as if she were listening intently. The truth was, her mind was a million miles away—scoring the winning run in softball, running for class president, or starring the lead in the school's latest play.

But this Sunday, things would be different for Susan. First of all, there was a new person sitting next to her on their pew. She had never seen this girl before, and Susan knew everyone. The girl appeared to be about her age. Friendly. Polite. Neat. The girls had even exchanged brief, awkward smiles before the service started with the forceful blare of the organ.

Susan watched this new girl with interest. She stood when it was time to stand. She sat when it was time to sit—just like everyone else. But when it came time for the sermon, she didn't stare into space. Susan was amazed. *What will she do to make it through this week's talk?* Susan wondered to herself. Susan felt the old temptation to zone out for the next half hour, but she just had to find out what this girl would do next.

At that moment the girl did the most incredible thing. She pulled out a small notebook and a pen. Her notebook had the name "Kelly" inscribed on the front. *Aha!* Susan thought. *She writes letters to people! That's it! She catches up on notes to friends!* Susan was proud of herself for figuring out the mystery.

To Susan's surprise, however, Kelly titled the page "Sermon Notes," of all things. She actually took notes on what the pastor said? Susan casually looked over to investigate what Kelly was writing.

"Sermon title." "Scripture text." Kelly had it all neatly written on the page. Susan watched as Kelly listened intently and jotted down the pastor's points as he spoke. She even wrote down a note about a good illustration the pastor used so she could remember it later. It wasn't a fancy report or anything, but it seemed to keep Kelly's attention and Susan's, too!

After the benediction, Susan introduced herself to her mysterious new pew partner. "I saw you taking notes on the sermon," Susan said, trying to hide her amazement. "That's uh, um—" Susan searched for the words—"really cool. How do you do it?"

Kelly smiled at Susan and replied, "It's nothing fancy! I just write down what sounds like something I should remember." Kelly showed Susan how she collected notes from every sermon in that notebook. "It helps me understand what I'm hearing," she said to Susan. "When I write it down, I remember it better, and I can look back at my notes later."

Susan was inspired. She planned on taking notes next week—and sitting next to her new friend, Kelly!

Questions

- What was different about this Sunday for Susan?
- Why did Kelly take notes during the sermon?
- Why do you think it's easier to remember things when you write them down?
- What do you usually do during the sermon in church? What can you do differently to get more out of it?

Bible Discovery

Read these Bible verses: Proverbs 4:13, 20-22; 13:13-14; 16:20.

Bible Point

We are responsible for the godly instruction we are given. Listening carefully and writing good notes on a sermon are good ways to follow through on our responsibility. In that way, we are better able to remember and actually use what we hear and learn in church.

Bottom Line

To get the most out of church, listen carefully and take notes on the sermon.

## *Great Sunday*

When Susan went to church the next week, she could hardly wait for the service to begin. She and her new friend, Kelly, sat in the third row. A few days earlier, Susan had asked her mother to buy her a notebook like Kelly's. She even got one with her name printed on the outside. She had already titled the first page "Sermon Notes" and wrote down the date. Following Kelly's advice, Susan kept the notebook near her Bible so she would not forget it Sunday morning.

With her Bible in hand and her new notebook nearby, Susan felt as though she was ready for church. Before the service, she and

Kelly talked quietly together, sharing experiences from the week before. Suddenly the organ signaled the start of the service, bringing the girls' conversation to a sudden halt.

As the choir members filed in, singing along with the organ's tune, Susan straightened her back against the hard oak pew and took a deep breath. *Here we go,* she thought. *Concentrate!* Susan commanded herself.

After a few minutes, Susan felt like she was in a whole new experience. *This is going to be a breeze,* she thought. *I can't wait to use my new notebook.* She soon discovered, however, that it wasn't easy to stay so focused. Many things were competing for her attention.

First of all, she noticed that the woman in front of her was constantly coughing. *Cough. Cough, cough. Cough!* Susan was afraid the woman would never stop! She looked out of the corner of her eye at Kelly. But Kelly did not seem to notice. And if she did, it didn't seem to bother her.

During the prayer time, Susan was distracted by the shrill cry of an unhappy baby somewhere in the back. "Take the baby out, for heaven's sake," Susan muttered through clenched teeth. She looked at her watch—only ten minutes! It seemed like an eternity.

*When is the sermon?* Susan wondered, her energy and enthusiasm draining out of her as quickly as they had come. She glanced over at her younger siblings and felt a twinge of envy as they colored away on their bulletins.

During the singing, Susan had to make a concentrated effort to focus on the words of the hymns. She didn't understand some of the words, so her mind began to wander. Susan had never noticed all the distractions in church before. But then again, Susan had never paid this much attention before.

*Just get to the sermon!* Susan found herself wishing. But even as she tried to take notes like Kelly had taught her, Susan often doodled in the margin with her pen and then discovered that she had missed a point or two.

After the service, Susan talked with Kelly about the experience. "It seemed like I noticed everything around me, and they were all distractions," Susan complained. "It was tough to stay focused!"

Kelly knew exactly what Susan was talking about. She replied, "I know that God has something for me to get out of church each week. That makes me try harder to focus when there is so much to get me off track."

Susan and Kelly promised right then and there that they would pray for each other to be able to cut out distractions during church and focus on God. It wasn't going to be easy. But they knew that helping each other was the best way to cut out the distractions.

### Questions

- What distractions did Susan notice at church?
- How did Kelly say she responds to distractions during the service?
- How are you typically distracted at church?
- What is your plan for dealing with distractions during the service?

### Bible Discovery

Read these Bible verses: Psalm 86:11; Proverbs 18:15.

### Bible Point

It's not always easy to get something out of our church experience because many distractions pull us away from worship. God wants us to worship him with our whole heart and mind, and he will help us cut out the distractions.

### Bottom Line

To get the most out of church, ask God to help you tune in to him and tune out distractions.

# 33 How to Have Fun

### *Try It—You'll Like It!*

It was the middle of July, and, quite frankly, Randy was ready for school to begin. As he considered the next four weeks before football camp, he couldn't imagine how he was going to fill his days. Already the pool routine was old. He was tired of roller-blading around the neighborhood, and he had even completed his entire summer reading list. Randy was bored!

He plopped onto the sofa and flicked on the TV. Nothing but reruns, but at least it was *something* to do to pass the hours. His mom, who had been out watering the garden, came in, took one look at him, and walked over and shut off the TV. "Randy, I think you can find something better to do with your time," she said sternly. "Why don't you take a walk over to Emmet's and see what he's doing?"

Emmet was the son of his mom's friend from church. Randy didn't know him that well—and he really didn't feel like getting to know him—but it would take up some time walking over and back. Reluctantly, Randy got up and left the house.

Emmet was excited to see him. "Hey, Randy, come on in. I've got something to show you."

Emmet led Randy upstairs to his room. In the corner was a collection of model airplanes, rockets, and spacecrafts. "I've been working on these all summer," Emmet said, holding each one up and explaining what it was. "I took a class at the local hobby shop on how to build them, and now I can do them on my own. This one took me about eight hours to finish."

Randy admired them all. He had to admit that the models did look kind of neat. "Next week," Emmet informed him, "I'm going to take an archery class. I've never tried it before, but it looks like fun. So what have you been doing this summer?"

"Well, not much, exactly," Randy began. "I've basically been hanging out around the pool or at home. I haven't really done much of anything, I guess."

Emmet's mom walked into the room, carrying a pile of folded clothes, just as Randy finished talking. "Oh, we remember those days, don't we, Emmet!" she said with a sympathetic smile. "A couple summers ago, Emmet was in a similar slump. He had been to the pool and had read all his books. He was driving me crazy because he didn't know what to do. That's when we got the idea to use our vacation as an opportunity to expand our horizons."

Randy looked a bit skeptical. "It sounds somehow like class," Randy muttered, forgetting that he was just about ready to go back to school.

"That's what I thought until Mom explained it to me," Emmet said. "You see, before vacation even begins, we sit down and make a list of things I would like to try that I've never done before. It can be anything! Just let your imagination run wild—that's the fun part."

"But then," his mom interrupted, "I get to see what's possible and what's not. A trip to the Amazon to search for parrots is definitely not on the list this year!"

Emmet laughed. "No, I didn't actually get to the Amazon, but I did check out a few books on the rain forest, rented a computer game about it, and went to the zoo's rain-forest exhibit. I had my own mini-expedition without even leaving town."

Randy had to admit it *did* sound like fun—certainly better than watching reruns. When he went home, he decided that he would make up a list of ways to expand his horizons. But first, he wanted to learn how to make one of those cool model jets.

### Questions

- What does "expand your horizons" mean?
- What do you do when there's "nothing to do"?
- How can you learn to be "content" in any situation?

### Bible Discovery

Read the following Bible verses: Ecclesiastes 5:19; Philippians 4:11-12.

### Bible Point

God gives us the ability to enjoy his blessings and the

strength to be content in whatever situation we find ourselves. Our attitude determines our outlook.

Bottom Line

Have fun by expanding your horizons.

### *Find the Fun!*

Mr. Holman walked into the classroom. A few boys were throwing paper around the room, while a group of girls giggled and talked in another corner. "OK, kids, it's time to get ready for our Sunday school lesson. We're going to have fun today!" he announced.

A chorus of groans went up in the room. "We never have fun." "What's the fun of learning another Bible story?" "Can't we watch a movie today?" The rumblings went on.

"Whoa—hold on there. It sounds like a mutiny in this classroom," Mr. Holman said, walking to the front of the room. "It sounds as if we have a difference of opinion on what's fun and what's not. Let me hear from you first—what do you think is fun?"

Immediately the answers came flying: "Watching movies." "Playing games." "Playing Nintendo 64!" "Doing crafts."

Mr. Holman smiled at some of the answers. "That's a wide variety of answers," he remarked. "But what if I told you how to look for the fun in *any* situation?"

The class stared back at Mr. Holman doubtfully. "I don't know about that," said one boy. "That doesn't sound like much fun."

"On the contrary—sometimes *looking* for the fun is half the fun of any activity," Mr. Holman answered. He went over to the white board and printed in large letters *F-U-N*. "This is a little challenge I always use when I find myself needing to put some fun into my day. *F* stands for *find*—find the fun in a situation. Maybe your parents are taking you to the boss's house for a picnic. You don't know anyone there, and you're sure it's going to be a complete bummer. What can you do to find the fun?"

"Maybe you could find someone interesting to talk to," suggested Elizabeth.

"Or you could organize a game if there are other kids there," said Joe.

"Bring a book along," said another.

"Those are great ideas," said Mr. Holman. "The idea is not to wait for the fun to begin—start it yourself. That brings us to *U*. The fun all begins with you and your attitude. If you walk into a classroom and have already decided it's not going to be any fun, you've already lost. How much fun you have in any situation depends on you and your attitude. For example, how could some of you change your attitude about Sunday school?" Mr. Holman asked.

The class was silent, until one of the boys who had been throwing paper raised his hand. "I guess I could at least wait to hear what you're planning to do before I begin complaining."

Another offered, "I could remember that we usually *do* have some fun by the time we leave."

Mr. Holman nodded. "You see, already things are starting to look a bit different. *N* stands for *now.* Don't wait for someone else to come and entertain you. Find the fun for yourself now. Don't let a bad attitude ruin an opportunity to have fun with others or to enjoy whatever you're doing. Change your attitude *now* before it's too late!" Mr. Holman encouraged. "Now that brings us to our Sunday school lesson—and before you groan again, remember to look for the FUN first."

### Questions

- Why does attitude play a part in how much fun a person has in a situation?
- How can someone have fun in a situation that looks completely hopeless?
- What do the letters *F, U,* and *N* stand for?
- When did you have fun where you least expected it? What made it such a fun experience?

### Bible Discovery

Take a look at Ephesians 4:23-24 and 5:10, 15-17 for a view on the type of attitude and behavior that pleases God.

### Bible Point

Adopting the right attitude will go a long way in how much enjoyment we get from any situation. God wants us to have a thoughtful, truthful attitude, always seeking to know what pleases God. We should be careful to adopt an attitude that is pleasing to God.

### Bottom Line

To have fun, go into a situation with an open mind and look for the fun in any situation.

## *Join the Fun*

Margaret was an exceptional artist. She had loved to draw even as a child. As she got older, her talent developed. The only trouble was that no one but her parents and her teachers at school even recognized that Margaret was so gifted. Margaret was painfully shy. She dreaded speaking in front of the class and avoided large groups of people as much as possible. She barely spoke to the other children at school except when she had to, and many of them thought she was a snob because she took such pains to avoid them.

Consequently, Margaret didn't have many friends. It didn't really bother her that much because she had her art. Margaret would spend hours in her room, painting and drawing, enjoying the solitude of creating.

All that was in danger of changing, however, when Susan moved in next door. Margaret had never met anyone like Susan, an outgoing, vivacious girl who was friendly to everyone, even Margaret. It didn't seem to bother Susan that Margaret didn't respond to her friendly greeting each time she saw her. Susan always had a bright smile for everyone. She was in many of Margaret's classes and had quickly become one of the more popular girls in school.

So when Susan sat down at Margaret's lunch table one day, Margaret was dumbfounded. "Hi, how you doing? Mind if I eat lunch with you?" Susan chattered as she sat down without waiting for a reply. It was a good thing, too, because Margaret was speechless. "I've been noticing that you're a really good artist. I saw some of the paintings you did in class the other day, and they were really terrific. How did you learn to draw so well?"

Secretly Margaret was thrilled that someone had noticed her work, especially someone like Susan. But she was also terrified of saying something stupid. She mumbled a few words in reply and then got up and ran out of the lunchroom. As she walked home that afternoon, Margaret got upset at herself. She liked Susan and would like to know her better, but she had blown it. Susan couldn't possibly bother spending time with anyone like her. Fortunately for Margaret, she was wrong about Susan.

The next day, Susan again approached Margaret at lunch. She joked as she sat down next to her. "Don't worry, I'm not going to stay and eat lunch or anything. I just wanted to know if you would be interested in working with several of us on the scenery for the school musical. I'm in charge, but I don't know the first thing about painting scenes. I thought you would be great as part of the team. It really will be fun."

Margaret gulped. She had never done anything big like that before, and the idea intrigued her. But the thought of joining a group scared her to death. Susan waited patiently while Margaret struggled to reply. "I really don't know. I usually work by myself. I'm not sure I can draw something like that," she told Susan shyly.

Susan smiled broadly, encouraged that Margaret at least hadn't run away this time. "Well, I'll be there to help, and the other kids are really nice once you get to know them. I think you'll have a good time—and you'll get to do something you really love, too! My mother always said that anything you do is always more fun when you do it in a group. What do you think?"

Margaret wasn't totally sure about what Susan's mother said, but it might be worth a try. If things didn't work out, she could always go back to her room and draw for herself. But somehow, looking at Susan's warm, cheerful face, Margaret was gaining confidence that she wouldn't do that this time.

### Questions

- When is it more fun to participate with others than to do something alone?
- How can others make an activity fun?
- How would you convince Margaret to join the stage crew? How would you convince someone you know to join an activity in which you currently participate?
- Think of your particular talents and abilities. How can you enjoy them and have fun with a group?

### Bible Discovery

Read the following Bible verses: Psalm 133; Ecclesiastes 4:9-12; Hebrews 10:25.

### Bible Point

God wants us to live together harmoniously, sharing our thoughts, feelings, and time with others. There is more to be gained when we join with others, helping each other and sharing a common bond.

### Bottom Line

To have fun, get involved in a group.

## *Help Others*

Peter rolled over, slammed the button on his alarm, and sleepily tried to remember why he had to get up so early. It was summer, he recalled groggily, so it couldn't be school. Why was he supposed to get up? Then it dawned on him, and Peter gave a loud wail of protest. Today was the first day of his church's Vacation Bible School, and his mom had signed him up to help with the four-year-old class.

He remembered the day his mom had come home with this little "surprise." She had acted as though she had signed him up for soccer camp or something really cool. "Oh, Peter, it's going to be so much fun. You'll really have a great time. I know you'll love it," she had assured him. *Fat chance,* thought Peter as he grumpily got out of bed. What in the world was he going to do for three hours with fifteen four-year-olds? Suffer, that's for sure.

If his mom noticed his bad mood, she gave no indication during breakfast. While Peter moped around, getting his breakfast, his mom chatted cheerfully about the VBS program and the teacher he was going to be assisting. "You're going to love Mrs. Walker. She is just great with the kids and is really creative. I'm sure you're going to enjoy working with her. You'll learn a lot," she told Peter.

Peter grunted a reply into his cereal bowl. The only thing he *was* sure of was the absolutely rotten time he was going to have.

When Peter arrived in the classroom, it was even worse than he had imagined. The theme that week was a safari adventure. Mrs. Walker greeted him, dressed like a safari guide. Worse yet, she had a safari hat for him! Peter tossed it to the side, mumbling that he would put it on later—much later. Quickly Mrs. Walker explained that Peter should help the children find an activity to do when they arrived for the first ten minutes. *That sounds easy enough,* thought Peter confidently. He could handle that.

Things *were* going smoothly until Jake arrived. Peter had an easy time directing the boys and girls to the Play-Doh table or the art center or the building-block area. But Jake wasn't so easily distracted. He wanted no part of making a building or drawing a picture. And he definitely didn't want his mother to leave the room. When she finally left, Jake broke out into loud sobs. Peter quickly looked for Mrs. Walker. She was busy getting three little girls settled at the art table. It looked like it was up to Peter. Quickly he glanced around. Spying his safari hat on the floor, Peter grabbed it and placed it on Jake's head. Immediately Jake stopped crying, momentarily surprised.

"Come on, Jake," Peter encouraged, seizing the moment. "Let's go find some monkeys and tigers and elephants." As he led Jake around the room, stopping to make noises like a monkey or an elephant, more of the children joined in. Soon they were a jumbled, laughing mass of children as they all tried to do their best imitation of a monkey.

Mrs. Walker beamed over at Peter. "Good job, Peter," she said.

The rest of the morning went quickly. Peter found himself enjoying helping the children with their crafts, playing the games, and preparing their snacks. He found himself followed by a crowd of children everywhere he went. Before Peter knew it, the mothers were arriving to pick up their children. When Jake's mom arrived, Jake ran over to Peter and gave him a hug. "Can I wear your hat tomorrow, Peter?" Jake asked him.

Peter gave him a huge smile. "Sure, we'll go looking for more animals tomorrow," he promised.

Peter's mom walked in just then. "Make a new friend, Peter?" she asked.

"Lots of them," Peter replied. "You know, I hate to admit it, but you were right. Helping out *is* fun. I have a feeling this week is going to go much faster than I thought."

### Questions

- Why can helping someone else be fun?
- When did you find helping others fun? How did it match your expectations?
- How can you learn to take the focus off your own needs?
- When you are helping others, what should your attitude be?

### Bible Discovery

Read the following Bible verses: 1 Corinthians 13:4-5; Ephesians 4:32; 2 Peter 1:5-7.

### Bible Point

When we take the focus off our own needs and look for ways to help others have fun, we will discover the joy that comes from serving and being patient and kind to others.

### Bottom Line

To have fun, help others.

### *Laugh a Little*

Rusty was the last one to get his ice skates laced up. He sat on the bench a moment and took a deep breath. Rusty had never ice-skated before, but his church's youth group had voted to go ice-skating as their winter social. From the beginning, Rusty had been dead set against going, but gradually his friends had talked him into it. Now here he sat, and where were his friends? Rusty looked out on the ice. Everyone he could see was either gracefully gliding by or tearing down the ice as if they were running down the street. Rusty looked woefully at his feet. What had he gotten himself into?

It was time. Holding onto the side of the rink, Rusty put one tentative skate on the ice. Now the other. Gripping the side, he slowly began to advance down the ice, never letting go of his only support. A couple of his friends whizzed by him. "Looking good, Rusty! Ready to join us out here?"

Rusty smiled and waved at them, nearly losing his balance in the process. He grabbed the wall again and steadied himself. *Whoa—that was close,* he thought. Rusty began pulling himself along the wall, making his way around the rink.

As he neared the starting point, his friend Jason skated up beside him. "How you doing?"

Not wanting to look like a wimp, Rusty answered, "Just fine, just fine. It just takes a little getting used to, that's all. I'm ready to go now." With that, Rusty let go of the wall and took a big step out onto the ice. The next thing he knew, his legs were flying into the air, and he landed with a big thump right on his backside.

One of the girls, sensing his total embarrassment, came over and reached down to help him. "Come on, skate with me a while," Lynn offered. "You'll get the hang of it."

Rusty rudely brushed her hand aside. "I don't need any help. Skating is for nerds anyway. I don't know why I even bothered," he said angrily.

Lynn shrugged her shoulders and skated off. The other kids left, too. Rusty finally got back on his skates and agonizingly made his way back to the bench.

As he was unlacing his skates, Mr. Jones, the youth group leader, sat down besides him. "Taking off your skates already?" Mr. Jones asked. Rusty just nodded, not looking up. "Boy," Mr. Jones said, "I can remember the first time I went skating in college. What a klutz! I was so macho I didn't even bother with the wall. I took a big step onto the ice and went sailing clear across the rink. I ended up crashing into this older couple. I was totally embarrassed."

Rusty stopped unlacing his skates and listened. Mr. Jones continued, "After that, I just sat on the bench and watched everyone else have fun while I pouted and felt sorry for myself. It was awful. I vowed I would never ice-skate again."

"But you can skate now. What happened?" Rusty asked him.

"Well, that's the good part of the story. While I was sitting there, one of the girls in the group came up and offered to help me learn. Not only did I end up spending the evening with the best-looking girl in our group, but I learned to skate, too," Mr. Jones answered. "We still laugh about it today."

"We? Who's we?" Rusty asked.

"Well," Mr. Jones said with a smile, "that girl eventually became my wife. Not only did she help me learn to skate, but she also helped me learn to laugh at my myself and get over my embarrassment. I would have missed out on a lot if I hadn't joined in."

Rusty thought a moment and watched as a group of his friends went by, laughing. "Well, maybe I could try this again. Can you give me a hand, Mr. Jones?"

### Questions

- How do you feel when people laugh at you when you're trying something new?
- Do you find it easy or hard to laugh at yourself? Why?
- Why do you feel it is important to learn to laugh at yourself?
- Who do you know that always approves of you no matter what you do? Why is that important to know?

### Bible Discovery

Read the following Bible verses: Proverbs 11:2; Luke 12:6-7; Galatians 6:3; Philippians 2:3-4; 1 Peter 3:8-9.

### Bible Point

It is important to keep a proper perspective on ourselves, being humble and thinking of others more highly than ourselves. Then we will be able to laugh with others and at ourselves and have fun.

### Bottom Line

To have fun, don't take yourself too seriously!

# 34 How to Get Things Done

***Break It Down***

The spring floods that year had devastated Beth's town. No one, it appeared, had been untouched by the destructive waters that had spilled over the riverbanks. Beth's own family had suffered major damage to their house, but they were among the fortunate ones. Many families had lost everything—right down to the foundations of their homes—in the floodwaters. The town was slowly getting back on its feet, but there was still much to do. At youth group that evening, the talk centered on how the town was coping with this disaster.

"I feel so helpless," said one girl. "I just wish there was something we could do."

"Maybe there is," suggested Beth. "Maybe we could organize some work teams who could go around on weekends helping families with the big chores such as cleaning out basements, washing down the house, cleaning and disinfecting household items—that kind of thing."

The group enthusiastically responded to Beth's idea, quickly adding other services: collecting canned foods for needier families; offering short-term child care for families with small children so they could attend to business; soliciting donations from local stores for items such as garbage bags and cleaning supplies.

By the end of the evening, the group had come up with quite a list of services they could offer the community. Beth was feeling good that her idea had such merit, until it came down to selecting a person to organize the project. All at once, Beth felt all eyes on her. Surprised, she looked around and said in disbelief, "You don't want me to head this up, do you?" Beth had helped out with the school's food drive before and had plenty of baby-sitting experience, but this was totally different. This was a massive task. She couldn't possibly undertake it.

Unfortunately, no one else seemed to want to head up the project either, so it was unanimously decided that Beth would organize their flood-relief service project. Beth walked out of the meeting, the knot in her stomach growing bigger by the minute. What would happen if she failed? What if she let down her friends—or worse yet, the people of the town who really needed the help? How did she get herself into this? How was she going to get herself out of it?

Beth was quieter than usual on the ride home from youth group. After letting out her last friend, Beth's father turned and asked what was wrong. Dad listened as Beth explained the situation. "It's just too overwhelming. I don't even know where to begin," she wailed. "I'm going to call up Mr. Thompson when I get home and quit. I can't do this."

"Nonsense," replied her father. "You're letting the scope of the project scare you. No one expects you to get this done overnight. What you need to do is look over the various parts of the project and break it down into manageable sections. For instance, a baby-sitting service is one task, right? Are there other areas you can divide?"

Catching on, Beth replied, "There are the cleaning teams. We'll also have a food drive and store-donations drive. We'll need to do some publicity and some phone calling. Do you think we could use the church office as a headquarters?"

"That's the spirit," said her father. "I'm sure you can enlist lots of help from the deacons and elders at the church. With a little bit of planning and management from the beginning, you'll have this project up and running in no time."

Questions

- How do you think Beth could manage this project?
- How do you handle a task that appears too big?
- Why is it important to plan first before tackling a big project?
- When you planned for a project, what happened?
- How can God help us tackle big projects? What should Beth do before she even begins planning?

### Bible Discovery

Read Nehemiah 2:11-17 and 3:1-2, 28-32. Check out the process that Nehemiah went through in devising a plan to rebuild the wall around Jerusalem. See also 1 Corinthians 14:40.

### Bible Point

Before devising a plan for rebuilding the walls, Nehemiah spent several days in careful observation and thoughtful consideration. Then he divided the project into sections. Follow Nehemiah's example: Plan ahead and break down large projects into manageable sections.

### Bottom Line

To get things done, plan ahead and break large projects into smaller tasks.

## *Get Real!*

Troy's family was getting ready for the church picnic. Mom had packed the picnic basket with all of his favorite picnic foods, including her famous double-chocolate brownies. She was putting the last of the sandwiches in the basket when she called for Troy and his sister to get ready. Troy's sister came immediately down the stairs, but there was no sign of Troy. Puzzled, Mom went upstairs to see what was going on.

Knocking on the door, she got no response. Finally she walked in to discover Troy sitting at his desk, buried behind a small wall of books. "What's going on here? Didn't you hear me calling you? It's time to get ready for the picnic," Mom said.

Troy looked up. "Oh, I'm not going. I've got to work on my report for social studies. I'm going to read through all these books by Sunday evening. Then I can start writing my report and have it done by Monday."

Mom's mouth dropped as she looked at Troy. "You're going to read *all* these books by Sunday evening? There must be about fifteen here. How are you possibly going to get that done?"

Troy shrugged his shoulders. "I will," he said stubbornly. "You always tell me that I can do anything if I put my mind to it."

Mom had to smile at that one. "Yes, I guess I do. What I failed to add is that you can do anything you put your mind to on a *realistic* time schedule. I don't think even a speed reader could plow through all these books that quickly."

"But Mom," said Troy, "if I don't get through these books, I'll never get my report done on time. Now what am I going to do?"

Mom sat down and grabbed a piece of paper. "What you need to do is learn to use your time wisely. Maybe trying to read fifteen books over the weekend is not the best use of your time in getting this report done. I think you need a P-L-A-N," she said.

"To start with, you need to Prioritize—that's what *P* stands for. What are the most important things that need to get done? Before you start reading, maybe you should make a rough outline of the kind of information you will need for your report. Then you should look at which books present this information in the best and most precise way. That way you'll only have to read portions of a book. While you're thinking of your priorities, make a List of everything that needs to be done for your report (that's the *L* in PLAN). List *everything,* right down to typing the paper and assign a timetable for when you can reasonably expect to have it done. That way you can budget your time wisely."

Troy grabbed the paper from Mom and began jotting notes. Mom stopped him and said, "Not so fast. There are two more things you need to consider. One is to Add some extra time into your schedule, so that if something takes longer than you expected, you won't be rushing at the last minute. And that brings us to *N*—Now. Get it down right away! Don't procrastinate or you'll find yourself cramming everything at the last minute."

Troy looked at his half-written list. "Well, I better get started on my PLAN now. Maybe if I budget my time right, I won't have to spend the whole weekend in my room!"

### Questions

- How can making a reasonable timetable help a person get work done?
- Why is it important to plan extra time into getting a project done?
- What is your usual style of working on a long-term project? Do you wait until the last minute, or do you plan ahead of time?
- How can you make better use of your time when working on a project?

### Bible Discovery

Read these Bible verses: Proverbs 10:4; 12:11; 16:3.

Bible Point

Time is a gift from God. We must learn to seize the opportunities given to us and use our time wisely to work diligently and be productive.

Bottom Line

To get things done, use your time wisely.

## *Focus*

During her campaign for class president, one of Mandy's promises had been to institute a schoolwide recycling-and-beautification effort. In recent years, the school's grounds had become trash filled and neglected. The school definitely didn't make a good first impression on its visitors. There also was a good deal of waste in the school cafeteria and in the classrooms. No one was recycling the soda cans, and there was no effort to recycle the reams of paper tossed out each day.

As class president, Mandy had worked hard with several classmates and the principal during the summer to design a working plan. Each class was assigned a certain area of the school yard to keep trash-free. A committee of three students and three teachers worked over the summer, planting flowers and sprucing up the bushes already planted. Mandy had a crew in place to plant bulbs this fall for the spring. Each classroom was given a recycling bin for paper. Numerous receptacles for recycling cans had been placed throughout the cafeteria and commons area.

As school got underway, Mandy felt good about the committee's efforts. She had taken a large task, had broken it down into manageable sections, and had established a reasonable time schedule for accomplishing their goals. Things were proceeding smoothly, and Mandy was sure the program would be a complete success.

By the second month of school, however, Mandy began to notice a change. The grounds were beginning to fill with litter again. She saw discarded soda cans in the trash rather than in the recycling receptacles. Teachers were becoming lax about recycling paper. In many classrooms, no one was bothering to empty the recycling bins, and paper was overflowing onto the classroom floors.

Mandy decided to call an emergency meeting of her recycling committee. She was met by a flood of complaints. "It's too hard. Nobody even pays any attention to the recycling receptacles." "Why bother picking up the trash? As soon as we get it done, someone's out there making more." "None of the teachers are even bothering to help out. In fact, they're complaining about how the recycling bins are causing more trash." By the end of the meeting, Mandy was completely discouraged. The bright future of her recycling program looked dismal.

Before leaving school, Mandy went in to talk with the principal, Mrs. Branch. "I think we're going to have to drop the recycling effort," Mandy told her. "Everyone is complaining, and no one seems interested anymore. It's a complete failure."

"I'm aware there has been some opposition. But there always is when anything new is introduced. You can't let the opposition distract you from the main objective," Mrs. Branch said. "Look at everything positive that has been accomplished so far. The school grounds look better than they have in years. You have outlined a very good recycling program. Everything is in place. We just need to refocus our efforts and look for ways to resolve some of these problems."

On the way home from school, Mandy thought about what Mrs. Branch had said. The recycling effort *had* accomplished a lot, and some committee members still were enthusiastic. Maybe what they needed was a campaign to educate everyone about the program. Or better yet, she thought excitedly, they could have a contest for the best recycling poster. Mandy picked up her pace. She couldn't wait to get home to call her committee chairperson and get started.

### Questions

- How do you handle opposition to your plans?
- What else could Mandy do in this situation? How would you advise her?
- How can you keep your focus on a task when opposition hits?
- Why do you think people sometimes oppose new ideas or programs? What are some ways to combat those attitudes?

### Bible Discovery

Read Nehemiah 4:1-14. Look for how Nehemiah handled opposition to his plans for rebuilding the wall. See also Deuteronomy 1:27-30; Isaiah 50:7; Philippians 3:12-14.

### Bible Point

Accomplishing a large task can be tiring and, at times, discouraging, particularly in the face of opposition. The only cure for discouragement and fatigue is to work hard and continue focusing on God's purpose and provision for accomplishing a goal.

Bottom Line

To get things done, work hard and keep your goal in focus.

## *Handoff*

As a community service project, Phil's soccer team had decided to host a one-week soccer camp for young children. Members of the team, along with some high school players and coaches, had signed up to assist in leading various clinics.

Phil had agreed to help his coach organize the event. He was given the responsibility of publicizing the camp and handling registration. During the past several weeks, Phil had distributed posters at the various elementary schools and parks. He had made sure that kids who preregistered would be assigned to age-appropriate groups. He and his mom had designed a registration form for walk-ins. So far, the camp had attracted about fifty children. There had been a lot of details to take care of, but Phil was confident that everything was in place. Tomorrow would be the real test of his organizational skills!

Phil arrived about twenty minutes before the camp officially opened. He couldn't believe his eyes at the scene before him. Already a long line of kids waited to register. Another group of children and parents stood off to the side, waiting for their assignments. Phil quickly looked for some extra registration forms and name tags. He hastily set up the table and began the long process of registering each child. The group waiting for their assignments began to get testy. Hurriedly, Phil left the registration table and tried to get the right kids with the right coaches. By the time he had that completed, a number of parents still waiting to register were clearly annoyed. Some began to complain. Others gave up and left. Helplessly, Phil sat down and registered those still in line. By the time he had all the children registered, the morning session was nearly half over. Phil was exhausted.

That's when the coaches came to complain. "Phil, I've got three four-year-olds in the seven/eight group. You're going to have to assign them to another slot," one said. Another asked why he had twenty kids in his group when the other coaches had only twelve. Phil's head began to hurt. The morning had been a total disaster.

Phil dreaded facing his coach. He felt he had really let him down. So much for his organizational skills, Phil thought.

While he was taking down the registration table, Coach Mac walked up. "Seems like we had a few problems this morning, Phil. What happened?" the coach asked.

"I'm sorry, Coach, but I couldn't handle the crowd. I didn't expect that many people to register this morning. I needed to split myself in two," Phil said apologetically.

"No, what you needed were a couple pairs of extra hands," Coach Mac replied. "I think your planning lacked one essential ingredient—delegation. You tried to do too much by yourself. No one alone could have handled all those people this morning. But if you had asked a couple of your teammates to take some of the responsibility, we might have had a fighting chance at getting *all* those kids registered.

"Sometimes in a big project like this we tend to think that we're the only one capable of getting the job done. Sometimes that's true. But more often than not, there is someone out there just as capable—and willing—to help out," the coach continued. "How about we try again tomorrow, but this time, ask a couple of your friends to lend a hand? What do you think?"

Phil smiled gratefully. "That sounds great to me. I'll get started on it right away. I know just the person to get these groups organized."

### Questions

- What makes it difficult to delegate tasks to another person?
- What are some of the advantages of delegating responsibility and authority to others? Disadvantages?
- When you're involved in a group project, how do you feel when someone gives you an important job to do? How about when someone hogs all the work?
- Think of a situation where delegation might not be the best solution.

### Bible Discovery

Read Exodus 18:12-26. Analyze Moses' situation and how he resolved his problem. Also read Acts 6:1-7 for another example of this principle.

### Bible Point

Sometimes when we are responsible for a project, we think

we're the only one who can do the work. But we can learn what Moses learned: Proper delegation can multiply our effectiveness while allowing others a chance to contribute.

Bottom Line

To get things done, recruit others to help.

## *Work Hard!*

Jeff was a good student at school although he never had to work hard for his grades. With a minimum of studying, he was able to stay on the honor roll—and keep his parents satisfied. So when his science teacher handed out the guidelines for this year's science project, Jeff thought, *No sweat. Piece of cake.* Last year, he and his friend had worked together on a project (admittedly, Jeff's friend had done most of the work), and they had received the highest honor. This year the rules were a little different. Everyone had to work alone. Still, Jeff was not concerned.

As the weeks progressed, from time to time Jeff's mom would check with him to see how things were going. "Just fine, Mom. Don't worry about it," Jeff would reassure her. "Mr. Hamilton gives us time to work on our projects at school. Mine's going great." Satisfied, she would drop the matter for another couple of days.

About a week before the science project was due, Jeff's mom walked into his room, clearly alarmed. "Jeff, I just ran into Ken's mom at the library. She said Ken has been at the library every night for the past two weeks, working on his science project. Are you *sure* your project is going to be finished? I haven't seen you work on it yet."

Jeff got up from reading his book. "Mom, it's OK. Ken always thinks he has to put in all this extra work. I told you, Mr. Hamilton lets us work on it at school. I've been doing some research at our school library. My project will be finished on time, just like Ken's," he promised her.

It was true. Jeff had done *some* research at school. He had looked up a couple of scientific articles via the Internet and had a general idea of what he was going to do. He could get it all done this weekend. But when the weekend came, Jeff got a chance to attend a football game with his best friend. He gave the science project a fleeting thought but was confident that he could squeeze everything in on Sunday afternoon.

After spending all day Sunday and most of the evening working on his project, Jeff overslept Monday morning. He quickly got dressed, gulped down his juice, and ran out the door before his mother could see the "finished" product. It was a bit messy, Jeff had to admit, but Mr. Hamilton was pretty easygoing about those kinds of things. Besides, this was a science, not an English, project.

The next evening was open house at Jeff's school. Parents were invited to visit classes, participate in some activities, and view the science projects. Jeff did all he could to talk his parents out of attending, but they insisted on going. After visiting the art room and the computer lab, his parents entered the commons where the science projects were displayed. One of the first ones they saw was Ken's project, displaying a blue ribbon for organization. "My, some of these projects are really good," his mom remarked. "Where's your project, Jeff?"

Jeff hemmed and hawed but finally led his parents to a far corner of the room. There on the wall hung Jeff's project—a hastily scribbled poster with crooked handwritten labels that had obviously taken little research. It was quite evident that this "project" had been thrown together at the last minute. After a few moments, Jeff's mom said quietly, "You know, Jeff, it's obvious to anyone who sees this project that you did not put in the work at all. This is not even close to your best effort. I think you owe Mr. Hamilton an apology—and a new project. If you are going to undertake anything, it is worth it to always work hard and do your absolute best. You can't expect to put in a few hours of work and get good results."

Miserably, Jeff nodded his head. "I'm sorry, Mom. You're right. Mr. Hamilton won't even accept this. But I do promise this time I will work hard on it. I think I've learned my lesson."

### Questions

- When you turned in something that was less than your best effort, how did you feel about your work?
- How do you feel when you have turned in something you've worked hard on?
- Why is it important to always do our best, even if the task is not very important?

### Bible Discovery

Read the following verses: Proverbs 12:14; 28:19; Ephesians 6:5-9.

Bible Point

God expects us to always do our best in whatever we attempt. He will reward our hard work and effort.

Bottom Line

To get things done, work hard.

# 35

# How to Find What You Need in the Bible

### *God's Library*

"How about if we go to early church all summer and then come home?" Henry suggested to his mom. He was thinking of all the things he could do on the long summer Sundays.

"Well, Henry," Mom answered, "going to early church is fine with me, but we won't be coming right home afterward."

Henry wasn't surprised by Mom's response—she was a firm believer in attending Sunday school. "Oh, Mom," Henry grumbled, "summer and Sunday school just don't go together."

"I agree," said Mom. "No Sunday school for you this summer."

Now that response *did* surprise Henry. He could hardly believe his ears! Then Mom went on. "There's a Junior Bible Class this summer, and Mr. Wilkens is teaching it. It will be just right for you."

Mr. Wilkens was a favorite teacher with the kids. His classes were interesting, and he made learning fun. After everyone was settled on the first Sunday, he said, "We're going to visit and explore the greatest, most important library in the world this summer. You will get to know it very well and be able to find all kinds of things in it. Do you know where it is?"

The kids looked at each other and shrugged their shoulders. Surely, Mr. Wilkens wasn't talking about the town library—it was far from great and important.

Then Mr. Wilkens held up a Bible. "This is it, right here," he said. "The Bible is God's library of books. There are only sixty-six books in this library, but they can help us know about God and his plan for our life. The Bible has verses that help us when we're sick, sad, or worried. It also has great songs and prayers. And, of course, it tells us all about the good news of salvation. Now let's see how well you know your way around God's library."

Mr. Wilkens distributed Bibles to those who needed them. Then he wrote a Bible reference on the chalkboard and challenged everyone to find it in less than a minute. Only Emily succeeded. Henry was still frantically searching for it when Emily started reading.

"To help find what you need in the Bible, you need to learn the books of the Bible," Mr. Wilkens said. "There's also a list of the books and page numbers in the front of most Bibles. That list tells you where each book begins, but you still need to know the order of the books."

The kids read through the list of Bible books several times. Then Mr. Wilkens taught them a song about the books of the Bible. They practiced looking up more verses, and Henry actually found one in less than a minute.

*Wow! I'm learning how to find things in this library,* he thought. He couldn't wait to challenge Mom to a book-finding contest.

### Questions

- What did Henry think about summer Sunday school?
- How did Mr. Wilkens's class differ from a typical Sunday school class?
- How is the Bible like a library?
- What can you find in God's library?

### Bible Discovery

Read these Bible verses: Colossians 3:16; 2 Timothy 3:16; Hebrews 4:12.

### Bible Point

The Bible is God's inspired word given to us to teach and counsel us in how to live God's ways. It's hard to play a game without knowing the rules or to build something without having the directions. In the same way, it's difficult to find things in the Bible if you don't know the location of the books. As a family, take turns naming a book of the Bible. Then see how quickly it can be found.

### Bottom Line

The first step in finding what you need in the Bible is learning the books of the Bible.

### *Addresses*

During the week, Henry and Mom took turns seeing who could find selected books in the Bible the fastest. By the next Sunday, Henry felt more confident about knowing the books. He still couldn't say all of them in order, but he knew that Exodus was toward the front of the Bible and Romans was toward the back.

After the opening prayer, Mr. Wilkens asked, "If you go into any library, the books are divided into two main categories. What are they?" With a lot of guessing and help from the teacher, the kids finally came up with the correct answer: fiction and nonfiction.

"The Bible has two main categories, too," Mr. Wilkens said. "They're not fiction and nonfiction because everything in the Bible is true—nonfiction. The two parts of the Bible are the Old Testament and the New Testament. The Old Testament tells about things that happened before Jesus was born. The New Testament tells about Jesus' life and the early church."

The class found the two parts in their Bibles and in the table of contents in the front. Then Mr. Wilkens wrote the names of ten Bible books on the chalkboard and had the students write down whether the books were from the Old or New Testament. While the kids were working, he said, "I am inviting all of you to come to my house for ice cream and cake next Saturday." Lots of smiles and clapping greeted this announcement.

Mr. Wilkens continued. "I live in Prescott. See you about three." Prescott was the neighboring town about five miles down Highway 10.

"Prescott's a pretty big town," Henry said. "How can we find your house? We need the rest of your address."

Mr. Wilkens smiled and said, "Aha! You're right. It would be pretty hard to find me without a house number and street. Not to worry! I'll give you all the details before you go home.

"Finding something in the Bible is sort of like finding a house in a city," Mr. Wilkens said. "If you know only the name of the Bible book where a verse is from, it's pretty hard to find it. You need to know the rest of the reference. I like to call it the Bible address. The name of the book is like the city; the first number is the chapter—like the street. The last number is the verse—like the house number. In order to find what you need in the Bible, you need to know its address."

The kids practiced finding familiar Bible verses for the rest of the time.

Mr. Wilkens was at the door as the kids left. He handed each one an invitation to his house. It had the *whole* address on it and even a map. No one was going to get lost looking for that ice cream and cake!

Questions

- How did Henry's mother help him practice learning the books of the Bible?
- What are the two main parts of the Bible?
- What three things do you need to know to find something in the Bible?

Bible Discovery

Read these Bible verses: Acts 17:11; Romans 15:4; 2 Timothy 3:15.

Bible Point

The Bible contains God's truth and his promises to us. Knowing the Bible "address" of stories and verses helps you find them.

Bottom Line

You can find what you need in the Bible by knowing its Bible "address."

## *Treasure Hunt*

When Henry arrived for Junior Bible Class the next Sunday, Mr. Wilkens was nowhere to be found. What he *did* find was a huge sign made to look like a treasure map. On one corner was a picture of a tree with this message: "Meet us at the tall, old oak tree next to the parking lot. If you want to find the treasure, be there by 9:30."

"Rats!" Henry said to himself. "Hope I make it." Henry was running late—it was already 9:30. So he scurried down the hall, out the door, and around the corner to the parking lot. And there they were—Mr. Wilkens and the rest of the kids. Henry tried to catch his breath as he plopped down on the grass under the tree.

"Hi, Henry," Mr. Wilkens greeted him. "We're going on a treasure hunt this morning."

Mr. Wilkens divided the class into two teams and gave each team their first clue. Each team had different clues and took different routes. They followed all their clues until they came to the treasure. The treasure was hard candies and folded pieces of paper. Mr. Wilkens directed them to each take one piece of paper but not unfold it until they were back in the classroom.

After they all trooped back into the classroom and settled down, Mr. Wilkens told them to unfold their papers. Mumblings of "What?" "I don't get it." and "What are Philistines?" floated around the room. Henry's piece of paper contained the word *truth.*

Mr. Wilkens said, "You seem a bit confused, so let me explain. Each of you has a word that can be found in the Bible. I want you to see how many Bible verses you can find with your word in it."

"This seems like mission impossible," Henry said to Mr. Wilkens.

"It might seem that way, but it's not," answered Mr. Wilkens. "Even if you know only one word of a Bible verse, you'll be able to find it. It's a kind of treasure hunt—only we use a concordance instead of clues. We can find what we need in the Bible by using a concordance."

Then Mr. Wilkens went on. "A concordance is sort of like a dictionary without definitions. It lists words alphabetically and tells where to find verses with the selected word in them." Then Mr. Wilkens showed the kids where to find the concordance in their own Bible. He also showed them how to use a large concordance.

Henry looked in the concordance for his word: *truth.* He was amazed at how many Bible verses had that word in them. "It seems that *truth* is a very popular Bible word," said Henry. "I could read one 'truth' verse each day for a year and still have some left over."

### Questions

- What was unusual about Junior Bible Class this Sunday?
- What is a concordance? Have you ever used one?
- How can using a concordance help us find what we need in the Bible?

### Bible Discovery

Read these Bible verses: Psalms 33:4-5; 119:105; Luke 11:28.

### Bible Point

Everything in the Bible is true. The Bible can light our way and teach us how to live. Sometimes finding a verse in the Bible is like a puzzle, because we may know only one or two words of it. That can be enough if you use a concordance to look up those words. Then the pieces suddenly fall into place.

### Bottom Line

You can find what you need in the Bible by using a concordance.

## *Customs and Curiosities*

"I'm glad Mr. Wilkens is having this Bible class," said Henry. "I'm learning about lots of things to use to find things in the Bible. I wonder what we'll do this Sunday."

"It probably will be interesting," said Mom.

And indeed it was! When Mr. Wilkens walked in, he looked as if he had stepped back in time several thousand years. He wore a knee-length robe with a wide belt around his waist. A long piece of cloth was wound like a turban around Mr. Wilkens's head. On his feet, he wore sandals.

"I'm dressed similar to a Bible-time man," Mr. Wilkens explained. He told why this clothing was so suitable for living in Israel. "It's very hot there, so loose clothing and sandals are cooler. The turban protects the head from the hot sun. In case of a sandstorm, one end can be unwound and wrapped around the nose and mouth," he said. "The most interesting piece of clothing is this belt called a girdle. It serves as pockets in which money, food, a dagger, or even a sword was carried."

"I always wondered why the people dressed like that," said Henry. "That's neat. How did you get so smart about this stuff?"

Mr. Wilkens laughed. "I'm not really that smart, but I know where I can find information about Bible-time customs and curiosities. You can find out about all kinds of things in the Bible by using Bible dictionaries and Bible history books. And it just so happens that I brought some with me today."

Mr. Wilkens gave each kid a subject to look up and tell the rest of the class about. Henry found out about Bible-time burials. He learned that the bodies were washed, rubbed with spices and perfumes, and then wrapped from head to toe in long strips of cloth. People were buried very soon after they died because of the heat and there was no embalming. The bodies were often buried in caves instead of in the ground. "That really helps me understand the story of Jesus' raising Lazarus from the dead," said-Henry.

Pam read about Palestinian homes, and Josh learned why big water pots always sat by the door. "Their feet got mighty dirty wearing sandals on the dusty roads," he said. "All the moms probably said, 'Wash those feet before you come in the house.'"

On the way home, Henry told Mom about food shopping in Bible times. "The women had to walk all over town, buying a different food at each stall," he explained. "And there were no price tags. What you paid was decided by how good you were at bargaining and how anxious the merchant was to sell his things."

"Well, we need milk and fruit," said Mom. "I'm glad I can get them both at one place. Wonder if the cashier will bargain on the price."

Questions

- What was the most interesting part of Mr. Wilkens's clothing?
- Have you ever dressed up as a Bible-time person?
- How can using a Bible dictionary or a Bible history book help when you read the Bible?

Bible Discovery

Read these Bible verses: Genesis 29:26; John 19:40; Romans 15:4.

Bible Point

The Bible often informs us about Bible-time customs; some may seem strange or even weird to us today. But when we learn more about Bible times, we can better understand some of Jesus' teachings.

Bottom Line

You can find what you need in the Bible by using Bible dictionaries and Bible histories.

## *Important Stuff*

It was the last Sunday of the Junior Bible Class, and the kids were sorry to see it end. They had learned lots of great tips on how to find what they need in the Bible. Mr. Wilkens had also made them aware of other resources such as concordances, maps, charts, Bible dictionaries, and Bible history books. Using these resources would make Bible reading more real and understandable.

When all the kids had arrived and were settled in, Mr. Wilkens asked, "Why was the Bible written?"

"So we would know about important believers," said Sue.

"So we would have a history of the believers," guessed Frank.

"So we would know about Jesus and his life and teachings," suggested Henry.

"All of you are right, but no one is completely right," said Mr.

Wilkens. "God had the Bible written so all people can know his plan of salvation—so we can learn about Jesus' death and resurrection. The Bible tells us that when we trust in Christ, our sins are forgiven, and we will live with him forever. The parts of the Bible that tell us how we can be saved are called the Gospels.

"There are also parts of the Bible that tell us how sinful we are and what we have to do to obey God. These are called the Law; the Ten Commandments are an important part of the Law."

"What about teachings like the Lord's Prayer, the parables of Jesus, or the Old Testament stories?" asked Henry.

"They are all important and can teach us many things," Mr. Wilkens said. "Many of those stories have law or gospel in them too. How would you find these teachings or stories when you need them?"

Some kids thought they would use the concordance, and others thought they could memorize where they were found. Cherie suggested making a list of the references to keep in her Bible.

"Excellent idea!" said Mr. Wilkens. "That way it's always available and can be used easily and quickly. A good way to find what you need in the Bible is to make a list of where some important stories and teachings are found."

Mr. Wilkens and the class found the Bible references for the Ten Commandments, the Lord's Prayer, and the story of Jesus' death and resurrection. They also found other gospel passages, favorite parables, and some well-known Old Testament stories. Mr. Wilkens listed all the references on the chalkboard, and the kids copied them on paper to put in their Bibles.

As they left, Mr. Wilkens reminded them, "You own the greatest, most important, library anywhere. Check out its books often. They make for good reading."

### Questions

- Why was the Bible written?
- What does the Law do?
- What is the gospel?
- How can making a list of where some important stories and teachings are found be helpful?

### Bible Discovery

Read these Bible verses: Exodus 20:1-17; John 3:16; Romans 5:8; 2 Timothy 3:15.

### Bible Point

The Bible shows us how to be saved. Knowing where some of the main teachings and stories of the Bible are found can be very helpful. We can read the Ten Commandments and know how sinful we are. Then we can turn to verses and stories that tell us of God's love and forgiveness; that's the good news of salvation.

### Bottom Line

You can find what you need in the Bible by making a list of where some important stories and teachings are found.

# 36
# How to Know What You Believe

### *All in the Family*

Terri's mom had been finding out the history of their family called a genealogy. She knew where their ancestors moved from, who married whom, and even when they settled in the state Terri lived in. So Terri was prepared when her youth group leader, Ginny, asked the group to do their religious genealogies. She wanted each young person to trace back three generations on each side of the family. Did their ancestors go to church? Were they part of a certain denomination?

The kids had two weeks to do this. They were to talk with their parents and grandparents, if possible. If their parents didn't attend church, that was OK. The kids still needed to trace back and see what their family's religious history was like.

For Terri that was pretty easy. Her dad's father had been a preacher, as had his father before him. Her mom's father wasn't a preacher, but she had gone to church with him and Grandma a lot. Terri was surprised to discover that her mother's grandparents didn't go to church at all.

Terri finished gathering all her information the night before the deadline. She had made some notes and took them with her to youth group.

Terri was amazed by all the different stories. Some of the kids were the first ones in three generations of their families to even go to church. They were the exceptions, however. Most of the kids had somebody in each generation who had been pretty active in church. Many were still in the same denomination.

Ginny said, "We learn the most about what we believe from our family. As we grow up we decide if we are going to keep those beliefs or change them. So the first step to understanding your own belief system is to understand the belief system of your family."

Terri asked, "Why is it that some kids do exactly what their parents did and some don't?"

"That's a good question," answered Ginny, "and there are probably a lot of answers. Let's ask somebody who is in that situation. Tammy, you come to church here, but you said that no one for two generations back in your family ever went to church. Why didn't you do what they did?"

Tammy answered, "I guess because somebody asked me to go to church. Maybe no one ever asked them. Also, I saw that my parents have nothing to trust in when things go wrong. They get really stressed out and unhappy. The people I met here at church get stressed, but they trust that God will help them."

"Great answers," said Ginny. "Sometimes we change our beliefs because of opportunity. Someone introduces us to another way. Sometimes it's because we see what faith does in the lives of other people, and we come to see things differently. But one way or another, we'll always see a little of our parents' influences. So it is helpful for us to know what our parents believe."

### Questions

- Does Terri's family go to church?
- How do parents show kids what they believe?
- How do parents influence their children spiritually?

### Bible Discovery

Read these verses: Deuteronomy 4:9-10; Joshua 24:15; Proverbs 1:8; Acts 16:31-34.

### Bible Point

Families often have very similar beliefs because they have similar experiences. God tells parents to teach their children and grandchildren about their belief in God. You may not always believe exactly as your parents do, but the first step to knowing your own beliefs is understanding what your family believes.

### Bottom Line

To know what you believe, understand what your family believes; then let God lead you as you grow in your faith.

### *Teacher God*

Anthony was in Terri's youth group. He had been there last week when they discussed the spiritual heritage of their families. Anthony had gone home depressed.

Anthony's family didn't seem to believe much of anything. He had started going to church because a bus had come through his neighborhood a few years ago, and the driver had given the kids candy. Now everyone was asking him questions about what he believed about God. If he were honest, he would have to say that he just wasn't sure.

Ginny, the youth leader, had noticed that Anthony had seemed down. She called Anthony and asked him to shoot baskets that evening at the park. Anthony was always up for basketball.

After a couple of games of "horse," Anthony decided to tell Ginny how he felt. "My parents don't believe anything. How am I supposed to figure it out? Most of the other kids in our group have one person in the family to talk to about God, but I don't have anybody. I'm afraid I'll never really understand this church stuff."

"I think you're forgetting one thing," Ginny responded. "You have God on your side. When you accepted Christ as your personal Savior last summer at camp, you began a relationship with him. He certainly wants you to know and understand him better. He will help you."

"How will he help me? How can God talk to me and help me?" Anthony asked.

"Through his Word, for one thing," answered Ginny. "But even before that, just praying and asking God to teach you what to believe will strengthen your faith. Just the act of believing in him enough to talk to him will help. Then you learn even more of what to believe about him—that he's here and wants to help you. Those are two great truths to believe in."

They continued to shoot baskets, so Anthony could think about what Ginny had said. Finally Anthony asked, "So you're saying that I can ask God what to believe about God? Will that really work?"

"I'm saying that you can ask God to help you with anything that concerns you," Ginny answered. "If knowing what to believe concerns you, then yes, ask him to help you with it." With that, Ginny swished a shot from half-court.

That night Anthony asked God for help in figuring out what he believed and how those beliefs should affect his life. Anthony also remembered to thank God for the good things in his life, for his friends at church, and for parents who cared about him even though they didn't know a lot about faith. He prayed for his parents, too, that God would help them in their lives.

Questions

- What is faith?
- What was bothering Anthony?
- What do you believe about God?

Bible Discovery

Read these verses: Exodus 33:12-13; Psalms 25:4-5; 86:11; 119:66-68.

Bible Point

People of faith trust God for everything. They trust him to help them make decisions, and they trust him to teach them how to believe. Moses did. David did. You need to also. Ask God to teach you about himself and about what you should believe about him.

Bottom Line

To know what you believe about God and life, don't forget to ask God himself for help.

## *Study, Study, Study*

In a few weeks it would be Youth Sunday at Pam's church. The youth would teach Sunday school classes, take up the offering, and lead in prayer in the worship service.

Pam's assignment was to teach an *adult* class, Mrs. Wright's class. Pam was rather nervous because she knew Mrs. Wright was a great teacher. So Pam called Mrs. Wright and asked if she would help her study. They made plans to study together on a Thursday night. Pam's mom dropped her off at Mrs. Wright's house and said she would come back in a couple of hours.

Mrs. Wright had a special room where she studied for her lessons. When her husband was alive, it had been his study. She used it because it had a lot of bookshelves. She had already pulled several books off the shelves so she and Pam could use them easily.

"You use all this to study the Bible?" Pam asked.

"Oh yes," said Mrs. Wright. "There are so many good Bible-study helps these days, and I try to use as many of them as possible. How do you study the Bible, Pam?"

"Well, I just read it, and if there is a word I don't know, I look it up in the back of the Bible," Pam answered.

"What if it's not listed in the back of the Bible?" Mrs. Wright asked.

"I guess I just figure that I'll learn it later," answered Pam with a smile.

"Let me show you a few tricks. Let's look over the lesson that you will teach," said Mrs. Wright. Then she and Pam read through the Scripture for that week. Next they made a list of the parts that Pam didn't understand. They used the Bible dictionary to look up objects and words from the Bible that Pam didn't know about. They used the Bible handbook to tell them who wrote that Scripture and why it was written. They picked out a word that described what that passage was about. Their word was *grace*. Then they used a big concordance (a lot bigger than the one in the back of Pam's Bible) to look up verses with that same word.

When Pam went home that night she knew *much* more than when she had come. She thanked Mrs. Wright. She also borrowed a couple of books from her so she could study some more.

"Remember, Pam," Mrs. Wright had said, "as you read the Word of God, ask yourself, Why did God say that? and What does that mean for my life today? After answering those questions, you will be ready to obey God. You will also be ready to teach. Teaching is helping other people discover those answers too."

### Questions

- What does it mean to study the Bible?
- Why is Bible study important?
- What tools can help us in Bible study?

### Bible Discovery

Read these verses: Ezra 7:10; Psalm 119:27; Hebrews 4:12.

### Bible Point

God communicates through his Word, so we need to read and study it like Ezra and the psalmist did. When we study, we pull out all the truths in that story—truths about God's love and what he wants to do with our lives. We ask questions about what we are reading and how he wants us to live, and then we find the answers to those questions.

Bottom Line

To know what you believe, study the Bible, asking God to teach you his truth. Using modern Bible-study tools can also be helpful.

## *Honestly*

Cal didn't like going to Sunday school. He dreaded it every week. He didn't think he believed the same things as the other kids in his class, but he didn't feel that he could be honest with them about that. What would they think? Would they kick him out? Would they dislike him? Because he never talked honestly, he didn't enjoy it or get any of his questions answered.

One Sunday afternoon the teacher, Mr. Lewis, invited the whole class out to the lake for a cookout. Cal wasn't sure he would like this any better than Sunday school, but he heard that Mr. Lewis had a boat, and he loved boats, so he went. On the way up in the van, Cal sat beside Frank. They went to the same school, so they talked about sports and classes.

"I've never heard you talk this much, Cal," Frank said. "Why don't you ever talk during Sunday school? I figured you were shy or something, but you don't seem shy now."

"I'm not really shy," Cal said. Then he just dropped the subject.

After the cookout, Cal and Frank were floating in the water, waiting for their turn to ski.

Frank asked again, "So why *don't* you talk much in Sunday school?"

Cal was so relaxed floating in the water with the sun on his face. Maybe that's why it was easier to be honest. He said, "What if I don't believe the same thing the rest of you do? What will happen then? That's why I don't say much. You all seem so sure of what you believe, but I'm not. I don't want to get kicked out or anything."

"Kicked out! Kicked out?" Frank started laughing and doing flips in the water. "Cal, nobody gets kicked out of Sunday school. You don't have to worry about that."

"But all you guys' parents bring you to church," Cal replied. "I just come with my grandma. I don't know as much about the whole Christian thing as you do."

Frank had stopped doing flips now. He wanted to help Cal feel better about this. He said, "We don't know as much as you think,

Cal. When you get to know us better, you'll find that out. Besides, if you never talk about stuff, you'll never know what you believe because it'll all be in your head. If you talk about it, we can give our ideas, and Mr. Lewis can help us figure it out.

"I tell you what, Cal. Anytime you come up with a question you don't want to ask in class, just tell me. I'll write it on a note and give it to Mr. Lewis. If I do that, will you be brave enough to join the discussion when we discuss it?"

Cal knew that he had made a friend. He promised Frank that he would join in. And he felt so relieved to know that he couldn't get kicked out of Sunday school because he was starting to like it more already.

Questions

- Why wouldn't Cal talk in Sunday school?
- How did Frank help him feel better?
- How can being honest help a person know what to believe?
- What things do you hear at church that you aren't sure you believe in?

Bible Discovery

Read these verses: Mark 9:23-24; Romans 4:18-25.

Bible Point

Pretending to believe is not the same as believing. God will help us with our doubts and questions. We'll never find answers to our questions unless we open up and ask the questions. To find answers about our faith, we should be honest with God and with those who can point us to the truth.

Bottom Line

To know what you believe, be honest about your questions and doubts.

## *Making a Statement*

In the worship services at Randy's church, the congregation would say specific prayers and readings together. Some of the prayers and readings were in the bulletin. Some were in the hymnal. Some people looked at the words, and some didn't even have to open a book because they knew the words by heart.

Randy attended special classes on the beliefs of the church on

Sunday nights for one month. The teacher explained the church's beliefs and the meanings of each of the prayers and readings. One of the readings was called a Statement of Faith.

The teacher said, "A statement of faith is just a set of sentences that state our basic beliefs. We use this one as a church, but you can make your own statement of faith."

After discussing a sentence in the church's Statement of Faith, the teacher had each person in the class put that belief in his or her own words. Eventually each person would have a personal statement of faith. The teacher said that each morning they should look in the mirror and say their statement of faith to remind them to follow God that day.

Randy worked hard on his statement. He liked the one his church used, but he also liked the idea of having his very own. When all the class was finished, they sat in a circle and read their statements. This was Randy's:

- I believe that God created me and loves me.
- I believe that Jesus lived on earth and died for my sins. I believe he arose from the dead.
- I believe that God helps me through the Holy Spirit, who came when Jesus went to heaven.
- I believe that God wants me to read and obey his Word.
- I believe that I will live forever with God in heaven because I have trusted in Christ as my Savior.

Randy felt good knowing that he could say the things he believed. When he got home, he read his statement to his parents. His mom asked if he wanted her to print it out on the computer and frame it. That way he could keep it by the mirror in the bathroom, but it wouldn't get all wet. Randy thought that was a good idea.

By the next week, Randy had his statement memorized. As the class began, the teacher asked how many could say their statement of faith by heart. Several raised their hands including Randy.

Then the teacher said, "As you grow, you may want to add to your statement. You might learn truths that are so important to your faith that you want to make them part of your statement. That's OK. Just always remember to use your faith to worship and serve God and to help other people. That is what our faith is meant to do."

### Questions

- What is a statement of faith?
- Why did Randy write his own?
- What beliefs would you put in your own statement of faith?

### Bible Discovery

Read these verses: John 6:68-69; Acts 15:11; Romans 6:8-10; 1 Thessalonians 4:14.

### Bible Point

These verses are statements of faith. It's important to know your own statement of faith, to state in a few sentences your beliefs about God's existence and Jesus' death and resurrection. Write out your own statement of faith and memorize it.

### Bottom Line

To know what you believe, write a personal statement of faith.

# 37

# How to Be a Success in Life

### *Eyes on the Prize*

Ben had made the basketball team. *Thank you, Lord,* he silently prayed as he walked into the gym for the first team practice. He and the other boys took some shots until they heard the sound of a whistle.

"Listen up, guys," said the man with the clipboard and whistle. "I'm Mr. Peterson, coach of the eighth-grade team. Congratulations on making the squad."

The boys nodded and looked around at each other with satisfied smiles.

"You've made the team, but that's only the beginning," the coach explained. "If your only goal was to get on the team to be popular—well, there's the exit door." Nobody moved a muscle. "Each of you should have personal goals for improving your game, and we will have goals as a team. Now let's see what you can do." Then the coach guided the team through a layup drill.

A few hours later, Ben was wolfing down dinner with his family. "Whoa, there," said his mother. "Slow down a bit and tell us about your first practice. Did you work hard? Will you have a good team? How did you do?"

Ben swallowed and then smiled. "That's a lot of questions. Well, practice was good. Coach Peterson said something kind of surprising, though, something about goals. He said that each player should have personal goals and that we would have goals as a team. I got the feeling he didn't just mean winning games."

His father commented, "It's easy to think that playing sports only has to do with the final score when the buzzer sounds, with winning and losing. But remember when you were working on your free throws before you tried out for the team? That was a goal. You decided that you would improve and eventually make ten out of ten. And you achieved that goal."

"Having goals to work toward is part of life," his mother added. "It's like that saying 'Keep your eyes on the prize.' The heroes and leaders of the Bible did the same to achieve success in God's eyes."

Ben took another bite of mashed potatoes and then said, "Hmmm. Now that I'm a free-throw expert, I'll have to find another goal."

"You might practice throwing your dirty socks *into* the hamper this week," his mother said with a smile.

### Questions

- How do goals help people succeed?
- What basketball goals might Ben work toward?
- What life goals do you think Ben's mother might be remembering from the Bible heroes she mentioned?
- What important goal do you have?
- How difficult is it for you to "keep your eyes on the prize"?

### Bible Discovery

Read these Bible verses: Genesis 6:11-22; Matthew 16:21; Philippians 3:12-14; 1 Timothy 6:11-16.

### Bible Point

The men and women of the Bible who achieved success in God's eyes had goals and worked toward them. Jesus set his eyes toward Jerusalem to fulfill God's purposes for him. Paul focused on becoming the man of God he was meant to be. We must also keep our eyes on God's prize for us.

### Bottom Line

To be a success in life, set and work toward goals.

## *Smart and Hard*

Daniel and Dennis were preacher's kids. Other than that they were just like any other kids. They got an allowance, and sometimes they worked a little extra around the house for some extra money. Their chores were probably a little different from what other kids their age had to do. For instance, they would help fold and stuff bulletins for the Sunday morning services. Their dad never had time because he was preparing his sermons. Mom never had time because she was cooking supper and doing the wash. So Daniel and Dennis took on the task.

Their dad said that he would pay a penny for each bulletin they folded and stuffed with the announcements. He gave them each a stack, and off they would go. Although Dennis was younger than Daniel, he would always finish first and do the most. *Every time!* Daniel could never figure out why, because he was working as hard as he could.

Dad also wondered how Dennis always stuffed more bulletins. One day he called the boys in and had them stuff and fold the bulletins in his office. He put them back to back and let them go at it. Soon he realized that while both boys worked just as hard and both boys worked just as long, Dennis worked smarter. Daniel would pick up each bulletin, fold it, place each piece of paper in it, and then put it in another pile. But Dennis would fold and stack all the bulletins first. Then he would pick up the papers, open the bulletin with one hand, and stuff in the papers one at a time, moving the bulletins to a new stack as he went. That may seem like a small difference, but it really saved time. Dennis was like a stuffing/folding machine. Daniel was like a huffing/puffing little boy.

That day, Dad and the older son learned from the younger son. They all finished stuffing the bulletins together and went out for ice cream. While they were slurping up their sodas, Dad explained that he hoped they would always try to work *smart* as well as *hard*. That way they would get ahead. He also hoped that the next time Dennis found a great way to do something, he would share it with Daniel.

### Questions

- What is the difference between working smart and working hard?
- Why is it important to work smart as well as hard?
- Why was Dennis's way smarter?
- When do you work smart?

### Bible Discovery

Read these verses: Joshua 1:7-8; 1 Samuel 18:5, 12-16; Ecclesiastes 9:10.

### Bible Point

Many people in the Bible worked diligently to find success. Two of the most successful were Joshua and David. They took their responsibilities seriously and worked smart as well as hard. They did everything they were supposed to do, and they did it in the smartest way possible. God blessed their efforts. If you work smart and hard, God will bless your efforts too.

Bottom Line

To be a success in life, learn to work smart *and* hard.

### *Go, Team, Go!*

"I am so tired of working on a team!" said Bart. "In every class and on every project, we have to do things with a team. It takes twice as long, is three times as frustrating, and turns out half as good as if I had done it myself. Why don't they just let us do our own work?"

Bart said all this as he walked through the kitchen, threw down his books, and headed up to his room. His mom heard him, but she was too busy to respond right then. She waited until Bart came back down for supper.

"What new team are you on?" she asked.

"It's a social studies project," answered Bart. "Each team will make up a city and a problem that city faces. Then we'll take another team's city, and, as city planners, we'll try and find a way to solve that problem. This would be so much more fun on our own."

Usually Bart's dad had to work late, but he happened to be home for supper that night. After hearing Bart complain about his project, he said, "I can see why they make you work on teams."

"Please tell me!" said Bart.

"Bart," Dad answered, "school is supposed to prepare you to be an adult. As an adult you will have a job, a career. In that career you probably won't sit in a room by yourself and solve a problem. Instead, you will work with people, each with his or her area of expertise. You will need to work together to solve a problem, finish a project, accomplish a task, or whatever. You will have to bring up issues that relate to your area of expertise, and they will speak for what they see from their areas of expertise. It isn't always pleasant, but it usually makes for a better solution. Our world is too complicated for a lone ranger to solve problems. Teamwork is vital."

Bart stared at this dad. "Are you telling me that my whole working life is going to be like school—teams working on projects?"

Dad smiled at Mom and replied, "Hey, even marriage and family involve teamwork. Just think of the mess we'd have here if Mom and I didn't work together." Turning back to Bart, he continued.

"If you're going to accomplish anything, Bart, you're going to have to handle projects of some kind or other. If you're going to find the best solutions you can, you must be able to work with a team of people who can lend some of their knowledge to the solution. Some days won't be any better than your teams in school. But when you find that solution and it really helps people instead of just earning you a grade, you'll like it a lot better."

Bart decided that it was a good thing that he was getting practice doing what he would need to do in his career. But he still thought he'd look for a job that had as few people on a team as possible.

Questions

- What is a team?
- Why didn't Bart like working on a team?
- In what ways does a family depend on good teamwork?
- What makes a good team member?
- What kind of a team member are you?

Bible Discovery

Read these Bible verses: 1 Chronicles 12:16-18; Esther 2:21-22; Philippians 2:3-4.

Bible Point

The Bible tells about heroes who worked with others to accomplish their goals. People like Esther, David, and Paul joined with others people in their efforts, and they changed the world. They knew that success meant depending on others and sharing the glory. That's an important part of being a success today.

Bottom Line

To be a success in life, learn to be a good team member.

### *First Things First*

Michelle had some choices to make. She was changing schools, and her new school had a lot more options in the classes she could take. She also had many extracurricular activities to choose from, probably too many. She needed to decide between year-round swim team and gymnastics. She also had an offer for a part-time job baby-sitting after school, but she didn't know if she could handle it with her schoolwork. These were just some of the decisions Michelle needed to make. Her life was suddenly becoming much more exciting but also much more stressful.

Michelle was having trouble sleeping. She wasn't eating well either. Michelle's mother had died a few years ago, so she decided to talk to Paula's mom about what she was going through.

"I've noticed that you seem preoccupied lately," Mrs. Grant said. "You *do* have a lot on your mind, don't you!" For the next few minutes Michelle explained her feelings of busyness and stress.

After Michelle had finished, Mrs. Grant said, "Michelle, you feel overwhelmed, and I'm not surprised. Let's make a list of the decisions that you need to make."

Michelle was surprised at how short the list was. She *felt* as though it probably would go on for pages. They reviewed the decisions one at a time. A few were easy, once Michelle saw them on paper, but most were still on the paper even after she had reviewed them.

"I'll tell you what," said Mrs. Grant. "You take one decision a day and commit that decision to the Lord. Ask him to make it plain what you should do. Pray about it from morning until evening. Then make the decision and trust him to lead you. By the end of the week you will have made the decisions, and you will have given God time to guide you. Allow him to lead you to make the right decisions. That's how the Bible says we are supposed to handle it anyway."

For the next seven days, Michelle prayed about one decision a day. Then she made that decision and moved on. She trusted God to somehow make it plain to her. It was much easier to think through the decisions one at a time instead of all of them at once.

The next week Mrs. Grant took Michelle and Paula out for lunch. Michelle filled them in on all the choices she had made, and they celebrated God's guidance in her life. "It's so much easier to make one decision at a time. And it's so much more pleasant to make a decision when you've given God time to guide you. I hope I remember that with all my decisions!"

"Just call us," said Mrs. Grant. "We'll remind you."

### Questions

- Why was Michelle worried?
- In what ways can decisions be scary to make?
- How can making one decision a day help relieve stress?
- What can you do to determine God's guidance?
- About what decisions are you worried?

Bible Discovery

Read these verses: Psalm 118:24-25; Proverbs 3:5-7; 16:3.

Bible Point

Scripture reminds us over and over to ask for God's guidance *before* we make big decisions. We need to trust God's plan for us. We need to commit all our work and activities to him and seek to know that we are living the way he wants us to. Then we will find success.

Bottom Line

To be a success in life, commit all your ways to God, trust him, and walk in his paths.

## *Learn to Learn*

Larry felt horrible. He had one of the main roles in the school play. Last night he forgot his lines not once, not twice, but three times. The other cast members were irritated with him, and it was the one night that both sets of his grandparents had come. How humiliating!

He went to Mr. Keye, the drama teacher, and asked if the understudy could go on for him.

"Larry, why in the world would you want to have your understudy replace you after you have worked so hard?" asked Mr. Keye with a bit of alarm.

"Because I messed up," Larry answered. "You don't need someone who is going to forget the lines. That messes everyone up."

Mr. Keye took off his glasses. "Let's talk about a few things, young man."

*Oh no,* thought Larry, *this is going to take awhile.*

"First of all," Mr. Keye began, "you feel like a failure, but you did not fail. It's true that you didn't have the best of nights. So let's talk about why that happened."

"I thought I knew the lines," explained Larry, "but I got distracted by all the guys waiting backstage to move the scenery."

"Well then, let's talk about some ways we can keep that from happening again," Mr. Keye responded.

"Mr. Keye, if I could keep it from happening, I would have last night . . . ," Larry began, but he could tell that his answer was unacceptable. Mr. Keye kept waiting. "Well," Larry continued, "I guess I could put cue cards on the desks. The desks are out on the stage each time I am."

"OK, what else?" Mr. Keye asked.

"I could turn more toward the audience so I wouldn't notice all the guys backstage."

"Yes, and let me add that you can make a greater effort to concentrate when you are up there. You have to concentrate on *your* job only. You cannot afford to think about what everyone else has to do, like the tech crew. Concentration is just as important in being an actor as the acting. Tonight, Larry, I expect that you will go on and may even make a mistake or two."

"Oh, great," Larry said, "even you don't even believe I can do it."

"Yes, I do believe you can do it. But it's not important to me that you do everything perfectly. It is important, however, that you learn to keep your wits about you on stage rather than run away because you are afraid of failing. Here are some cards. Go make a few notes, OK?"

Larry hated to admit it, but Mr. Keye was right. Instead of feeling bad, he just needed to figure out how to do a better job. Larry made his cue cards.

That night everything went great.

### Questions

- How did Larry feel about the first night of the play?
- How had he failed?
- What can be learned from failure?
- When did you fail?
- How could you learn from failure?

### Bible Discovery

Read these verses: Job 6:11-13; Proverbs 15:22; 16:20; Hebrews 12:3.

### Bible Point

Many people who followed God failed sometime in their life. Solomon, who wrote many of the proverbs, failed. Even King David did too. But each of these people learned from failure. They learned not to repeat the same mistakes. They used their failures to better equip them for success.

### Bottom Line

To be a success in life, learn from your failures.

# 38 How to Deal with a Crisis

***Positively!***

"Class, today we're going to talk about disappointment. We all experience disappointment in different ways. Let's list some of those ways on the board," said Mrs. Thompson.

Students began shouting out various ideas: "Parents splitting up," one said. "Losing a game," piped another. "Being cut from the team." "Bad grades." The list went on and on. Soon the board was filled with many very hurtful disappointments.

Susan felt as though one of the phrases on the list was staring straight at her—*bad grades.* It seemed that no matter how hard she tried, she just couldn't understand math. Last semester she got a D. This semester didn't seem any better.

Just then, Mrs. Thompson interrupted Susan's thoughts. "This is a pretty discouraging list, all right. But now I want you to come up with encouraging phrases that help you meet these disappointments head-on. For example, you could say about peer pressure, 'I won't let pressures press me out of shape.' Or if you lose a game, 'I won't let defeat defeat me.'"

The class began to catch on as students put together clever positive phrases that dealt with each disappointment. Susan even caught herself suggesting: "I won't let struggles strangle me."

Mrs. Thompson explained, "Having a positive attitude and a catchy phrase won't solve our problems, but it will help us deal with them. This is the first step in dealing with heartache, disappointment, and loss."

Then Mrs. Thompson pulled out a volleyball from behind her desk (it looked inflated but really wasn't). She said, "A lot of people are like this ball. They look great on the outside. But when problems come—" she paused and dropped the ball, and it went *plop* on the floor—"these people fall flat. They don't have what it takes to bounce back. Instead, they should be like this." She brought out another volleyball, this one inflated, and continued. "When troubles hit, these people may be knocked down." She paused, dropped the ball, and caught it. Then she continued, "But they bounce back.

"That's my goal for you. I want each of you to be the kind of person who can take it when things fall apart."

Susan understood. She knew that she had a lot of work to do in math, but she wasn't going to give up. She would maintain a positive attitude and not give up.

#### Questions

- What disappointments would you have suggested for Mrs. Thompson's list?
- What's your definition of positive thinking?
- Why is a person's attitude so important?
- What phrase can you come up with to help you through a disappointment that you listed in question one?

#### Bible Discovery

Read these Bible verses: John 16:33; 2 Corinthians 4:8-9; Philippians 4:8, 13.

#### Bible Point

Problems can overcome us, or we can overcome them. God never abondons us in our troubles. He will help us maintain a positive attitude.

#### Bottom Line

When faced with a crisis, maintain a positive attitude.

### *The Move*

"Lunch is over! Please report to your next class." The crackling voice of the school secretary droned through the lunchroom speakers as students scrambled to clear away their lunches. Jaimie shoved the rest of his chips and an empty plastic bag into his pop bottle, making room at the last minute for a wadded-up napkin to top off his "work of art." He tossed the bottle creation into his lunch bag, shoved the whole thing into his backpack, and walked out of the cafeteria into the bright sunlight.

He wondered how the day could seem so bright and cheery when inside he felt so gloomy. Last week his parents had announced the bad news: Their family was officially moving. For some time now, his parents had entertained the idea of moving out East, but Jaimie hadn't taken it seriously. *No way,* he thought, *we'll never really move.*

Jaimie's younger sisters had been bawling about the possibility from day one, but he had said and felt nothing. The very idea of saying good-bye to his friends at school was more than he could stand. So even after the final decision had been announced, Jaimie pretended it wasn't true.

When Jaimie got home, he tossed his backpack into one of the seats in the dining room, went upstairs to his room, and popped in a CD. Hours later, Jaimie heard a knock on his door. "Come in," he shouted over the music. Jaimie's dad walked in, carrying Jaimie's backpack in one hand and turning down the stereo with the other. "Sorry, Dad," Jaimie offered. His father had warned him before about leaving his backpack around the house.

"Son, I want to show you something," he said.

*Uh-oh! Here comes the speech,* Jaimie thought. Instead of being upset, however, Jaimie's dad smirked and pulled out Jaimie's pop bottle with all the shoved-in leftovers from lunch.

"What does this look like to you?" his dad asked.

"A . . . a . . . bottle?" Jaimie answered.

His dad chuckled and said, "Well, yes. It is a bottle . . . but it reminds me of you in a way." Now Jaimie was really confused. "You see, Son, when something changes in our life, we can deal with it in one of two ways. We can work through our feelings of sadness and even anger, or we can try to keep our feelings bottled up inside. If we don't let our emotions out in healthy ways, we end up shoving them down inside us—just like you did with this bottle." He put the bottle down and continued. "Jaimie, I know the idea of moving upsets you. But if you're not honest about your emotions now, they'll end up hurting you more in the long run."

Jaimie looked at the tightly packed contents of the bottle. He knew what his dad was talking about. He had shoved his real feelings about the move down so deep it was hard to feel anything anymore. Jaimie began to tell his dad how he felt. At first, he expressed disappointment and then anger. Finally, he just sat there and cried.

All during this outburst, Jaimie's father looked at Jaimie and just listened. Then he gave Jaimie a big hug, and they cried together.

Although Jaimie still didn't want to move, he felt much more at peace having expressed his emotions. Jaimie was glad his father had showed him that it's necessary to express our feelings.

Questions

- Why did Jaimie keep his true feelings inside at first?
- What did Jaimie's father encourage him to do?
- Why was Jaimie's bottle a good illustration of his feelings?
- What made Jaimie feel better?
- What advice would you give to a friend about expressing emotions?

Bible Discovery

Read these Bible verses: Psalm 56:8; Matthew 5:4; John 11:35.

Bible Point

Emotions are not right or wrong; they just are. God created emotions, and he knows our every feeling. What we do with our emotions, however, can make a big difference in our life. Instead of bottling up feelings of grief, fear, anger, sorrow, etc., we need to recognize them, express them, and deal honestly with them. Bottled feelings can cause all sorts of physical, psychological, and social problems. God wants us to be in touch with our feelings instead of shoving them deep inside.

Bottom Line

When faced with a crisis, stay in touch with your feelings and express them—they're God's gift to you.

## *The Tryout*

"Good luck!" Marsha called to Kim as they passed each other in the hall. Today Kim would find out the results of last week's tryouts for the cheerleading squad at school. The competition was tough—two dozen girls were competing for the same ten openings on the squad. *I've just got to make it,* Kim thought to herself as she made her way to the PE office to see the posted results. Her heart quickened as she spotted a crowd gathered around a list posted outside the office. Kim anxiously looked for her name on the list. Her name was not there—she didn't make it.

The rest of the day seemed like forever as she rehashed the list of names in her mind. *Why didn't I make it? It's not fair,* she thought repeatedly all day, but she told no one.

When Kim got home, she went straight for the kitchen, breezing past her mother in the hallway. "How was your—" her mother began. But Kim was already in the kitchen before her mom could finish her question.

Grabbing a soda and a bag of chips, Kim solemnly trudged out of the kitchen and plopped down on the floor in front of the TV. "What's wrong, honey?" her mom gingerly pressed.

"Nothing," Kim grunted. Inside, she desperately wanted to tell her mom about how she felt—rejected, foolish. But the words just wouldn't come—she was too proud to let anyone know how upset she was. Her dream of being a cheerleader was finished. Whom could she turn to? Who would understand?

Later that evening, Kim's mother came to her one last time before Kim went to sleep. "I can't help but think something is wrong," Mom began. "You know you can talk to me. Kim, sometimes we need help to get through a tough time. God doesn't want us to keep things inside when we're hurting. That's why he gave us parents and other people we can trust. Talking about our hurts helps us get through them."

Mom's urging was just the nudge that Kim needed. She poured out the feelings of hurt and anger that she had been trying to hide. Afterward, Mom assured Kim of her love, and they prayed together. Before leaving the room, Mom said that in the next day or two they could talk about other activities that Kim could get involved in.

Kim was so glad that she had talked to her mom about her disappointment. As painful as it was at the time, talking about it made Kim feel better.

### Questions

- How would you describe Kim's feelings after she discovered that she hadn't made the cheerleading squad?
- What do you usually do when you're hurting or disappointed?
- To whom would you talk about your problems? Why?
- Why is it good to stay in touch with others, to talk to someone about your concerns?

### Bible Discovery

Read these Bible verses: Psalm 94:19; 2 Corinthians 4:8-9; Matthew 26:38-39.

Bible Point

God wants us to turn to family and friends we trust so they can help us through tough times.

Bottom Line

When faced with a crisis, stay in touch with others. Talk with someone who knows you well and whom you trust.

## *Calling God—911*

"Great! Jessica leaves just when I need her the most!" said Jessica's best friend, Laura, as she angrily hung up the phone and put her chin on her folded hands. Laura had called Jessica to tell her she was having the "worst day" of her fourteen-year-old life. In between rings, Laura remembered that Jessica had left that morning for a family vacation.

The day had started with Laura's mom informing her that Stryper, her cat, had left a little accident that Laura would have to clean up. Then her little brother had sneaked into her room to play and had scratched her favorite CD. To top it off, Glen, the guy she had liked all year, finally called—only to ask for another girl's number.

"Who do I have to talk to now?" Laura said to herself. Frustrated, she rolled off her bed, went to the living room, and flopped onto the couch in front of the big-screen TV. After ten minutes of channel surfing that failed to drown her sorrow, she went back into her room. Blasting her next-favorite CD until her mother yelled for her to turn it down, Laura tried to get her previous conversation with Glen out of her mind. But it was no use. She even tried telling her woes to Stryper as the poor cat lazily basked in the sun. But that sure didn't help. Feeling more and more depressed, Laura slouched down in her chair in front of her desk and opened up the drawer. Maybe she would write some letters. Suddenly she spied a crumpled slip of paper shoved in the crack of her top desk drawer. "What's that?" Laura said.

"'Give your burdens to the Lord, and he will take care of you'" (Psalm 55:22) she read aloud. It was a memory verse from last year's Sunday school class. Laura felt a little embarrassed as she realized that she hadn't yet turned to God for help. She mustered up her strength and with a heavy heart began, "God? Are you there? I need somebody to talk to . . ."

Laura's problems tumbled out as she told God exactly how she was feeling. That timely verse reminded her that God is always available for her whenever she needs him. He takes no vacations. And his line is never busy.

Questions

- Why do you think Laura turned to God last instead of first?
- To whom do you turn first when you have a problem?
- When did prayer help you through a problem?
- Why does prayer make a difference?

Bible Discovery

Read these Bible verses: Psalm 55:22; Philippians 4:6-7.

Bible Point

Having a close relationship with God means that we can talk with him about anything. In fact, that's what prayer is all about—just talking with God. He wants us to turn to him in prayer, especially when we are hurting. He will give his peace and comfort.

Bottom Line

When faced with a crisis, stay in close touch with God.

## *The Plan*

In wrapping up youth group, Morgan, the youth leader, turned to James 1:2-4. Then she had a student read aloud: "'Dear brothers and sisters, whenever trouble comes your way, let it be an opportunity for joy. For when your faith is tested, your endurance has a chance to grow. So let it grow, for when your endurance is fully developed, you will be strong in character and ready for anything.'"

Next, she asked for suggestions from the group on what the passage was teaching.

Several kids voiced their opinions. "We should be happy when troubles come," said Julie. "Problems can help us grow," offered Walter. "Endurance means we can be ready for just about anything that comes our way," summarized Sally.

After the meeting Morgan noticed Heidi sitting off to the side, away from the rest of the group gathered around the refreshments. She walked over and pulled up a chair next to Heidi. "What's up?" she asked.

"Oh, nothing," answered Heidi. "I was just thinking about the verses in James and what everyone said."

They talked for a bit more, and suddenly Heidi burst out, "It's so easy for them to say 'we should be happy' and 'problems help us' and other stuff, but they don't have *real* problems." Then Heidi explained, sobbing, that her grandmother was dying of cancer, and she felt so terrible and powerless.

After talking with Heidi for a while and praying with her, Morgan set up a time for the two of them to talk more. She thanked Heidi for being honest with her feelings and for sharing them with her. Then she encouraged Heidi to keep in touch with God and to lay out a plan.

"What do you mean, a plan?" asked Heidi.

"I mean I want you to think about what's next. What are you going to do now? What is God going to teach you through all of this?" she answered. "God has something good in store for you, even in this very sad and scary time. It's your job to trust him and ask him to help you know what to do next. For instance, you can pray for your grandmother and take advantage of the time you have together."

"Thanks," Heidi said as she blew her nose. "You've given me some good ideas to think about. I know Grandma wouldn't want me to just sit around being sad!"

### Questions

- Why was Heidi so sad?
- What steps had Heidi already taken during her talk with Morgan?
- Why did Morgan encourage Heidi to ask "What's next?"
- Why is it important to lay out a plan when facing difficulties and trials?

### Bible Discovery

Read these Bible verses: Philippians 3:13-14; James 1:2-4.

### Bible Point

After adopting a positive attitude, staying in touch with our feelings, others, and God, the next step is to look for ways to take positive action, to lay out a plan. Instead of feeling sorry for ourselves and wallowing in the past or present troubles, we need to look to the future and what God has in store for us.

### Bottom Line

When faced with a crisis, lay out a plan, asking, "What's next?"

# 39

# How to Explain What You Believ

### *Lost and Found*

Jason and Scott have been best buddies since the first grade. They have shared a lot of good times together—camping out in the back-yard on hot summer nights, playing marathon baseball games, in-line skating all over town. They've also shared some tough times—the difficulty waiting to see what would happen after Jason's dad lost his job, the death of Scott's dog, the struggles of adjusting to middle school.

There have been more good times than bad—at least up until now. For weeks Scott has been acting really weird—moody, often angry at Jason for no particular reason, keeping to himself. Now Jason understands why. Yesterday, Scott told him that his parents are getting a divorce. Scott's dad already has moved out of th house, and his mom is thinking of moving back to her home-town about one hundred miles away. Jason still can't quite grasp what's happening, but it's clear that Scott really needs some help.

Jason has been thinking about this all week. How can he possibly help his friend? What can he say or do for Scott? Finally, Jason decides to find a quiet moment to ask his church's youth group leader, Mr. Nelson, after Sunday school. Mr. Nelson is a cool guy and is always available to listen.

After just about everyone has left the room, Jason grabs Mr. Nelson and quickly tells him about Scott. "What do you think I should do? It just seems like Scott is so lost. He really needs someone to guide him through this," Jason tells him.

Mr. Nelson looks at Jason and smiles. "You know, I think Scott already has a good friend who cares about him. But you're right, Scott needs someone more powerful, more wise, and even more loving to help him right now. Have you thought about introducing Scott to Jesus?"

"Well, I've invited Scott to youth group from time to time, but I know he doesn't think much about church stuff," Jason replies. "I guess what it comes down to is I really don't know how to talk to him about God."

"Well, let me share with you a new way to pray for your friend. Each letter reminds us of how we can pray. You already know the *P*—**P**eople whom you know who are lost and don't know the Lord. Right now, Scott is on your heart. But there probably are other friends at school who don't know Jesus." Jason nodded. Most of his friends at school were not believers.

"Start by praying for these people by name. Next comes *R*. Tell God the **R**eason why they need God in their lives. You already told me why Scott needs Jesus—to help him through this difficult time. Now tell God the *A*, or **A**nswer, you're seeking for Scott or what you want God to provide for him. It could be strength for Scott or comfort. Whatever it is, let God know.

"Now we come to *Y*. That stands for ***Y**ou*—what are you willing to do to help Scott? Maybe that will mean sharing a personal struggle you've had and how God helped guide you. Ask God to show you how to become more actively involved in Scott's life and to remind you to pray for Scott regularly," Mr. Nelson said. "And remember, God *wants* to establish a living friendship with Scott, even more than you do. He's in the business of searching for lost people, just like he found you and me."

Jason smiled. "*P-R-A-Y*. That's pretty basic when you think about it! Thanks, Mr. Nelson."

### Questions

- What five friends at school need to hear about Jesus?
- What are some ways God could use you to reach out to your friends?
- Take time, using the P-R-A-Y technique, to write a short prayer for one of your friends.

### Bible Discovery

Read these Bible verses: Luke 15; Ephesians 2:1-6; 1 Timothy 2:4.

### Bible Point

All of us, at one point, were lost in our sins. But God sought us out, and he continues to seek and care for the lost.

Bottom Line

Before you try to explain what you believe, realize that God cares about your lost friends.

## Real Love

"I just don't get it," Kara grumbled, taking a seat at the youth group meeting.

"What's up, Kara, what don't you get?" Mr. Nelson asked.

"Well, week after week I invite my friend Sarah to come to youth group, and she always has some excuse as to why she doesn't want to come. This week—get this—she said she had to clean out her closet. Nobody *wants* to clean out a closet. Why doesn't she want to come?"

"That is a pretty desperate excuse. Let's see. What exactly do you tell Sarah about being a Christian?" Mr. Nelson prodded.

"Umm, well, I tell her about the cool songs we sing in church and what a great bass player we have. I tell her about the wacky games we play in youth group—especially the one about stuffing all those marshmallows in our mouths. That's a real hoot!"

Mr. Nelson smiled at Kara. "Those are all good things that we enjoy at church, but have you told Sarah about God's love for her?" There was a long pause. Finally, Kara had to shake her head. "No, I guess I really haven't done that."

"I don't think you're the only one who has a hard time communicating God's love for others. Let me take a quick poll of the youth group." Mr. Nelson addressed the group. "What are some ways you communicate God's love to your friends?"

The group shouted out a few answers: "I try to act nice to everyone." "I talk about going to church with my friends." "I wear a cross every day." "I carry my Bible around."

"OK, let me ask you this: Can you imagine the U.S. ambassador to France trying to communicate an important message without saying anything—just trying to *act* in such a way that hopefully someone would get it? He wouldn't last very long in that post if he did that," Mr. Nelson said.

"Sometimes we Christians try to do exactly that. God has called us to be his ambassadors, but frequently we hope that non-Christians can pick up the message that God loves them just by looking at us. A good ambassador needs to speak up!"

"But, Mr. Nelson, if we start talking about Jesus, our friends will think we're weird," Mike pointed out. Others in the group nodded in agreement.

"That's a valid point," Mr. Nelson said, "but maybe the three *M*s can help you." He wrote three big *M*s on the board. "The first *M* is for Mind-set. A good ambassador simply doesn't care if others think he or she is crazy. This good ambassador is more concerned with telling others about God's love for them. The second *M* is for Motivation. A good ambassador is motivated by God's love. Because God loves us, we need to get the message out to others! And the last *M* is for the Message—we need to speak out!"

"But, Mr. Nelson," Mike broke in again. "What exactly do we say? We just can't run around and shout at people, 'God loves you.'" The group laughed as Mike proceeded to do exactly that.

After Mike finally sat down and the room quieted again, Mr. Nelson said, "You're right, Mike, and that was a terrific demonstration. You just can't run around blabbing at everyone. You need to have a personal message.The best place to look for what to say is in the Bible. Who knows any Bible verses that talk about God's love?"

A few people volunteered: "John 3:16." "Romans 8:38." "1 John 3:1."

Mr. Nelson nodded. "Good, those are excellent verses to use. The key now is to use those verses in specific situations when our friends need to be reminded of God's love."

Mr. Nelson turned to Kara. "Can you think of a specific situation where your friend Sarah might need to know about God's love?"

Kara thought for a moment and then slowly replied, "Well, she's been fighting with her mom a lot lately. Maybe the next time she has a big fight, I can use one of those verses."

"Good for you, Kara! I think we may see Sarah here before long! And we may have a marshmallow or two around for her."

### Questions

- What barriers stand in your way in telling others about Jesus?
- How can you become an effective ambassador for God?
- What Bible verses might you share with a friend?

### Bible Discovery

Read these Bible verses: Matthew 28:19-20; John 4:35; 2 Corinthians 5:11-21.

### Bible Point

God wants us to serve as his ambassadors and not be afraid to speak out about his love.

Bottom Line

To explain what you believe, use Scripture verses to tell your friends about God's love.

## *The Bad News*

Mr. Nelson was arranging the chairs for youth group when Michelle walked in. "Hi, Michelle, you're awfully early," Mr. Nelson greeted her. "Want to help me get the chairs ready?"

Michelle began dragging a couple of chairs into the circle, then sat down on one. Mr. Nelson looked at her, "Something on your mind?"

Michelle began slowly, "I've been thinking a lot about this one friend of mine. She's been in a lot of trouble at school—and at home. Her parents are always on her for her bad grades, and that just makes her hate school even more." Mr. Nelson nodded understandingly.

"Well," Michelle continued, "I've been praying for her, and I've even told her about how much God loves her, like we've been talking about. Barbara always says that's nice, but she really doesn't need God right now. I try to tell her that we all need Jesus because we're sinners, but Barbara says she's a good person and hasn't killed anyone, robbed any banks, or anything like that. I just can't get her to understand why she needs Jesus."

"That is a tough one," Mr. Nelson agreed. "Nobody wants to hear that he or she is a 'bad' person—or a sinner. There are a lot of people like Barbara who think that they are basically good and that's good enough for God. But the Bible tells us differently. God tells us that *all* of us have this problem called sin and that no one will ever be able to get into heaven on his or her own merits. That's why we need Jesus.

"In order for people to realize they need Jesus, however, they need to recognize their own sin problem. Wait a minute, I have something here that might help you explain this to Barbara." Mr. Nelson got up and fished in his desk for a piece of paper. On the top was the heading "Sin Quiz," and below it were ten questions about the past week, such as:

- Did you or someone you know use bad language?
- Did you or someone you know talk back to a parent?
- Did you or someone you know gossip or bad-mouth someone?
- Did you or someone you know get angry?

"The point," Mr. Nelson continued as Michelle read the quiz, "is that sin doesn't have to be a big one—like murdering someone or robbing a bank. Sin is a wrong attitude; it's anger, pride, lying, and jealousy; it's fighting with your brother or sister or even your mom. Look at that quiz again. Even if you can answer no to nine out of ten, you still flunk the test in God's eyes. God doesn't grade on a curve. And everyone flunks."

Michelle grabbed the quiz and jumped up. "I can't wait to get to school Monday and give Barbara this quiz. She won't be able to deny she's a sinner now," she said.

"Hold on a minute," Mr. Nelson spoke up. "Before you go telling Barbara how *bad* she is, you need to understand one more thing. As witnesses for Jesus, we have to demonstrate *our own* willingness to deal with sin."

Michelle looked puzzled. "What do you mean?"

Mr. Nelson walked up to the chalkboard and wrote in big red letters, *SIN-cere.* "We need to demonstrate that we are honest in dealing with our sin. The first three letters will help you remember how to do this. *S* stands for **S**orry, admitting the things we do that are wrong and not trying to hide them. *I* stands for '**I** was wrong,' accepting the responsibility for our sin and asking God to forgive us. And *N* is for **N**ew ways of doing things, so we don't keep on sinning.

"If you're willing to ask those friends you might have hurt for forgiveness, or are willing to change the way you do things in order not to sin, that will have a huge impact on them," Mr. Nelson said. He looked up at the clock. "And now, if we don't start hustling, we'll never be ready for youth group!"

### Questions

- Why is it important to be sincere about dealing with our own sin problems?
- How would you explain to a friend about sin?
- Look at James 1:19–2:17. What wrong attitudes and actions are mentioned in this passage? How well do you stack up against this list?
- What do you think is the purpose of knowing what God considers wrongful actions or attitudes? Read James 1:23-24 for a hint.

### Bible Discovery

Read these Bible verses: Genesis 3:1-19; Romans 1:18; 3:23; James 2:10.

Bible Point

Since Adam and Eve disobeyed God in the Garden, sin and its consequences have plagued human beings.

Bottom Line

Before you try to explain what you believe, admit and deal with your own sin.

### *And Now the Good News*

Anna and her friend Marie were discussing the latest movie when Mr. Nelson walked into the room. He caught the last part of their conversation. ". . . and then, the good guy comes back—only you don't know he's a good guy until the final part—and rescues the hostages from the aliens. Only it really was a trap to capture the spy, which is really the good guy, but the bad guys didn't know that. It was a great ending!"

"Boy," Mr. Nelson interrupted, "that sounds like a pretty complicated plot. I think I'm going to have to see this movie to understand it for myself." As the group quieted down, Mr. Nelson continued, "You know, that's how some people treat the gospel—like it's too complicated to tell others so they'll have to read it for themselves. Let me ask you, Where would you begin to tell others about Jesus and what he did for us?"

The answers came back: "With his birth." "With his teachings." "With his death." "With his miracles."

Mr. Nelson grinned. "See? It could be real confusing for a person who never heard anything about Jesus. There is just too much to tell about his life and all that he taught. Why, as adults, we're still learning about Jesus and how to live the Christian life. Try telling all that to a friend over lunch, and you're going to lose that person's interest for sure.

"But I can show you one Bible verse that sums up the entire gospel," Mr. Nelson said. The kids in the youth group erupted.

"No way!" "You can't be serious." "I don't believe it." "How can you do that? You just got through telling us there's too much to tell about Jesus."

"Hold on a minute, and I'll show you. We can break down the gospel into three basic facts: (1) God's love for us; (2) our sin problem; and (3) Jesus' sacrifice. Now all we have to do is find a way to lay out these facts in a short amount of time," Mr. Nelson explained.

Then he went over to the chalkboard and wrote in big letters *ROMANS 6:23*. "Can someone read that for me?"

Michelle began reading: "'For the wages of sin is death, but the free gift of God is eternal life through Christ Jesus our Lord.'"

"Take a good look at that verse. Everything we need to know, to summarize, and explain the gospel is right there in that one verse," Mr. Nelson told the group. "Let's break down the verse into two parts: Our Story and God's Story. He wrote those headings on the chalkboard. Unfortunately for us, the first part of the verse, 'For the wages of sin is death' is our story." Mr. Nelson wrote the words, *wages, sin* and *death,* under the heading *Our Story*.

Mr. Nelson continued. "*Wages* usually refers to money received in payment for a job. In this verse, *wages* refers to what we earn for doing the job of sinning. God has made it very clear that sin deserves only one type of payment—eternal death. That's not a very pretty picture, is it? And in the end, the payment is the same for everybody.

"But the good news is this isn't the end of the story. We move on to God's Story. Thankfully, God's story is much different. God's story is about *gifts* and *God* and *eternal life.* God gives gifts. Everything God does—from creating us to providing all our needs to dying for us—is a gift. And the gift that God gives, of course, is eternal life.

"There are two parts to that eternal life," Mr. Nelson explained. "One is right here and now—the good, worthwhile living as one of God's children. The second part is in the future when we get to live with God and our Christian friends in heaven. The question then becomes is how can I make God's story, *my* story.

"Look at those two columns again. I don't think anyone truly wants to be in that column," Mr. Nelson said, pointing to the words *wages, sin,* and *death.* "I think we all would rather receive God's really cool gift. That can be done by looking at the last part of the verse, 'through Christ Jesus our Lord.' By declaring Jesus our Lord, we can have this fabulous gift—even while we deserve the wages of sin! Pretty awesome, isn't it?"

"That's great, Mr. N, but how do we make it sound real to our friends?" asked Michelle. "I think my friend Barbara is really ready to know about Jesus, but I just don't want to quote a Bible verse at her."

"Good point," Mr. Nelson replied. "By adding your own personal touches—such as why you became a Christian, when you did, and what you did to become a Christian—you can give your own testimony based on Romans 6:23. My challenge to you this week is to rehearse a personal testimony using this Bible verse and share it with one friend or family member."

Questions

- What would you tell a friend about Jesus? What is the Good News?
- Why do we deserve death for our sins?
- Prepare and share your own personal testimony based on Romans 6:23. Have another family member share a personal testimony.

Bible Discovery

Read the following Bible verses: Romans 5:12; 6:23; 1 Corinthians 6:9-10; Galatians 6:7-8; 1 John 5:11-12.

Bible Point

Every person deserves eternal death as punishment for their sins, but God's gift is eternal life through Jesus Christ.

Bottom Line

To explain what you believe, use a "summary verse" such as John 6:23 to frame your testimony.

## *Putting It on the Line*

Michelle was pacing back and forth across the youth group room, glancing nervously at the clock every few seconds. She was waiting for her friend Barbara to show up for the banquet. She was excited that her friend finally was coming to see what youth group was all about. Michelle had been praying that Barbara would come visit youth group for months, and now it was about to happen.

Michelle sighed nervously as she glanced at the clock once again. As she turned to continue pacing, she encountered Mr. Nelson standing in her path. "I cannot watch you one minute longer," Mr. Nelson said, smiling. "What is the matter with you? You look like the tiger at the city zoo. Who or what is making you so antsy?"

Michelle grinned self-consciously. "Sorry, I didn't think anyone noticed me," she said. "But I'm waiting for my friend Barbara. Remember we talked about her a few weeks ago? We've been having some good conversations lately about God and church and all that stuff. She's finally agreed to come visit our youth group. I just want to make a good impression on her."

"Is that all?" Mr. Nelson asked gently.

"Yes—no—I mean no," Michelle said. "There is more. You see, I've been praying for an opportunity to tell Barbara about God's invitation to her, and I'm hoping we can talk about it tonight after the banquet. I just don't want to blow it or sound like I'm a preacher or anything. I guess I'm afraid of losing Barbara as a friend or of sounding like I don't know what I'm talking about."

"Well, I've heard you explain the gospel to others during youth group before, so I don't think you should worry about that. But it is a natural human tendency to be concerned about what our friends will think of us," Mr. Nelson began. "Explaining the gospel involves risk—and that's just what I want all of us to think about as our friends come to this special event."

The group gathered around Mr. Nelson. "Many of your friends will have questions after tonight's activities. It's going to involve a risk on your part. Let me explain what I mean." Mr. Nelson wrote *R-I-S-K* on the board. "*R* stands for **R**espond. You want to respond to the person's concerns, not just forcing your Christian life and beliefs on people. Answer your friend's questions at his or her level.

"That doesn't mean we don't talk about our faith. On the contrary. *I* stands for **I**ntroducing your values. State what you believe honestly and clearly. Remember these are our friends. We share our opinions, our beliefs with them on any number of issues. Why not our faith?

"*S* stands for **S**ay what you believe—your own personal testimony. We talked about this when we discussed Romans 6:23. Do you have a personal testimony? Could you give it to a friend if he or she asked you tonight? We need to be prepared to give our testimony," Mr. Nelson continued. "That brings us to *K*—**K**eep it short and simple. You don't have to give a fifteen-minute sermonette on your personal faith in Jesus. Be yourself and you'll be OK."

Michelle took a deep breath. "Thanks, Mr. Nelson. I think it's going to be OK. I'm ready to take that RISK now."

### Questions

- What are some fears that that prevent you from telling others about Jesus?
- If someone asked you about what you believe, what would you say?
- Why would your friends know that you are a Christian? Why wouldn't they know?

### Bible Discovery

Read the following Bible verses: Luke 12:8-9; Acts 1:8; Romans 1:16; 1 Peter 3:15.

### Bible Point

As witnesses for Jesus Christ, believers should be ready and willing to tell others the gospel.

### Bottom Line

To explain what you believe, prepare ahead of time so you'll know what to say and how to say it.

# 40

# How to Improve Your Grades

## *ANPAT*

One morning as Emily entered Miller Junior High, she noticed a colorful new poster on the main bulletin board. The heading HOW TO IMPROVE YOUR GRADES immediately caught her eye. The rest of the poster said "Learn of five ways to help you get better grades. See Ms. Jacobs for details. ANPAT."

*Anpat? What in the world is Anpat?* wondered Emily. *Maybe it's a vitamin to make me smarter. I sure could use it.* Emily was thinking about her not-so-good grades—especially in science and math.

When Emily asked Ms. Jacobs about the poster, Ms. Jacobs explained that a Grade Improvement Seminar was planned. There would be five sessions discussing how to get better grades. Interested kids would meet for an hour after school in the library.

Ms. Jacobs said, "I hope you can come. I'll give you a permission slip for your parents to sign."

It sounded kind of boring to Emily, but she really wanted to know about ANPAT. She decided she would at least go to the first meeting—if Mom and Dad said OK.

Emily's parents thought the seminar was a great idea. So Monday afternoon found Emily in the library with about twenty other kids. The mysterious ANPAT was written on the board.

"These letters stand for five ways to improve your grades. Today we're going to talk about the first, *A*. But to start out, we're going to play a game of Simon Says."

The students wondered how this would help them improve their grades.

"Now remember," Ms. Jacobs explained, "you only follow my directions when I say, 'Simon Says.'"

After about five minutes of playing and a lot of goof-ups, Ms. Jacobs had them sit down.

"What did you have to do to be good at this game?" she asked.

"Really listen to the directions," answered Bill.

"You're right," Ms. Jacobs agreed. "We could say that you had to pay attention. And the first *A* in ANPAT stands for Attention. To improve your grades you need to pay attention to directions and information. What are some things that may keep you from paying attention?"

Speaking from experience, the kids came up with such things as daydreaming, being bored, someone talking to them, thinking of something else, doing something else, or being tired.

Ms. Jacobs pointed out that there were different kinds of instructions to pay attention to. Some directions are spoken by the teacher; some are written, like on a test or homework assignment.

Then Ms. Jacobs said, "You can pay better attention if you remember two things: Always listen to or read directions very carefully, and ask questions if you don't understand. With written instructions, go back and reread the directions and make sure that you follow them."

Ms. Jacobs encouraged students to think of a personal signal they could use when their attention was drifting. She suggested using a word or short phrase—something easy to remember.

Emily was thinking about her personal attention signal as she headed out of the library. *Smack!* She and Bill ran right into each other.

"Oops! Guess I wasn't paying attention," apologized Bill. Then he and Emily both laughed.

### Questions

- Why was Emily interested in the poster?
- Why is it important to pay attention to directions?
- What things keep you from paying attention?
- What do you think Emily's personal signal will be? (Find out tomorrow.)

### Bible Discovery

Read these Bible verses: Proverbs 23:12; Matthew 11:15.

### Bible Point

When Jesus said, "Anyone who is willing to hear should listen and understand!" (Matthew 11:15), he was really telling the people to pay attention to what he was saying. Paying close attention to spoken or written instructions can keep us from making a lot of mistakes or missing out on really important information.

Bottom Line

Improve your grades by paying attention.

## *A "Notable" Day*

Emily was curled up on the couch, but her mind was thousands of miles away solving a mystery in the highlands of Scotland. She was reading about the latest adventures of a teenage detective named Daphne.

Mom came into the room and asked Emily to fold the laundry. Emily nodded her head. When Mom came back ten minutes later, she wasn't pleased to see the pile of laundry still unfolded.

Mom lowered Emily's book and said, "Emily, Mom says fold the laundry. Please pay attention to what I'm saying."

Emily was embarrassed. "I'm sorry, Mom," she said. "We were discussing paying attention in school at yesterday's seminar session. I guess I need to do it at home, too."

As Emily folded socks and shirts, she tried to think of a personal signal. All of a sudden she thought of the perfect one—Simon Says.

"Each time I catch myself not paying attention, I'll think *Simon Says,"* she decided.

Science class was a good testing ground for Emily's signal because it was hard to pay attention to the lecture about the many parts of a plant. *Simon Says* came to the rescue five times during the hour, and Emily actually learned some interesting facts.

At Friday's seminar session, each person revealed his or her personal signal and if it had worked. Then Ms. Jacobs handed out sheets of paper and pencils. She explained, "I'm going to talk about in-line skating. Write down the important facts so you can answer questions about what I say."

Ms. Jacobs talked about the care of skates, equipment needed, and safety rules. When she had finished, she asked the kids to read their notes. Some had only a few notes, and some had tried to write down everything. Emily discovered that she had written down some insignificant facts instead of the important ones. Very few kids could answer the questions.

Then Ms. Jacobs said, "You may have guessed that today's

session is about Note taking—the *N* in ANPAT. You can improve your grades by taking good notes. As you found out, this isn't easy to do. It's hard to listen, pick out the important stuff, and write it down all at the same time. Today we're going to learn how to make note taking easier and more useful."

Ms. Jacobs listed these things to listen:

- The subject—what the teacher is talking about.
- The key number—how many different areas will be covered.
- The important information about each area.

As practice, Ms. Jacobs gave two short talks, one about Alaska and the other about car racing. Everyone took notes, using the three steps. When compared to their first set of notes, there was quite a difference. They were ready to try it in class on Monday.

*I'll be just like Daphne, teenage detective,* thought Emily. *I'll use my trusty notebook and pencil to write down clues. Then I'll solve the mystery of the teacher's talk.*

Questions

- Why do you think Emily chose "Simon Says" for her personal signal?
- Why is good note taking important for improving grades?
- What do you find to be the hardest part of note taking?
- How could Ms. Jacobs's suggestions be helpful to you?

Bible Discovery

Read Luke 1:1-4 and 1 John 1:1-4.

Bible Point

Writers like Luke and John carefully wrote down the truths that God had told them. It is important to know how to take good notes so we can remember important things, both in and out of school. Good note taking will also save time as you study for tests, and you will learn more.

Bottom Line

Improve your grades by taking good notes.

## *Time and Place*

Armed with a notebook and several sharpened pencils, Emily felt ready to take notes all day. Well, at least in science class. Emily liked the teacher, Mrs. Raymond, but she sure did talk a lot! Emily tried to remember everything Mrs. Raymond said. But quite often what she did remember didn't show up on the tests. Emily was sure that she could take better notes now that she knew what to listen for.

"Today we're going to talk about destructive storms," began Mrs. Raymond. Emily scribbled "destructive storms" across the top of her paper.

Mrs. Raymond continued, "We'll concentrate on four of them—tornadoes, hurricanes, typhoons, and blizzards." Emily's pencil scooted across the paper, and a smile spread across her face. She was getting the idea of this note taking.

Each time the group met for a seminar session after school, they were more enthusiastic and eager to tell about using the suggestions they learned. Today they were showing each other and Ms. Jacobs the notes they had taken in their classes.

"I think you're finding that improving your grades can actually be exciting," said Ms. Jacobs. "We have three more skills to learn this week, and today we're going to identify the *P* in ANPAT. It stands for *place.* To improve your grades you need a special place to study daily. Where do you do homework?"

"On the floor in front of the TV," said Craig.

"At the kitchen table—near the refrigerator," volunteered Tom.

Emily added, "On my bed with papers all over."

Ms. Jacobs then asked, "You can also improve your grades by choosing a time to study daily. *When* do you do homework?"

The answers covered every time from after school to before the bus comes or whenever it can be squeezed in.

Ms. Jacobs said, "Let's talk about *time* for homework. It's important to pick a time every day when you study. An hour is a good amount. When you don't have an hour's worth of homework, use the time to read or review what you have learned. Make it a habit to use the same hour every day."

"A special *place* for homework is also important," continued Ms. Jacobs. "The best place is a desk or table, away from family, TV, and other distractions. You need a place where it's quiet and where you can concentrate. This quiet and private place could be your room. But don't try to study on your bed. Your mind will wander, and you may fall asleep."

Ms. Jacobs encouraged them to find their own special place and time for study at their homes. She suggested that they ask their parents to help them out.

*Well, I have a desk in my room,* Emily thought. *But first I need to find it under all the stuff burying it. I guess it's Operation Uncover tonight!*

Questions

- Why is having a special place to study important?
- Why is having a special time to study each day important?
- What was bad about Emily's study place?
- What time and place will you choose to study each day?

Bible Discovery

Read Mark 6:31-32 and John 9:4.

Bible Point

Jesus often went off by himself to think and pray. We can follow his example when we study each day. Studying at the same time each day in a special quiet place away from distractions will help you concentrate on your homework.

Bottom Line

Improve your grades by choosing a time and place to study daily.

### *Homework Check*

After dinner Emily attacked her buried desk. The papers, notes and other debris filled a large garbage bag. It was the first time the desktop had been bare in three months.

Setting aside an hour each day was harder for Emily. She liked to do lots of things, and an hour seemed like a long time. Finally, Emily picked from eight to nine each evening as her study time.

Sitting at her clean desk in a quiet room seemed strange, but she stuck with her homework with only one five-minute break. At the end of the hour her math assignment was finished. *Hey, this is great!* thought Emily. *Think I'll reward myself with a dish of ice cream.*

Wednesday's seminar session started with each kid telling about his or her special time and place for study. Everyone had made some changes and found that it *was* easier to concentrate.

"All the things we've talked about so far have involved only you," said Ms. Jacobs. "You need to pay attention, take notes, and have a special time and place to study. Today we are going to bring someone else into the picture."

Ms. Jacobs pointed to the second *A* in ANPAT as she explained, "This A stands for Adult. You can improve your grades by having an adult check your homework." This produced a groan from the group.

"That would make me feel like a little kid," said Jerome.

"I don't like other people reading what I wrote," complained Ashley.

"I hear what you're saying," replied Ms. Jacobs, "but let's really think about this. Sometimes our eyes and minds trick us. We know what we mean, so we think we're writing it clearly. But when someone else reads it, they may not understand it. Wouldn't it be better to have Mom or Dad point this out than to have a teacher give you a poor grade?" Most kids nodded in agreement.

Ms. Jacobs continued. "Often your mom or dad can give suggestions on how to make changes that will improve your work. They can also point out if you've misread the directions or forgotten to do something. Letting an adult check your homework is sort of like having your own private editor. They can help you do your best to make your work good and to improve your grades."

Ms. Jacobs asked them to have an adult check their homework for the next two nights and then tell about it at the last seminar session on Friday.

Emily decided to ask her dad to check her work. *He will use his engineering brain and catch all the little details,* she thought. *I wonder if I'm ready for this.*

### Questions

- What happened when Emily studied for an hour at a clean desk?
- How can having an adult check your homework improve your grades?
- How would you feel about having an adult check your homework?
- How do you think Emily will cope with Dad's check over? (Find out tomorrow.)

### Bible Discovery

Read Proverbs 12:15 and 13:10, 13.

### Bible Point

The Bible says to respect the opinions and advice of older people. Having adults check homework can be very beneficial. Because they are older and more experienced, they can spot problems or errors more easily. They can also make helpful suggestions on how to correct and improve homework.

### Bottom Line

Improve your grades by having an adult check your homework.

## *Test Time*

Emily had to write a report on a favorite historical character. She chose Sam Houston because she liked the history of the Old West. Emily had done research, taken notes, and typed the report. When she was finished, she reread what she had done and ran a spell check. *Looks great,* she thought. *Now Dad can check it, and then I'm done.*

When Dad gave the paper back to Emily, he said, "I like what you wrote, Emily. It's interesting. But I think that if you rework the ending, it will be even better. The paper is sort of confusing the way it is. I would be happy to help you."

Emily felt disappointed and upset when she looked at her marked-up paper. She almost felt like not making any changes at all. Then she remembered what Ms. Jacobs said—better to have Dad's corrections than a poor grade. Taking a deep breath, Emily said, "Thanks, Dad. I guess I need some help."

Emily learned that the other kids had similar experiences when they asked an adult to check their papers. Ms. Jacobs reminded them that that was the purpose of the check and encouraged them to keep doing it.

"Today is our last seminar session," Ms. Jacobs said, "and we're going to learn about the *T* in ANPAT. The *T* stands for Tests. You can improve your grades by doing better on tests. Everything you've learned in this seminar can be used when you study for tests. But you can also learn how to get better at actually taking the tests.

"How many of you get a sinking feeling in your stomach and feel afraid, even when you know a test is coming?" Ms. Jacobs asked. Every hand shot up in the air. Some kids said that they couldn't eat breakfast or that they got a headache when they had to take a test.

Ms. Jacobs continued. "Your teachers need to give tests to see what you have learned. And your test scores really affect your grades. You *do* need to study thoroughly. But today I'm going to give you some suggestions that will help you know how to take tests and, thus, do better."

Ms. Jacobs listed and explained these helps:

- Relax—take a deep breath and clear your mind.
- Read—before you start, read (and listen to) instructions.
- Scan—scan the whole test and do the easy questions first.
- Choose—after you have answered all the questions you know, come back to the others. Choose an answer or write something; don't leave anything blank.
- Check—check everything before you turn in the test.

Emily was sort of sad to have the Grade Improvement Seminar end, but she felt that she was much better equipped to improve her grades and better prepared to take tests. "Wait till Mom and Dad see my next report card," she told one of her friends. "It will knock their socks off!"

Questions

- Why do you think Emily felt as she did when Dad checked her paper?
- How can learning to take tests improve your grades?
- How important are tests in your school?
- How do you feel when you have to take a test?
- Which of the suggestions given will you use for test taking?

Bible Discovery

Read James 1:5.

Bible Point

Tests can be upsetting, but they are an important measure of what you have learned. Before you do anything else when you take a test, pray for God's help and guidance. Wisdom comes from God, but we must do our part and be prepared.

Bottom Line

Improve your grades by learning how to take tests.